Date Due   53872

JUN 08 1993			

COMEDY AND AMERICA

Kennikat Press
National University Publications
Literary Criticism Series

General Editor
John E. Becker
Fairleigh Dickinson University

MARTIN ROTH

COMEDY
AND
AMERICA

The Lost World of Washington Irving

National University Publications
KENNIKAT PRESS   //   1976
Port Washington, N. Y.   //   London

Manufactured in the United States of America

Published by
Kennikat Press Corp.
Port Washington, N.Y./London

Library of Congress Cataloging in Publication Data

Roth, Martin.
    Comedy and America.

    (Literary criticism series) (National university publications)
    Includes bibliographical references and index.
    1. Irving, Washington, 1783-1859–Criticism and interpretation. 2. Comedy–History and criticism.
3. Irving, Washington, 1783-1859. A history of New York. 4. New York (State)–History–Colonial period, ca. 1600-1775. I. Title.
PS2088.R6   818'.2'09   76-6870
ISBN 0-8046-9132-0

TO
ALICE, DULCINEA,
MARGARET, AND SEBASTIAN

CONTENTS

PREFACE

This book grew out of an act of curiosity, a desire to understand the nature and shape of Washington Irving's American period, which culminated in *The History of New York* in 1809, although a coda appeared in 1819: his two most successful tales, "Rip Van Winkle," and "The Legend of Sleepy Hollow." I soon discovered that this body of writing was not a short-lived exercise in the adaptation of various strains of English and European comedy to America, but a coherent, though intuitive, attempt to create an American literature; and the terms of that attempt were appropriate to a native literature, however artifical and derivative they may have seemed to generations of critics. Irving's American period was one of the real beginnings of our national literature (perhaps the most important one), and Irving's bequest to the major writers of nineteenth-century American literature is deeper and more meaningful than it is generally supposed to be. The subject of Irving's relationship to that richer literature would obviously provide my anticipated audience with a book more pertinent to the announced interests of American literary study. Discussion of this relationship depends to such a great extent upon the prior study of Irving's use of the comic tradition that I have ventured to treat it directly only in the last chapter of this book, and there only as a series of speculative generalizations and partial treatments awaiting more precise definition in the future.

The first investigation took me abroad for long periods of time, and the results have not been happy for Irving. In some chapters he is allowed only the briefest entrance; in others, devoted specifically to his American works, he is often overshadowed by the comic authors whose company he keeps. But if writers like Rabelais, Addison and Steele, Swift, Goldsmith, Fielding, Smollett, and, above all, Laurence Sterne, are his proper measure, it is inevitable that they will overshadow their American relative.

The point of departure for any study of Irving's American period is a close examination of the comic influences which shaped his work and the comic traditions to which the works variously refer. Irving's derivations ultimately testify more to an acute sense of the modalities of the comic than to the individual influence of comic writers.

There has never been an adequate study of Irving's exercises in comic expression. The early critics, who casually referred to an American Addison or Goldsmith, were answered in the 1930's by another group of critics, who asserted, with an equal air of authority and equal brevity, that Irving's roots were American, demonstrably so if we would only recover and thoroughly study a small body of facetious magazines and essay serials written in America in the latter half of the eighteenth century. Discussions of *The History* invariably mention echoes of Cervantes, Swift, and Fielding, but these youthful borrowings of Irving's are so often regarded in an apologetic or indulgent light that there can be no corresponding insight into why an author might positively choose to weave his art out of threads spun by earlier comic writers. This is a curious aversion in a century when so much vital literature, from Eliot and Joyce to Borges and Nabokov, demands that we regard quotation as a form of artistic reality superior to the outworn myth of actual experience.

Major and minor comic writers are definitely present in Irving's American works to an extent that has not been suspected. In several of the chapters that follow, *Salmagundi* will be examined as a vocabulary and grammar of comic characters, tropes, and fictions.

These presences are important *because Irving is using them.* He is self-consciously trying on a variety of comic voices, working through a wide range of comic fictions, in an effort to find or forge a voice and fiction that would serve an American comedy. This American comedy came about in *The History of New York* more deeply and prophetically than any contemporary reader of *The Contrast, Modern Chivalry,* or even *Salmagundi,* had any right to expect.

Irving's work through *The History* represents a relatively bold and vital gamble on behalf of an American literature that was still to be. Irving's gamble lost; yet he had a more complex sense of the terms and implications of the wager than Cooper, who succeeded timidly where Irving failed. Irving's American experiment failed partly for the obvious reasons: his literary isolation and his personal shortcomings in imagination and intellect. He did not create an American literature, but he did write an American book which offers, as one of its meanings, the reason for that failure.

The History dramatizes an attempt to create an America in which the imagination might take root and ultimately flower, because the qualities of that America are conducive to such a growth. Irving's colonial Dutch, however, are defeated by an alien civilization — that of the Yankees — a race belonging to no land, neither the England which they so intemperately left nor the America in which they never truly settled. We must not regard this defeat as the record of an actual passage in American history, for Irving's art is an attempt to counter that history, to unwrite it and substitute for it, symbolically, a culture that holds more promise than the historical society of 1809.

Marcus Cunliffe may have had something of this in mind when he asked if Irving was "so much to blame in judging his History a dead end, when it was only a false start?"[1] It was not a false start; it was a start whose terms we have failed to recognize. We may not feel any kinship between Irving's History and later works like Walden, "Song of Myself," and Moby Dick; but in several significant respects they belong to the same order of imaginative nationalism, which attempts to destroy the history that is in order to create a culture.

Irving's Dutch are defeated because Diedrich Knickerbocker, the author of that counter-history, fails to create in art a viable alternative to historical America. Throughout his career, Irving exhibited an attitude of ambivalence toward the efficacy and value of imaginative activity. In the act of imagining, he implicitly raises the questions of whether the imagination can flourish in a new and barren land, and whether the result of that activity is worthwhile.

Irving's subsequent career is a commentary on his failure to anchor his art in America. After finishing The History, he was virtually unable to write for nine years. In the works of his middle period (1819–32), he timidly sought in England, on the Continent, and in Spain the values of a homeland to replace his lost America, and the shape of that search is remarkably similar to the exploratory patterns of his History.

If The Sketch Book and Bracebridge Hall (1822) represent Irving's search for a system of values that would replace those he had tested and lost in America, these books also illustrate how enervated his artistic demands had become. He eagerly accepts the sentimental myth of the English past and its equivalent, the English countryside. The sketches and tales that result testify both to the falsity and sterility of the England he is courting and to his own fear of informing them with his imaginative presence. He no longer has any artistic end to work for and asks only that he be accepted as a naturalized son by any civilization whose cultural values seem tangible and secure. In the opening of Bracebridge Hall, he apologizes for the timidity and bankruptcy of his literary aims and implicitly admits how self-indulgent his recovery of "commonplace" England is:

I am aware that I often travel over beaten ground, and treat of subjects that have already been discussed by abler pens. . . . In venturing occasionally on topics that have already been almost exhausted by English authors, I do it, not with the presumption of challenging a comparison, but with the hope that some new interest may be given to topics when discussed by the pen of a stranger.

If, therefore, I should sometimes be found dwelling on subjects trite and commonplace with the reader, I beg the circumstances under which I write may be kept in recollection.

Irving returned to America from time to time, but he continued to avoid its historical present. He revisited another defeated American civilization in the two sketches in *The Sketch Book* devoted to the Indians, and he visited the ahistorical West in "A Tour of the Prairies" (1835), *Astoria* (1836), and *The Rocky Mountains* (1837). He also repeated, in the matter-of-fact historical manner which Diedrich Knickerbocker had earlier rejected, Knickerbocker's own cycle of re-creation, in his histories of Columbus (1828), the companions of Columbus (1831), and then Washington (1855-59). Symbolically, America ends for Irving, as it does for Rip Van Winkle, with the American Revolution, the creation of the historical state.[2]

The most significant returns to America occur in *The Sketch Book, Bracebridge Hall,* and *Tales of a Traveller* (1824). Each of these works contains a small group of American sketches and tales attributed to the dead Knickerbocker. In them Irving explores again the nature of his imaginary Dutch community and, often, its inevitable defeat. In the best of these works he is asking what went wrong not with Dutch values but with his own early, American, art.

In its largest sense, this book is devoted to the beginning of American literature and to American forms that are not so different from the familiar shapes of our major nineteenth-century literature. This beginning is significant in many respects; among other things, Irving suggests that the literature of a *new world* can begin only with the creation of the world, the original beginning, and *The History* also dramatizes what such a beginning means.

This book is also, in a small way, about the American attitude toward the imagination. Irving anticipates Hawthorne and James in his ambivalence about imagining deeply on American soil. For Hawthorne and James, one of the primary determinants of this attitude was the instinctive recognition that neither the imagination nor those psychic depths from which it draws its power had taken an oath of allegiance to this clean, new democracy. Even in the land of the free, the artist, try as he might, could only truly produce forms of Old World guilt and Old World monsters.

Above all, this is a book about comedy. Irving's initial choice of comedy may have been an accident of temperament, but it remains virtually his only mode of literary expression through *The History,* and in that work it is identified as the proper mode for American literature. Our sense of comic taxonomy is confused and impoverished; for that reason, an attempt has been made in the chapters that follow to sketch the synthetic form, when practicable, but at least to isolate certain paradigms, of the conventional genres of comedy — polite satire, political satire, and domestic humor.

Under the tutelage of Sterne and Rabelais, Irving finally settled on a mode of the comic that has never been properly defined; it has hardly ever been identified. New names being hard to come by, I refer to it as *burlesque comedy. Festive comedy* might have been a more expressive term, except that the ceremonial vision to which burlesque comedy is most often devoted is balanced by a reductive and negative vision of a *world of words.* The paramount necessity of defining burlesque comedy from several angles of approach has resulted in two chapters on the aesthetics and the primary strategies of burlesque comedy. They may seem to interrupt the continuity of this study. I can only hope that the reader will see the necessity for this organization.

I have attempted to read or consult what I considered to be the pertinent scholarship or criticism for this study: works on Irving certainly, theories of the comic, and, to an extent restricted by necessity, studies of the major British comic authors and Rabelais. Many of these articles and volumes are not mentioned here, for I firmly determined that this work should be devoted to Irving, comic authors, aesthetic issues, and American literature, and not become a battle of the folios itself. I have generally not pointed out that a certain scholar or critic has made the same or a similar observation before me, and that I am aware of the fact as the footnote indicates; although there is a certain order of insight to which homage must be paid. I have tried never to argue down interpretations with which I privately disagreed. It has been my experience that the assumptions, sensitivities, and training of responsible critics lead to differing, not incompatible, interpretations. The charting of these differences seemed to me to be a superfluous effort when there was so much other work to be done. In one instance, particularly, I regret this decision. William Hedge's studies of Irving represent the first major attempt to see Irving's literature adequately, that is, critically; and I have not brought him into this study as often as I might have. I respect his work, and I considered his treatment and conclusions seriously when they differed from mine.

Many colleagues, known personally or through correspondence, have contributed to the content and organization of this study: Walter Blair, Bruce Granger, James Scoggins, Robert Streeter, and Stuart Tave. Bernard Bowron and Edward Griffin read an earlier version in its entirety and offered very helpful comments. Arthur Geffen provided me with detailed and invaluable suggestions for the key chapters. I would also like to thank the Graduate School of the University of Minnesota for providing the funds for the final revision and Margaret Powers for undertaking the extensive and thankless task of making that revision as accurate as it is. Finally, I express my gratitude to my wife, Martha, for four or five judicious readings of the various stages of this book; for her tolerance with a writer who refuses to admit, for a while, that any line he has written could be less than elegant; and for allowing our dining room to be appropriated for so many years by an unshaven man in pyjamas.

Chapter 9 contains a revised version of an article which originally appeared in *Modern Philology* for February 1969.

COMEDY AND AMERICA

CHAPTER ONE

INTRODUCTION TO BURLESQUE COMEDY

Richard Dorson has suggested that the twin myths of the land which inform American folklore are "the conceits of an Earthly Paradise and a Howling Wilderness."[1] These myths are no less important to an understanding of our formal literature, and, with the exception of Walt Whitman, no American writer has appealed more totally to the first of these myths than Washington Irving in Books II and III of his *History*. There, America as a land of abundance is identified with the traditional Land of Cockaigne, and the mode of its expression is what I have termed *burlesque comedy*. A slow and often stumbling movement toward burlesque comedy characterizes Irving's American period. It will be necessary to use this term frequently and to appeal to various of its generic characteristics. A discussion of comic modality must, therefore, come at the beginning of this work, rather than at the various stages of Irving's development where his writing reflects the successful absorption of the qualities defined here.

The division of prose comedy into the three genres or modes of *satire, humor,* and *burlesque comedy,* which I use in this study, is not due to the application of any theory of comedy, nor, I am unhappy to say, does it depend upon the work of any author in the field of comic aesthetics, with the exception of Stuart Tave, whose authoritative distinction between satire and humor seems to me to be a necessary point of departure for any successful study of comedy.[2] On the contrary, this chapter grew out of my frustration at being unable to make meaningful statements about Irving's comedy within the various comic aesthetics in existence.

The usual approach to the problem of comedy is to identify it as a theoretically continuous form, fiction, or attitude, usually termed comedy or satire, which is capable of categorical definition. This tendency is still another instance of our uncritical dependence upon Aristotle's *Poetics,* and it is ultimately vitiated by the impossibility of extending generalizations that were originally based upon an extremely restricted body of examples; basically, one suspects, one tragedy — the *Oedipus* of Sophocles — and the comedies of Aristophanes. Within such an undifferentiated category, the critic or philosopher attempts to make whatever distinctions and modifications that his sense of the author or work under discussion dictates, but, once one leaves the apparently safe ranks of Plautus, Terence, Molière, and Ben Johson; or Horace, Juvenal, Dryden, Pope, and Swift; such studies become increasingly devoted to strategies of modification which quite overwhelm the opening categorical assertions.

In Northrop Frye's *Anatomy of Criticism,* for example, surely one of the most ambitious and complex attempts to systematize literature, satire is treated as both a mythos and a form. As a mythos, it is defined as "militant irony"; "its moral norms are relatively clear, and it assumes standards against which the grotesque and absurd are measured." By the time we have reached Sterne and Dickens, however, "gaiety predominates in such satire." "We have an attitude which fundamentally accepts social conventions but stresses tolerance and flexibility within their limits. Close to the conventional norm we find the lovable eccentric, the Uncle Toby or Betsey Trotwood who diversifies, without challenging, accepted codes of behavior." At this point, satire is no longer militant; its moral norms, however clear, are no longer operative, and absurdity is no longer measured against standards.

As a genre, the *anatomy* or *Menippean satire,* satire refers to both a form and an attitude:

As the name of an attitude, satire is, we have seen, a combination of fantasy and morality. But as the name of a form, the term satire . . . is more flexible, and can be either entirely fantastic or entirely moral. The Menippean adventure story may thus be pure fantasy, as it is in the literary fairy tale. The Alice books are perfect Menippean satires, and so is *The Water-Babies,* which has been influenced by Rabelais.

One must conclude that *Alice in Wonderland* is a formal satire which lacks the satiric attitude.[3]

Eighteenth-century English literature provides a useful triad of authors — Swift, Fielding, and Sterne — whose works represent the three proposed modes of the comic. Stuart Tave has studied a major transition in English criticism from a sense of satire to one of humor as the essential comic mode.[4]

But among humorous writers, the comedy of Sterne and Rabelais shares essential qualities that are quite different from those of Fielding and Cervantes. A common way of recognizing this difference is to distinguish Rabelaisian and Cervantic humor (or satire). To answer the need for a third category, I have pressed into service the already existing term *burlesque*. Once *burlesque comedy*, or any equivalent term, is granted generic status, we can return to such works as *Gulliver's Travels* or *Tom Jones* and identify burlesque elements in those works: the lies of a lying traveller, the academy of mad pedants, and the topsy-turvical relationship between man and beast in the first work; the digressive interchapters in the second.

These three categories serve to differentiate the comic materials that fall within the scope of this study, and they form a triad which is adaptable to a number of traditional distinctions. They correspond, for example, to the three kinds of linguistic signs in Aristotle's *Rhetoric,* the necessary, the probable, and the tangential (or associational). Satire is necessary comedy insofar as it seems to posit a rational or absolutely moral norm in terms of which the grotesque or the ridiculous is to be measured. In satire, the constrictive law which stipulates that a miss is as good as a mile is always in operation. Humor projects a relative world in which moral qualities are never pure but are enmeshed with personal qualities, bents, and eccentricities that would be trivial or foolish if they were detached from the essential worth of the character possessing them. In the world of burlesque comedy, all moral reference is lacking. The details of Lilliputian life are either praise- or blameworthy because the fiction is designed to isolate absolute patterns of reason and unreason; Tom Jones's affair with Mrs. Waters is improper, but we absorb this in our sympathy for him, since it proceeds from a peculiar but acceptable system of behavior; Mr. Shandy's lying-in arrangements with his wife, even though they result in lifelong harm and disgrace to the child, Tristram, have no moral content whatever. To put it another way, when Gulliver pisses on the palace in Lilliput, the inhabitants are morally outraged, and the reader disapproves of this reaction as an instance of the absurd lengths to which a sense of propriety may be taken; when Gargantua was annoyed by the Parisians, he "pissed on them so fiercely that he drowned two hundred and sixty thousand, four hundred and eighteen persons, not counting the women and little children."[5] Obviously these statements belong to totally different worlds.

Considering the three narrators, the satirist is only rational; the humorist is compassionate; and the writer of burlesque comedy is fanciful, whimsical, or mad. There is a sense, to be discussed later, in which burlesque comedy can be regarded as a humorous extreme, where the humor celebrated is that of being receptive to humors of all kinds. Humor was generally felt to be a mild form of madness, or anticipatory of madness, and madness itself has a place in the comic theory of the eighteenth century. There are, however, enough distinctive burlesque elements to grant it a generic status as a mode of comedy.

I believe that burlesque comedy is the essential mode of comic expression. The category exists in fact as a series of undefined comic masterpieces, but there is, to my knowledge, no critical recognition of it as a genre or a tradition. The major works of burlesque comedy — *The Praise of Folly, The Anatomy of Melancholy, Gargantua and Pantagruel, Don Quixote, Hudibras,* "A Tale of a Tub," *Tristram Shandy,* and *Ulysses* and *Finnegans Wake* — tend, like Irving's *History,* to be large, sprawling, disorganized works, notorious for their resistance to categorical definition.[6] The usual response to these works is to treat them as mock forms, forms which play off of or explode the settled realities of literature.

There are, I suspect, two major reasons for this failure in our understanding of much of Western literature. First, burlesque comedy is dangerous, because a clear view of it might commit us to admitting the validity of madness and obscenity as positive human values. Secondly, it is an international tradition and violates the linguistic and territorial agreements we have made in the area of critical nationalism.

If the preceding contentions are in any way acceptable, a treatment of burlesque comedy would be valuable in its own right. But it is even more necessary when one considers that in our own century the burlesque impulse has moved from the periphery to the center of comic expression — for example, in the work of Joyce, Borges, Witold Gombrowicz, Vladimir Nabokov, Eugène Ionesco, Günter Grass, Valeriy Tarsis, Abram Tertz, William Burroughs. In a period when the motive of all art forms has been a desire to purify themselves, extended fiction has been unable to adapt the methods of painting, music, and poetry to any great extent.

The most fertile development in this form of literature in our century has been through the absorption of the earlier tradition of burlesque comedy, which allows extended fiction to move in the direction of pure literature by annihilating or confounding the extrinsic elements of plot, character, motive, thought, and feeling; and exploding constrictive formal determinants. Finally, a treatment of burlesque comedy is particularly important to American literature, for it is to this mode that some of our greatest works — *Moby Dick, Walden,* and "Song of Myself" — primarily appeal.

There is some comic theory which seems to recognize this genre; one example seems particularly relevant: Erasmus, in *The Praise of Folly,* imagines a reader "that may cavil and charge me . . . that these toys are lighter than may become a divine . . . and that I resemble the ancient comedy, or another Lucian."[7] He then gives a long list of works which he considers authorities for his present endeavor, beginning with Homer's *Battle of the Frogs and Mice*. Significantly, his catalogue omits Horace, Juvenal, Varro, all of the recognized authorities for satire, although Erasmus mentions both Horace and Juvenal in the work. Erasmus presumes a clearly understood distinction between the tradition of folly and the tradition of satire. He goes on to say, "let them suppose I played at tables for my diversion, or if they had rather have it so, that I rode on a hobbyhorse. . . . For what injustice is it that when we allow every course of life its recreation, that study only should have none? Especially when such toys are not without their serious matter."[8] Erasmus' suggested definition of burlesque comedy as the "recreation of study" is extremely pertinent to one aspect of the genre: the civilized world of organized learning dispersed and floating through mental space. Erasmus also supports the generalization that one of the plots of burlesque comedy is likely to be the conflict between pedantic folly and pedantic gravity.

Erich Auerbach's description of Rabelaisian comedy celebrates the value of a nonsatiric model:

> . . . Rabelais' entire effort is directed toward playing with things and with the multiplicity of their possible aspects; upon tempting the reader out of his customary and definite way of regarding things, by showing him phenomena in utter confusion; upon tempting him out into the great ocean of the world, in which he can swim freely, though it be at his own peril . . .
> . . . in Rabelais, creatural realism has acquired a new meaning . . . that of the vitalistic-dynamic triumph of the physical body and its functions. . . . As a part of nature, man rejoices in his breathing life, his bodily functions, and his intellectual powers, and, like nature's other creatures, he suffers natural dissolution.[9]

The burlesque impulse most often manifests itself in the celebration of human life as an organic part of a world of process, a world of elemental flow and continual recombination. This impulse can also be regarded as a projection of aspects of infancy. In Rabelais especially one can glimpse a literary transformation of infantile joy, of what Freud calls the oral optative state, when the child feels himself to be the giant center of a universe streaming with nourishment.

The substantive fiction of burlesque comedy, that is, the fictional universe to which most of its elements properly belong, is that of the fools' paradise. Sometimes it is projected as a fictional realm — Aristophanes' Cloud-Cuckooland, the medieval Land of Cockaigne, or the English Gotham; but Rabelais' Touraine, as well as Irving's New Amsterdam, can be easily recast in this mold. Cockaigne is the image and myth that corresponds to our sense of a totally integrated world, the world as an extension of the body and its pleasures. It is the world that Prince Hal knowingly labelled tedious: all the year — all the book, painting, symphony, etc. — spent playing holiday. This is the essential myth, but it is extremely difficult to sustain in literature. Pieter Brueghel can make us see only the meaning of festivity, through its presence or even through its aftermath — his lubbers lying asleep on the ground, their distended bellies pleasantly reincarnating the great omphalic bulge of the mushroom table where the nourishment had once been set. Literature must pretend to pursue its arguments and plots, but, at the end of Thomas Dekker's *Shoemaker's Holiday*, the play finds its real world in Firk's description of the holiday feast:

There's cheer for the heavens: Venison-pasties walk up and down piping hot, like sergeants; beef and brewis comes marching in dry-fats, fritters and pancakes come trowling in in wheelbarrows; hens and oranges hopping in porters' baskets, collops and eggs in scuttles, and tarts and custards come quavering in in malt-shovels.[10]

Cockaigne is the land of all delights. One account tells of rivers of wine, houses built of cake or barley-sugar, streets paved with pastry. Roast geese and fowl wander about with knives in their sides, asking to be eaten.

This stress on food is a primary feature of burlesque comedy, and it often takes the form of what can be called *food translation* — that is, the translation of high planes of behavior into kitchen terms, which is what happens to politics and law, for example, in so many of Aristophanes' plays and to warfare in Rabelais and in *Hudibras*. The tavern scenes of *1 Henry IV* are burlesque comedy — taverns are Cockaignes — and there is great tension late in the play, when the everyday, historical Hal asks the burlesque Falstaff for a weapon and is handed a "pottle of sack."

Cockaigne is a world of comic forms and movements. Its citizen, the lubber, is traditionally fat, round, and rosy. Although it is the scene of great comic animation, bodies bounce off one another. Although it is also the scene of comic violence, the world of Cockaigne possesses great curative powers: wounds and gashes, severed heads and limbs are miraculously cured, usually by the magical powers of food. And to this world belongs a distinct vocabulary of comic symbols — noses, pipes, breeches, whiskers, geese, owls, oysters, pumpkins, cabbages — all of which are treated as comic mysteries that transcend any overt anatomical reference.

Another aspect of the substantive fiction of burlesque comedy is that of the world upside down, topsy-turvy. In the little world of man, the corresponding structure is that of man arsy-versy, or ass over ears: this is the figure to which the scatology in burlesque so often attaches itself. Burlesque comedy addresses itself to a dissociation of sensibility much earlier than the one proclaimed by Eliot, which occurred when a psychic line was drawn above man's waist, and he was dissociated into aspiring spirit above and bestiality below. Burlesque comedy can be seen as a triumph of repressed creatural instincts. The clearest example of this in fiction is also in Shakespeare, in *A Midsummer Night's Dream,* where, for the space of the holiday, the bottom becomes top, the bottom becomes head, the ass becomes king.

In the eighteenth century and after, the scatological impulse is either disguised, buried, or associated with anger. Sterne and Irving are reluctant to speak of and for scatology, and it gets into their works through quotation and innuendo. Thoreau and Melville are both polite writers but in their works there are essential structures corresponding to this topic. In *Walden,* for example, Thoreau continually plays off his Concord against his animal neighbors, and it is from the latter that Thoreau gets better instruction, better models of behavior. In contemporary literature there is a movement toward a greater freedom in the treatment of scatology. In J. P. Donleavy's *The Ginger Man,* for example, there is an episode in which the husband is using the toilet on the second floor when the plumbing breaks down and scatters its contents on the wife in the kitchen below. The episode brings together two aspects of life which Rabelais saw as belonging together, which, as a continuum, held man together and even defined him.

The narrative fiction of burlesque comedy tends to be one of editing or translating a great but unknown literary masterpiece — some metaphor for the creative act that separates the act of composition from the fiction composed, which creates a distance between the author and the work. A common fiction is that of the editing of an ancient, recently discovered epic, romance, or history, by a rattle-brained antiquarian who cannot keep his own life and activities separate from the fiction of the work he is editing. The double focus and the fluent interaction that results between the fiction of composition and the world of the fiction represents an extreme form of self-consciousness in literature: a term used to designate any penetration of the narrator and the narrative situation into the work. In burlesque comedy, self-consciousness is the rule; it is the result of the narrator's madness, his inability to distinguish the various worlds of fact, fancy, and learning, and his consequent occupancy of all three at the same time. So, too, the peculiar animation of the burlesque world, while it is sometimes posited as objective law, is more often the result of the narrator's mind running riot. The parabases of Aristophanes, like the digressive chapters of "A Tale of a Tub," are formal variants of the fluid and capricious manuscript play of Rabelais, Cervantes, and Sterne. The most unique feature of Old Comedy is the parabasis, a section of the play in which the fiction is arbitrarily abandoned and the chorus approaches the audience across the stage and addresses them as actors speaking for the author.

The particular madness of the burlesque narrator is, to vary Erasmus' formula, that of study gone mad. The narrator's head is stuffed with a vast amount of learning, and it is in continuous turmoil. As a result, he digresses continually from the fact at hand to catalogues of similar learned facts, generally recovering as he is about to go under in the sea of learning that he has conjured into being. Burlesque comedy is always characterized by this quality of free-floating lore, and this is as characteristic of *Moby Dick* and *Walden* as of the more overtly comic works.

The mad or foolish pedant is not merely the creator and narrator of his comic paradise; he is also its champion. One way of relating the narrative and substantive fictions of burlesque comedy would be the following: the foolish pedant is usually engaged in a running battle of the books and learned arguments with his counterpart, the grave pedant, that sour and stringy ascetic with his pale, lean face and constipated intestines. The grave pedant attempts to undermine the substance and the festive atmosphere of the comic paradise through a narrow use of the mind and to sublimate it into a *world of words,* or measurements, like the Cloud Factory in Aristophanes; the logomachia of Sterne and the battle of the folios that threatens to absorb Hafen Slawkenbergius' nose; and Irving's logocracy. The narrator opposes to this the spirit of learning on holiday, learning gone mad, in an attempt to preserve the purity of his desired vision. I have, however, included works and structures like Swift's *Battle of the Books* and the third book of *Gulliver,* where a world of words stands unopposed by any contrary vision, within the genre of burlesque comedy.

In applying a name to a third mode of the comic, one must either coin a new term or reapply a term that is conventionally either too narrow or too broad. In his *Anatomy of Satire,* Gilbert Highet points to a mode next to satire, which, unlike satire, creates gaiety out of the ludicrous, and, "although temporary, is wholesome." Sterne presumably belongs in this category, as do Lucian and Rabelais, since they leave "scarcely any aftertaste of bitterness; it makes us feel no contempt; it is a Disney dream." He calls this mode "Comedy."[11]

The term *burlesque* seems most appropriate for this category since literary historians customarily apply it, in its narrow sense, to all three of the major works considered in this study: *Gargantua* as burlesque romance, *Tristram Shandy* as a burlesque novel, and *Knickerbocker's History* as a burlesque history.[12]

There is some traditional justification for the use of the term *burlesque*. In the preface to *Joseph Andrews,* for example, Fielding places his work within the category of "the comic," of which comic romance and comedy are two types. He states that most of the parts of his work are those appropriate to the comic, except "In the Diction, I think, Burlesque itself may be sometimes admitted." Fielding goes on to say that, although he has admitted burlesque in his diction, he has "carefully excluded it from out Sentiments and Characters; for there it is never properly introduced, unless in Writings of the Burlesque kind, which this is not intended to be. Indeed, no two Species of Writing can differ more widely than the Comic and the Burlesque." Our delight in burlesque, Fielding goes on to say, "arises from the surprizing Absurdity," and, like *Caricatura* in art, "all Distortions and Exaggerations whatever are within its proper Province."[13]

Most existing critical formulations for Irving's comedy are useless in attempting to describe his early works. These are usually generalizations based on the softened humor of his middle period. When applied retrospectively, with the addition of appropriate qualifying phrases, they tell us that what we find in the earlier works is a rough or unstable form of the mode he eventually settled into.

When the American comedy is treated separately, Irving is invariably found to be writing satire, although his satire is not quite satire, or unstable satire, or inadequate satire.

He employs all the standard neoclassical satiric devices; nevertheless, the temper of his satire from the first has much of the romantic in it. He lacks consistency as to the objects of his attacks, as if uncertain what his true norm should be. His satire usually creates an immediate sympathy for its objects. His innate and incorrigible antiquarianism casts a shadow of remoteness over his satire. The subjective element is never absent. He loves eccentricity for its own sake. His satire is not really didactic in purpose.[14]

The author is arguing that Irving represents a transition in America from neoclassicism to romanticism, but he also suggests, quite fallaciously, that, because a transition means a passage from one thing to something different, the transitional writer must necessarily be confused and inconsistent in his tone. Laurence Sterne also represents a transition from neoclassicism to romanticism, and Sterne is not confused and inconsistent in his comic tone.

Opinions of *The History* clearly illustrate the simplistic critical orientation which has been fastened like a straitjacket around Irving's early works. The poles of these formulations are usually Augustan satire and native American humor, and the huge middle ground of opinion holds one

11

of two closely related views: that Irving's *History* is essentially Augustan satire, which, however, anticipates certain qualities of later American humor, or that it is essentially native humor filtered through an Augustan temperament.[15]

The earliest and strongest voices raised against the essential (as opposed to the nominal) presence of satire are those of Irving and Paulding themselves. These authors had consciously accepted a comic theory which defined the highest type of comedy as a good-natured presentation of humors which evoked innocent mirth or salutary laughter in the reader.

The term *satire* is rarely used by Irving; when it is, it refers to an involuntary outburst of anger. The term *ridiculous* sometimes occurs, but the term *risible,* the good-natured substitute for ridicule, occurs more often. The most frequent comic term is the adjective *sportive.*

The burlesque narrator plays self-consciously with a variety of incongruous editorial masks, and one of these masks is that of the satirist. "Take my word for it," Irving wrote, "a little well-applied ridicule, like Hannibal's application of vinegar to rocks, will do more with certain hard heads and obdurate hearts, than all the logic or demonstrations in Longinus or Euclid."[16] But this is simply one in a range of momentary stances which beset an author whose mind has been slightly muddled by the current of comic theory:

. . . if, shutting their eyes to the many striking proofs of good-nature displayed through the whole course of this work, there should be any persons so singularly ridiculous as to take offense at our strictures, we heartily forgive their stupidity; earnestly entreating them to desist from all manifestations of ill-humor, lest they should, peradventure, be classed under some one of the denominations of recreants we have felt it our duty to hold up to public ridicule (*Sal.,* 483).

The term *burlesque* sometimes appears in the statements of Irving's detractors: Whitman, for example, called *The History* a "shallow burlesque, full of clown's wit."[17] It was, however, used in an approving sense by some of Irving's earliest reviewers. Recently, *The History* has been called Irving's "burlesque saga," and "one of the giant burlesques of literature"; this shift represents, it seems to me, a significant change in perception. For along with it, the names of Rabelais, Sterne, and Isaac D'Israeli have begun to appear more frequently in discussions of Irving's American period, as well as statements to the effect that in *The History* the world of actuality is turned topsy-turvy.[18]

In his chapter on the Knickerbocker period of American letters, William Hedges quotes a definition from *The Knickerbocker Magazine* of a literary quality called "Rabelaisianism." According to Perry Miller, New

York, "owed it to Irving":

. . . there is the same extraordinary display of universal learning, the same minute exactness of quotation, the same extravagant spirit of fun, the same capricious and provoking love of digression, the same upsetting of admitted ideas, by which trifles are seriously descanted upon, and bolstered up with endless authorities, until they expand into gigantic proportions, while time-honored truths are shuffled by with the most whimsical contempt.[19]

CHAPTER TWO

IRVING'S SENTIMENTAL JOURNEY

To understand Washington Irving's erratic and perplexed career as the first successful American man of letters, a decade of literary paralysis between 1809 and 1819 should be considered as the crucial period in the chronology of a lifetime devoted to literature. It is significant because of its sheer length, almost ten years during which Irving was virtually incapable of writing anything except random reviews and factual sketches — because he no longer had anything to write from or anything to write about.

The measure of this decade is what it separates, and these poles suggest how great the discontinuity was. The mad pedant Diedrich Knickerbocker died (although his posthumous voice attempted to assert itself, less and less convincingly, throughout much of Irving's subsequent writings), and in his place there eventually appeared a slight and muted idler, Geoffrey Crayon, Gent., a member of the British aristocracy whom *Burke's Peerage* has failed to record. England replaced America as the place and source of creativity, an England which, by focus and evocation, preceded the tumultuous events of 1776. Most significantly, this period corresponded to a radical shift in Irving's voice and literary sensibility: after 1809, Irving repressed a vital attraction to a robust mode of comedy and became instead that safe, often tepid, essayist and storyteller whose reward was a popularity that no other important nineteenth-century American writer would enjoy.

The biographical signpost for this decade was the death of Matilda Hoffman in 1809, but the cause of Irving's paralysis was the composition of a successful and meaningful American work, his *History of New York*. It came into being too easily, yet beneath the surface ease of composition psychic depths were stirred and articulated in structures that had to be responded to even if they could not be identified.

F. Scott Fitzgerald may have overstated the case generally when he said that there were no second acts in American literature, but it describes Irving well, and something similar happens to Melville and Twain, with the writing of *Moby Dick* and *Huckleberry Finn*. These writers are spoiled by success, because their consummate work expresses too much about the inner shape of their earlier work and the personal dimensions of their commitment to experience and to literature. Irving's *History* explained why he could no longer be an American author.

The breakdown of Irving's artistic career was, of course, more radical than Melville's or Twain's. He was less imaginative and less gifted than they, and he was more isolated; according to his sights he had no meaningful body of native writing either to reject or appeal to for support. His shock of recognition in 1809 was also more traumatic because his American period was so casual and thoughtless, even compared to the early journalistic career of Mark Twain.

New York, at the turn of the nineteenth century, was an ideal milieu for a good-natured, coddled, and very lazy youngest son of a family whose level of affluence softened the problem of a career. The years from 1802 to 1809 were a time of high spirits and sociability for Washington Irving. He responded to the charms and the follies of his birthplace with gusto. While the pleasures of the day sufficed, the future could take care of itself, and he put in its charge the difficult question of profession, both the profession of law, which he had desultorily chosen as his life's work, and the profession of letters, which he carelessly practiced.

From time to time during this period, Irving wrote. He wrote as he was prompted. The writing is all spontaneous — work carelessly, almost unconsciously, written. The decision to write each successive piece was a response to some external cause, some productive accident. Irving's later reaction to the works of this period — it begins to be heard almost immediately after 1809 — was one of intense shame. This is understandable insofar as the work is juvenile, but most of it is not. The uniformity of this attitude suggests that after 1809 he could no longer respond to his early comic impulses; one could almost say that he was afraid of them.

What dried up in Washington Irving was an impulse toward burlesque comedy. The works of his American period all strive to become burlesque comedy, but, until *The History,* the elements and qualities of burlesque comedy were channelled into satirical or humorous formats. Irving was unable to assess his performance within a given work. There is usually a great discrepancy in tone and mode between the beginning of a work and its end, because he unconsciously reshaped the work in the act of writing it. But no thought was given to these disparities; there was nothing that could be called revision until after 1809. His work at the beginning of a piece depends upon satirical or humorous models which are either nominally accepted or, what is much the same, closely parodied. By the end of a given piece, the burlesque impulse dominates his writing. The one exception is *The History;* but apart from this work, there is in this period a tension between the initial choice of format and a deeper, more instinctive, choice of influence, between modes of satire and humor and the spirit of burlesque comedy.

There are several ways of seeing the inner shape of the period. It was of course a period of Irving's increasing competency as a comic writer. It was also a period of the successive narrowing between model and impulse, which finally resulted in first-rate burlesque comedy. It was a period of increasing exploration of American subject matter. It was, finally, a period which saw the slow rise to consciousness of certain attitudes toward the present and the past. It seems that the more conscious these became, the more the former tended to bitterness and abuse, the latter to sentimentality and nostalgia. It is possible to isolate passages in *The History* which are written in the key of the works of Irving's middle period. The change, nevertheless, was definite and remarkable.

It is doubtful whether Irving could have developed further as a writer of burlesque comedy under any conditions. The two American tales in *The Sketch Book* suggest, however, how the early achievement could have been absorbed into a comedy of bittersweet regret. The examples of Rabelais and Sterne indicate that burlesque comedy may not be susceptible of development; it expresses itself in one monumental gesture of spontaneous gaiety.

Washington Irving's career as a comic writer began in 1802 when he contributed a letter serial signed by "Jonathan Oldstyle" to *The Morning Chronicle,* edited by his brother Peter. In 1804, he contributed a series of comic sketches to another newspaper, *The Corrector,* also edited by Peter. This second body of writing consists almost wholly of political lampoons, direct abuse of New York Republican leaders, designed, according to the simple political formula of the time, to promote the election of Aaron Burr to governor of New York.

In both instances, Irving tries on comic voices and gestures, which he knows to be traditional. The overt imitations, quotations, and allusions with which both works are fairly sprinkled leave no doubt that Irving also knows the authors and works that he is laying under contribution.

Washington Irving's literary career opens with a very young author looking for a voice. His earlier choices are obvious and conventional: the polite satire of the *Spectator* papers and the low political hoaxes and lampoons, usually anonymous, which attended the political battles in England and America in the late eighteenth century.[1]

It is not surprising that these first works are stiff and clumsy, but the apparent cause of their failure is not a lack of talent so much as an air of indifference or boredom. Irving is simply not interested in his impersonations and consequently grinds them out in a perfunctory manner. Only toward the end of each is there a sense of engagement between the author and his literary surface. Comic energy is released to animate the surface sufficiently to hint at some future promise as a comic writer. It is not a question of Irving finding a voice of his own. He drifts, in each case, toward the insane, dazzling accents of *Tristram Shandy*.

In the concluding number of *The Corrector*, Irving complained that he was "weary of the task of punishing . . . despicable objects"; and well he might be, for the joke of nastiness soon wore thin with nothing but the fun of the thing to sustain it. When he next wrote for the public in January 1807, he could sustain his joke for "twelve-month and a day." If he was not even then a master humorist, he was no longer an indifferent apprentice; in the intervening years he had undergone his initiation as a writer.

As if in preparation for this, Washington Irving embarked on a two-year odyssey into the European past less than a month after *The Corrector* stopped publishing. Although the European tour was not yet a regular extension of an American education, Ebenezer and William Irving felt that it was desirable to bundle off their younger brother for a while; the boy was constitutionally unwell and, like Peter, had no interest in a profession or career. Rather than giving a finish to his education, it was to be almost the only education he would receive. He sailed on May 19, 1804, with pencil, notebook, and a few select texts, including Joseph Addison's "Letter from Italy" and Laurence Sterne's *A Sentimental Journey through France and Italy*.

Considering the strategic position of Irving and his work in our literature and the debt that *Salmagundi* and *The History* would owe to continental burlesque comedy, his European tour was an appropriate mythic gesture. He went, not like the narrator of *Innocents Abroad*, to do battle by virtue of his greater freedom, but, like Henry James's Christopher Newman, to loot and expropriate.

For the third time in Irving's life, a body of occasional writing came about by accident. During his eighteen-month tour of France, Italy, the Netherlands, and England, he wrote letters home and filled a number of diaries and journals with travel notes.[2] Some of this material was extracted from travel books with which he had supplied himself. He had probably been ordered by his brothers, on good mercantile principles, to keep an account of what he learned; and the letters and the journal entries culled from these sources were partly receipts for their investment, but the returns were often couched in the laggardly tones of an unenthusiastic schoolboy: "As I am now about quitting Bordeaux it is probably necessary to say something about its history, its founders &c. &c. On this subject I shall be very brief for my information is chiefly picked out of French books that I cannot read very fluently" (51).

The letters and journals were primarily the accidental exercise books of an accidental writer. The attitude toward writing expressed in connection with *The Corrector* — "dashing away" and writing to order — applies to his entire American period. He set himself no exercises, nor gave a thought to the work to come until the occasion for it arose. Now chance had given him the occasion and the obligation of rendering his experience over two years.

The content of the letters and journals need not be considered, for very little of it gets into Irving's next two works. One or two anecdotes or observations would be used again in *Salmagundi*, or *The History*, but beyond those the letters and journals are not the source of materials used in Irving's later comic writing; they are exercises in comic style and construction. Even the lowest activity involved — the culling of lore to satisfy his brothers — was a rehearsal for a future literary task. The problem of incorporating masses of erudite notes would arise in the first five chapters of *A History of New York*, and Irving's instinctive but slight tampering with his materials in the journals is in the spirit of that later effort. The letters and journals also contain exercises in the comic use of allusion, in comic diction and syntax, and in the detachment of personality from emotion and of humorous content from experience.

Irving's course through Europe was largely determined by a need for comfortable society and a consuming fascination with the liveliness of crowded theaters, balls, promenades, parks and marketplaces. There was something irresistible in the chatter of foreign voices and the drape and flow of foreign shawls and gowns.

Irving's extreme sociability was a product of the self-indulgence of his early years in New York and a propensity to melancholy in solitude. Whatever the cause, his sociability in Europe distressed William: "Good company, I find, is the grand desideratum with you; good company made you stay eleven weeks at Genoa, where you needed not to have stayed more than two, and good company drives you through all Italy in less time than was necessary for your stay at Genoa" (Ltr., 140). Washington promised William, who stood *in loco parentis*, that he would attend, while in Paris, "A course of lectures at the Garden of Plants . . . on botany, chemistry and different branches of science, by the most experienced and learned men." But to Peter he confided, "I am almost afraid to own that I have not taken a single note since I have been in this metropolis" (Ltr., 149). Three months later, in London, he wrote to Peter: "Thus you see I shift from city to city, and lay countries aside like books, after giving them a hasty perusal" (Ltr., 152).

The most noticeable feature of Irving's travel writing — particularly in the letters, because they could continue the artificiality and playfulness of his American coterie — is the frequency of unassimilated quotations. In its place, this illustrates little more than the casualness of keeping a journal or a young writer's extreme dependence on literature; but, in the development of *A History of New York,* it is an important first stage in the achievement of a rich burlesque voice.

The most prominent literary source is Laurence Sterne. Irving was already familiar with the novels of Sterne, for he had alluded to both *Tristram Shandy* and *A Sentimental Journey* in *The Corrector.* He carried *A Sentimental Journey* with him to Europe as a guide book — a temperamental guide, however, not a practical one, for their tours crossed only in Paris. George Hellman first isolated the presence of Sterne in these writings: "In no index to any biography of Irving can Sterne's name be found, but it is now quite obvious that Irving had read 'The Sentimental Journey,' and it was largely in the mood of the literary Sterne (the selfish, licentious, cold-hearted English clergyman being very different, in actual life, from the engaging man of letters) that Irving travelled through France and Italy."[3] In a letter to William of September 13, 1804, he describes the spirit in which he undertook his journey; the passage is a patchwork of Sterne on the same subject:

For my part, I endeavor to take things as they come with cheerfulness, and when I cannot get a dinner to suit my taste, I endeavor to get a taste to suit my dinner. . . . There is nothing I dread more than to be taken for one of the Smellfungi of this world. I therefore endeavor to be pleased with everything about me, and with the masters, mistresses, and servants of the inns, particularly when I perceive they have "all the dispositions in the world" to serve me; as Sterne says, "It is enough for heaven and ought to be enough for me" (Ltr., 79).[4]

References to Sterne range from passages which indicate an almost total identification with the mood of *A Sentimental Journey* to allusions and quoted fragments from Sterne's two major works. One letter, in addition to quoting Sterne, echoes the vitality of focus and the notorious spirit of genial lasciviousness introduced to English literature by Sterne in *A Sentimental Journey:* "With such fascinating objects around me, think what a warfare there is between the flesh and the spirit, and what dreadful conflicts I have with the 'divinity that stirs within me.' You can't imagine how many narrow escapes I have every day, from falling in love."[5]

The most intriguing use of Sterne occurs in an entry for September 11, 1804, in Irving's journal:

> They [the innkeeper and his wife] told me he [the chief Engineer of the Department] was a grand man and ought to be well accomodated and that he wished to have my room as he had slept in it before & liked it the best in the house. I told the woman that I should not give my room up for all the engineers in the kingdom, that I was an American gentleman of character, & not inferior to any engineer in France — that I was however very willing to share part of my room & some of my bed to the _____ lady.[6]

This anecdote, probably an imaginary reconstruction of some incipient or tangential incident, is recast from the last chapter of *A Sentimental Journey,* in which Yorick spends the night at an inn lying within hand's reach of a young lady from Piedmont. What makes the connection almost certain is that in the journal entry for that day Irving had quoted with considerable accuracy, even underlining a word that had been italicized in the original, three passages from Sterne which occur within the last forty pages of *A Sentimental Journey.*[7]

Once one considers the possibility that Irving is responding to his own experiences in the spirit and substance of Sterne, another anecdote becomes suspect. It presumably occurred in April 1805, when, making his adieus to an Italian banker, he was asked in confidence, "Dites-moi, Monsieur, êtes vous parent de General Washington?" (Ltr., 133). A similar misunderstanding occurs in *A Sentimental Journey:* "The poor Count de B_____ fell but into the same *error* — *Et, Monsieur, est il Yorick?* cried the Count. . . . *Mon Dieu!* said he, embracing me — *Vous êtes Yorick!*"[8]

In addition to the influence of Sterne, many observations in the letters and journals depend upon literature for their expression. In an apostrophe to the French, for example, Irving hits off their national character with a line from Pope's "Essay on Man" (II, 276): "Happy people — 'Pleased with a feather — tickled with a straw,' you forget your national calamities at the sight of any new amusement however trifling" (83). It often seems that Irving feels no incompatibility between announcing that a sight or feeling is particularly striking and following that announcement with nothing more than a quotation: he channels the feelings aroused when entering "a superb & solemnly constructed edifice" (138), for example, through a quotation from *The Mourning Bride* (II.iii).

At times Irving's dependence upon literature goes beyond expression; it seems as if Irving is actually observing and feeling in terms of literary blocks. His account of the decaying city of Syracuse is simply a chain of phrases from a speech in *The Tempest:* "Syracuse – has gradually crumbled into dust. . . . 'The cloud capt towers – the gorgeous palaces, the solemn temples' are no more and 'like the baseless fabric of a vision' have almost literally left 'not a wreck behind'" (192).

A slavish dependence upon recorded voices characterizes these journals, and that itself would be a trivial observation except for the fact that this tendency also informs the narrative technique of Irving's comic works and, before them, *Tristram Shandy*. The comic writers that stand behind Irving speak with the voices of earlier literature. Sterne, for example, works into his performance whole pages of quotation and paraphrase – never within quotation marks and acknowledged only by the random appearance of the author's name in some other connection in the text – from "Rabelais, Montaigne, Cervantes, Butler, Burton, Bruscambille, Bercalde de Verville, and many others." And this, says A. D. McKillop, "has been a fascinating theme for the commentators ever since Ferriar in his *Illustrations of Sterne* (1798) undertook to expose the novelist as a plagiarist."[9]

Writers of burlesque comedy are generally charged with plagiarism, and in their defense they seem only to get angry, as if their need to identify with their earlier incarnations were too deep for argument. Irving was frequently accused of plagiarism, and, although he was an inordinately reticent man, he took the trouble to answer these charges. The charge of plagiarism, moreover, is frequently incorporated into the burlesque work and treated there in a self-conscious manner. After Irving, the tendency that was once called plagiarism has continued to characterize a certain order of writing in which the act of quotation asserts itself as a meaning – in *Walden, Ulysses, Finnegans Wake,* and *The Waste Land.*

The structure of received experience is more fundamental than its expression, and the patterns of interpretation imposed by Irving upon his European experiences are equally conventional. Most of Irving's recorded experiences in the letters and journals fall into three artificial categories: the literary, the picturesque or painterly, and the theatrical.

There was certainly more truth than jest in Irving's remark to Peter that he laid "countries aside like books." There is a self-conscious tendency in the letters and the journals to force experience into the structure of literary modes: the epic, the romantic, the Gothic, or the sentimental. Irving's treatment of Europe in terms of its storied associations was in no way unique; the feelings behind it were shared by many American writers. In 1805 he first made the distinction so familiar to readers of *The Sketch Book:* "Accustomed to our *honest* American Hills & dales where *stubborn fact* presides and checks the imagination in its wandrings you may conceive with what enthusiasm I haste to those 'poetic fields' where fiction has shed its charms o'er every scene."[10]

The epic frame was a normal convention of travel books, particularly in connection with places mentioned by Homer and Virgil, and Irving thrilled, in anticipation, to these associations:

I am now hasting to scenes of romance and poetic fiction which the ancients so much delighted in, and even thought them worthy of being the favorite haunts of Gods. Sicily, you know, is one of the particular spots of mythologic events, and has been sung into eternal celebrity. Every step will seem to me to be on enchanted ground, every breeze seem to waft romance and inspiration (Ltr., 91).

Europe was also swathed for Irving in the language and images of medieval and contemporary romance. At Gersau, he pictured to himself "issuing from the gateway the gallant knight that 'never [sic] was ydrad'" [*The Faerie Queene,* I.c.i.2] (257). And at Bordeaux the intricate ascent through a church reminded him "of some of those winding & perplexed passages thro which some of the heroes of modern romance wander when prowling about the interior of an old castle" (41).

In addition to these normal associations, there are others which seem to involve an inversion of experience, as if certain scenes, neatly framed and labelled, more properly belong in literature and art than in nature. Of an old castle near Langon, for example, Irving wrote: "It had a most picturesque appearance as the first gleams of morning fell on its mouldering towers. . . . The descriptions of Mrs. Radcliffe were brought immediately to my recollection; this would have formed a fine picture for her talents to work upon" (55–56). Of the graveyard at Gersau, he wrote, "what a rich chapter would Sterne have made of such a subject";[11] of an old monk at the convent of St. Martino who denied that one got sensual pleasure from the pictures of female saints: "Sterne would have gloried in describing him" (233); and he remarked, of a fair in Nismes: "Had Hogarth ever been present at one of them he would have found an excellent situation for his *enraged musician*" (69).

Irving, who had been an inveterate theatergoer prior to his European travels, attended theatrical and other exhibitions almost continually while on tour. "Hardly a town is mentioned without reference to its theater," as Williams and Tremaine McDowell say, and notations about evenings of entertainment crowd the journals at the expense of all other items of observation. He saw the celebrated French tragedian La Fond perform at Bordeaux, went to the ballet in Marseilles, and in Paris he attended the theater almost every night. The notebook Irving kept in London, besides a few London addresses and lists of botanical terms, is filled with the records of performances seen. The editors of Irving's *History* notice that "between November 9 and his departure for America, he records disbursements for nearly thirty plays."[12]

Irving found much that was theatrical outside of the theater. He found it in the Roman Catholic services in Rome, and the town of Nismes was itself like a performance, as Irving entered it to the "Drums & trumpets of shewmen & jugglers," the "whistles and pipes of children" (69). The very ocean might still be a scene of thrilling play, he remarked: "Had those happy days continued when the Deities made themselves visible to man . . . we might have been entertained by the *raree shew* of Neptune and Amphitrite and all their gay train of Nereids and Dolphins" (144).

The letters and journals are also a record of games and masquerades in which Irving participated: blindman's buff at Lady Shaftesbury's in Genoa, an amateur production of *Zavra* in the "Dillitanti [sic] theatre" of Mme. Brignoli, a masquerade in Syracuse, the carnival in Palermo, a masked ball in Termini, and *Le Tableau* at Mme. Gabriac's in Venice.[13]

With all this in mind, we may find it more than delightful and more than accidental that there is also a thread of personal masquerade in the letters and journals comparable to the succession of roles that Yorick dances through in his journey. One of Irving's roles in Europe was of a type of practical joker known in the eighteenth century as a "quiz," and it involved the acting out of farfetched or pathetic stories with the intention of duping the hearers.

The campaign of high masquerade in Europe was performed under the tutelage of a "singular little genius," a Dr. Henry of Lancaster, Pennsylvania, with whom Irving travelled from Bordeaux to Mèze. The doctor was an inveterate prankster, and Irving found his vein of humor sympathetic:

[He] was continually passing himself off on the Peasants for a variety of characters. Sometimes a Swede, sometimes a Turk, now a German & now a Dutchman. With a Farmer he was a Wine merchant, with a Shoemaker, a Tanner, with an officer he was a former captain in the American army. With others a professor in one of the German colleges & with others a secretary of the American minister who was travelling with dispatches to Commodore Preble in the Mediteranean (65).

Together the two Americans quizzed a group of seamstresses in Tonneins. Irving, they were told, was a young English prisoner awaiting death by firing squad or perhaps the guillotine (57). In another town Irving was a "young Mameluke of distinction, travelling incog.," and Henry was his interpreter (Ltr., 72). Henry bade Irving good-bye by telling him "when next we met I might probably find him a conjurer or high German doctor" (65).

The masquerade continued sporadically for the rest of the tour, but without Henry it descended to youthful teasing. In Syracuse, Irving went to a masquerade at the theater "dressed . . . in the character of an old physician," and spoke to the officers "in broken English mingling Italian and French with it, so that they thought I was a Sicilian" (195). Another episode occurred at Iornina, in Switzerland, where Irving and another companion, Joseph Carrington Cabell, "engaged with the landlady and her two daughters in the kind of conversation that would have delighted Laurence Sterne, Cabell teasing the mother about some swelling she had, and Irving, as he mounted his horse . . . calling back to the daughter, Marianne, who hoped that he would some day return: 'Alors je vous touverais mariée avec une grande goiture.'"[14]

Irving's letters and travel notes resonate at their best with a charming insincerity. Others have commented on this body of writing and drawn their own conclusions about the glimpse of a young Irving that it affords, but if there is a natural personality to be sensed in these pages, it is one that must be inferred from the succession of poses that actually fills each page. His personality, when it expresses itself, is a thoroughly artificial one, and its formation involves the translation both of expression and of experience into artificial forms.

Furthermore, the attitudes expressed in the letters and journals involve no moral and, I suspect, no real emotional commitment to experience; poses alternate with an easy fluency. Irving was under no obligation to take sides in the Napoleonic conflict, but, as Hellman says, he "arrived in France at a time so big with historical happenings," and "his comments on world affairs are . . . few and far between."[15] One of these political comments follows:

[I] inquired for the Church of Cordeliers that contained the tomb of the belle Laura. Judge my surprise, my disappointment, and my indignation, when I was told that the church, tomb, and all, were utterly demolished in the time of the Revolution. Never did the Revolution, its authors, and its consequences, receive a more hearty and sincere execration than at that moment (Ltr., 76).

Irving was also able to develop the knack of so selecting or so diverting observations that they fell within well-established burlesque contexts. The following examples all reappear in *Salmagundi* as elaborate burlesque motifs; they involve the elements of absurd genealogy, the play with origins going back to Noah, the comic associations of the priests of Fo, and burlesque physiology: "neither will I dwell upon the etymology of the name [Bordeaux] . . . both [two possible originals] you will perceive have equal claims to credibility, and both are almost as direct & unadulterated derivations as that of *Noah* from *Fohi"* (52); "The quarrels among the lower class in this country [France] are generally settled by the *tongue* and he that has the most volubility & strongest lungs carries the day" (96).

In "The Letters of Jonathan Oldstyle" and *The Corrector* Irving was never consistently able to achieve the detachment of the accomplished comic writer. This was due not to any moral or emotional commitment to the subject matter, but to his technical inability to sustain the particular mock tone he was projecting. The letters and journals provide many examples of a growing ability. The example that follows also indicates an ability to handle the rhythmic rises and falls of burlesque writing:

I cannot pretend to give you any detail of my adventures or account of the wonders of the vasty deep. . . . I shall only say that the sea has much degenerated since ancient days, for then one could hardly sail out of sight of land without meeting Neptune and his suite in full gallop, whereas I have passed across the wide Atlantic without seeing even a mermaid. Tis true we were one blustring night visited by Caster and Pollux at our mast head, and once or twice had a shoal of Grampuses in company, but as to the former, their godships have of late fallen very much into disrepute and as to the latter they are at best but *queer fish* of which we had enough on board already.[16]

The comic detachment from experience of the narrators of *Salmagundi* and *The History* first appears in the letters and journals. Irving cultivates this detachment in the records of his own skirmishes with danger or frustration. A crew of pirates, by whom Irving was abducted en route to Sicily, "would have shamed Falstaff's ragged regiment in their habiliments" (Ltr., 96). A shift of the wind during his ascent of Mount Vesuvius fills Irving's lungs with poisonous vapors: "Fortunately for us," he adds, "the wind shifted, as I sincerely believe that in a little time we should have shared the fate of Pliny & died the martyrs of imprudent curiosity" (241). The account of his twenty-one-day quarantine in Messina is as lively an example of detached play as the letters and journals contain:

Twould make your heart bleed my dear Andrew ["Quoz"] to hear how your venerable friend has been besmoked and befunked by villainous fumigations. I have been rammd into the hold with my unfortunate shipmates & stenched & stifled with a chaffing dish of burning dings & doctor stuff — I have been overhauld by Physicians, bullied by health officers and have even run a narrow chance of being shot & killed by a guard armed with a bayonet on the end of a broom stick.[17]

The letters written after Irving's return to New York until the time of the publication of the first number of *Salmagundi* on January 24, 1807, reflect a heightening of the artificial traits found in the European letters and journals. They contain, in addition, a more self-conscious use of pose, as if the detached personality of the journals had now become equally attached to various types of humorous characters.

In the examples that follow, Irving assumes the comic poses of the splenetic humorist and the physical butt. The differentiation is not conscious here. Irving had worked with both types in his previous literary productions, but he seems also to have adopted them for his personal use. They were to be among the major character types in *Salmagundi:*

The *pensive Petronius* [Peter] and myself smoked a sentimental or rather philosophic segar together yesterday afternoon, over the office fire. You would have been amused to have witnessed our melancholy confab. We had met together with the express determination to be miserable and to indulge in all the luxury of spleen. . . . We were lolling in crazy arm-chairs on each side of a grate, in which smoked a few handsfull of vile seacoal. Our deadly foe, the east wind, howled without, and our still more inveterate enemies, the ponderous fathers of the law, frowned upon us from their shelves in all the awful majesty of Folio grandeur (*PMI,* I, 169).

I have just received your [Gouverneur Kemble's] most welcome lines of the 24th, and being immediately sent out on an errand, I amused myself with reading them along the street; the consequence was, I stumbled twice into the gutter, overset an old market-woman, and plumped head and shoulders into the voluminous bosom of a fat negro wench, who was sweating and smoking in all the rankness of summer heat. I was stopped two or three times by acquaintances to know what I was laughing so heartily at; and, by the time I had finished the letter, I had completely forgotten the errand I was sent on; so I had to return, make an awkward apology to *boss*, and look like a nincompoop (*PMI,* I, 170-71).

In our literature, the American returning to his European past is either unable to register or interpret his experiences there or secures himself ahead of time against the terror of what he might experience — like James's poor Mr. Babcock with his Mrs. Jameson and his Graham bread and hominy, and the late George Apley. From a personal point of view, Irving's return in 1804-5 was childishly indulgent, anticipating the sentimental solipsism that would characterize his later return as a suppliant. From the point of view of the two American works he would write soon after his return, he had been informed by experience; he had thoughtlessly absorbed an artificial voice, attitude, and fiction of experience that was truly European. Such an education would have been impossible in America. And yet the fruits of this education were to become essentially American, in defiance of the public qualities of that new nation. Out of this experience, Irving was able to generate the first deeply charged American narrative voice in the national literature, and it was the voice of a childish neurotic and solipsist.

CHAPTER THREE

SHANDEAN AESTHETICS

The opening note of *Salmagundi* must have been a delightful surprise to its readers, for never before in America had there sounded a comic voice so free and so deft in its whimsical meanderings:

As everybody knows, or ought to know, what a SALMAGUNDI is, we shall spare ourselves the trouble of an explanation; besides, we despise trouble as we do everything low and mean, and hold the man who would incur it unnecessarily as an object worthy of our highest pity and contempt. Neither will we puzzle our heads to give an account of ourselves, for two reasons; first, because it is nobody's business; secondly, because if it were, we do not hold ourselves bound to attend to anybody's business but our own; and *even* that we take the liberty of neglecting when it suits our inclination. To these we might add a third, that very few men *can* give a tolerable account of themselves, let them try ever so hard; but this reason, we candidly avow, would not hold good with ourselves (27).[1]

Almost a century of repetition and variation had gone into the formation of this smooth pebble. Writers of serials traditionally devoted their opening essays to an explanation of their choice of title and role. There was also a later apologetic tradition in which reasons were given why the author would not concern himself with these details. Facetious serials of the eighteenth century mocked now one, now the other, opening strategy. Although the paragraph just quoted may be placed at one extreme of this set of relationships, the act of placement is too heavy for it. The paragraph contains little more than self-conscious verbal play. Its purpose is in its movement, in the ratio of sayings to unsayings, in the absurd pounce upon the word "trouble," and the flirtation with the reader in the enumeration of "reasons."

Salmagundi is mainly an eclectic portfolio of satire, humor, and burlesque comedy. It was begun as a parody of a contemporary American periodical, *The Town*. This intention was almost immediately abandoned, and its authors began, in a haphazard way, to play with well-known comic elements in the periodical serial tradition, political satire, and the English humorous novel. Apart from the initial parody, there was no plan for the magazine; whatever worked would be extended; whatever palled would be dropped and replaced by some new comic format.

The moments of comic achievement in *Salmagundi* almost always betray a more or less successful absorption of the attitudes of comic possibility toward language and the world which Irving and Paulding had found in the works of Laurence Sterne. The work could not consistently sustain this either, but when it did, burlesque comedy redeemed potential wastes of parody, irony, and satire. Even the best items in *Salmagundi*, however, reveal that disparity between format and treatment which had so far been the characteristic failing of Irving's comedy. In a few instances, toward the end of the work, a new, more flexible voice and form evolved, a comic form appropriate to the instinctively chosen model.

The comic aesthetic of *Salmagundi*, which is continually on display in the work, is an aesthetic of *whimsy*, and it was derived from the work of Sterne. But Sterne was himself working with an extreme variation of a theory of amiable humor which, during the eighteenth century, was modifying and replacing the system of Augustan satire with its emphasis on wit as the comic faculty, its aggressive theory of laughter, and its choice of vicious subject matter for comedy. "By the middle of the nineteenth century, it was a commonplace that the best comic works present amiable originals . . . whose little peculiarities are not satirically instructive, but objects of delight and love."[2] Sterne was at the center of the controversy between satire and humor, and, until the appearance of Mr. Pickwick, Tristram's Uncle Toby was the brightest name in the galaxy of amiable humorists.[3]

The first thing we are told about the Cockloft family, the tribe that populates *Salmagundi*, is that they are a family fruitful in *humorists* (61). Will Wizard, one of the three editors of the periodical, announces his character sketch of Launcelot Langstaff to be the portrait of a genuine humorist (189), and almost all of the admirable characters in the periodical are referred to at one time or another as humorists, although the claim is not often realized. The term is overused and misused, and its frequency testifies more to the attraction that the term has for Irving than to his grasp of it as a principle of character.

As the concept of humor drifted toward its late eighteenth-century significations, the term became more or less identical with the concept of the *oddity* or unique behavioral peculiarity, and the humorist came more and more to anticipate the Romantic ideal of the *original* or the *genius*.[4] The extravagances of the humorist were not the exaggerated traits of a foolish or ridiculous social class, but the identifying traits of the true individual: "every member of the [Cockloft] household is a humorist *sui generis*" (151), just as "the SHANDY FAMILY were of an original character throughout."[5] And Uncle Toby tells Tristram that he shall "neither think nor act like any other man's child" (*TS*, 6). In *Humphry Clinker*, Jerry Melford writes to his Oxford colleague: "I have got into a family of originals, whom I may one day attempt to describe for your amusement," and he describes his uncle, Matthew Bramble, as an "odd kind of humorist."[6]

In introducing Pindar Cockloft to the readers of *Salmagundi,* Langstaff boasts that Pindar has oddities "sufficient to eke out a hundred tolerable originals" (65). It is the highest recommendation that he can confer upon a colleague, and it is also the quality of the highest subject matter for comedy:

As I delight in everything novel and eccentric, and would at any time give an old coat for a new idea, I am particularly attentive to the manners and conversation of strangers, and scarcely ever a traveller enters this city whose appearance promises anything original, but by some means or another I form an acquaintance with him (71).

In both *Tristram Shandy* and *Salmagundi,* the basis of comedy is not so much humor in its centrality, as in one of its extreme forms, repeatedly identified in *Salmagundi* as *whimsy*.[7] The concept of whimsy can be considered a burlesque humor, since the humor involved is capriciousness, or humorousness itself. The *whimsical humorist* is an eccentric — a madman, really — whose bias is a tendency to respond to the impulse of the moment.

The development of comic character in the direction of uniqueness obviously has as its serious counterpart the emphasis on originality and diversity as aesthetic criteria in Romantic literature.[8] But it is even closer to the moral doctrine of individuality which followed so consistently from the primacy of the will in nineteenth-century philosophy. I would suggest that the character of the whimsical humorist is in many ways the comic equivalent of the hero, the extreme form of the individual, whose greatness is also an ability to drift with the currents of the moment. Emerson, for example, uses the language of comedy to characterize his notion of heroic individuality: in "Self-Reliance" — "I would write on the lintels of the door-post, *Whim";* and in his journal for 1832 — "He that rides his hobby gently must always give way to him that rides his hobby hard." And the cosmic giant of "Song of Myself" occupies his fiction best when he is seen as a variant of the whimsical humorist.[9]

The history of *whimsy* as a moral term corresponds to that of humor; originally associated with madness in a serious social context, it was slowly invested with amiable overtones in the eighteenth century.[10] Although the term *whimsy* rarely appears in the major serial periodicals of the early eighteenth century, when it does, it has either the older sense of a condemnable foible, or else it is washed clean of all specific meaning whatsoever; it is in a state of transition and slowly being prepared for future positive and valuable significations. In a letter to Mr. Spectator, a correspondent discussed "that sort of Men who are called *Whims* and *Humourists."* Beginning with the commonplace that humor is a typically English trait, responsible for the richness of English comedy, the writer depicted a practical joker and enjoined the editor to agree with him "that as there is no Moral in these Jests they ought to be discouraged, and looked upon rather as Pieces of Unluckiness, than Wit" (*Spec.,* No. 371). In *Spectator* No. 497, whim is equated with a wanton disposition, and in *Spectator* No. 632, it is a source of childishness in great artists: "with due Respect to these great Names [this tendency] . . . may be looked upon as something whimsical."

Sir Roger de Coverley may be a "good humour-ist," in the sense that his benevolence is related to other so-called odd character traits, but he is not whimsical, although the word is proudly applied to him. Sir Roger is whimsical in a carefully neutralized sense; he is "whimsical in a corrupt Age" (*Spec.,* No. 6): "His Singularities proceed from his good Sense, and are Contradictions to the Manners of the World" (*Spec.,* No. 2).[11]

On the other hand "these little Singularities . . . [are] Foils that . . . set off . . . his good Qualities" (*Spec.,* No. 112); his whimsicality, in other words, is either evidence of his virtue, or morally meaningless illumination for that virtue. His character is basically that of the exemplary man, the "good old Knight" (*Spec.,* No. 106). More often there is "Nothing . . . that indicates anything but an excellent Gentleman, not even a Foible" (*Spec.,* No. 106).

The aesthetic of whimsy or the principle of impulse is the comic basis of *Salmagundi,* as well as the source of all moral, intellectual, and artistic excellence within that comic world. Irving took the substance and direction of this comic theory from *Tristram Shandy,* and, although he often applied it hastily to motives and behavior which simply would not sustain such an interpretation, its presence in *Salmagundi* is unequivocal. Irving's debt begins on his title page; for his subtitle "The Whimwhams and

Opinions of Launcelot Langstaff, Esq. and Others" is an adaptation of Sterne's subtitle. The word *whim-wham* was not Sterne's coinage,[12] but Irving probably took this, his central term, from *Tristram Shandy,* where it occurs in the opening pages of the book, just prior to the chapter on "HOBBY-HORSES" (*TS,* 13).

With the exception of Anthony Evergreen, all the central characters in *Salmagundi,* as in *Tristram Shandy,* are identified as whimsical humorists. Wizard, speaking of Langstaff's love life, says that he "could no more live without being in love with somebody or other than he could without whimwhams" (193). And here is Langstaff on Wizard:

Such is the turn of my knowing associate; only let him get fairly in the track of any odd out-of-the-way whimwham, and away he goes, whip and cut, until he either runs down his game, or runs himself out of breath; I never in my life met with a man who rode his hobby-horse more intolerably hard than Wizard (416).

The Shandy family and its associates are similarly whimsical. Tristram assures his readers that his father is "a gentleman altogether as odd and whimsical in fifty other opinions [as in that of Christian names]":

In truth, there was not a stage in the life of man, from the very first act of his begetting, – down to the lean and slipper'd pantaloon in his second childishness, but he had some favourite notion to himself, springing out of it, as sceptical, and as far out of the high-way of thinking, as these two which have been explained (*TS,* 145).

Uncle Toby too has a "most whimsical character" (72), as does Yorick, the local parson:

. . . instead of that cold phlegm and exact regularity of sense and humours, you would have look'd for, in one so extracted [from the Danish]; – he was, on the contrary, as mercurial and sublimated a composition, – as heteroclite in all his declensions; - with as much life and whim, and *gaité de coeur* about him, as the kindliest climate could have engendered and put together (*TS,* 25).[13]

Character description in *Salmagundi* reaffirms this view of character as valuable in proportion to the richness and variety of its humors and whims. Ultimately, character becomes simply the manifestation of whimsy. The character sketch of Langstaff, for example, introduces him as a man "fertile in whimwhams," and the essay is a series of anecdotes and examples intended to illustrate Langstaff's quirks and pointed edges. This, however, is a "mere sketch of Langstaff's multifarious character; his innumerable whimwhams will be exhibited by himself, in the course of this work, in all their strange varieties; and the machinery of his mind, more intricate than the most subtile piece of clockwork, be fully explained" (187-96). The practice and the rationale for this equivalence between subject matter and technique had already been given in *Tristram Shandy*. As Tristram finds it necessary finally to draw his Uncle Toby's character, he explains five erroneous methods used by previous writers to present character and rejects them in favor of drawing his uncle's character "from his HOBBY-HORSE":

A man and his HOBBY-HORSE, tho' I cannot say that they act and re-act exactly after the same manner in which the soul and body do upon each other: Yet doubtless there is a communication between them of some kind. . . . By long journies and much friction, it so happens that the body of the rider is at length fill'd as full of HOBBY-HORSICAL matter as it can hold; — so that if you are able to give but a clear description of the nature of the one, you may form a pretty exact notion of the genius and character of the other (*TS,* 77).

Whim is the essential principle of character for Irving and Sterne, but it is also the principle of artistic creativity. Both Langstaff and Tristram know what their readers expect of them in the way of literary productions, yet both are helpless against their whimsical fancies: whenever "my whim is opposed to my opinion," Langstaff writes in an early editorial essay, "my opinion generally surrenders at discretion" (50). Apologizing to the reader for the number of chapters needed to get his father and Toby to the bottom of the stairs, Tristram pleads a similar necessity: ". . . let that be as it will, Sir, I can no more help it than my destiny: — A sudden impulse comes across me — drop the curtain, *Shandy* — I drop it — Strike a line here across the paper, *Tristram* — I strike it — and hey for a new chapter!" (*TS,* 281). *Salmagundi* is ended as a result of Langstaff's whim.

The psychology of whim need not concern us at any length here. As readers of Sterne know, it was based on the associational theory of knowledge which he derived from John Locke's *Essay Concerning Human Understanding.* Irving was aware of this theory, even knew it by name, but he did not understand it, as his attempts to imitate it indicate. The selections from the travel diary of Jeremy Cockloft were meant to be written associationally; Irving and Paulding must have felt that short diary notations accommodated themselves easily to such connections. The associations arrived at, however, belong more to the jestbook strain in *Salmagundi* than to the comic practice of Sterne:

. . . students can't dance — always set off with the wrong foot foremost —

Duport's opinion on that subject — Sir Christopher Hatton the first man who ever turned out his toes in dancing — favorite with Queen Bess on that account — Sir Walter Raleigh — good story about his smoking — his descent into New Spain — El Dorado — Candide — Dr. Pangloss — Miss Cunegunde[14] — earthquake at Lisbon — Baron of Thundertentronck — Jesuits — Monks — Cardinal Woolsey — Pope Joan — Tom Jefferson — Tom Paine, and Tom the ____ whew! (104-5)

The physiology of humor and whimsy, however, did inform *Salmagundi*. Whim and laughter were felt to be closely associated impulses, and, next to *whim* and its synonyms, there is no term so valuable as *laughter* in the comic vocabularies of Sterne and Irving. Both whim and laughter were produced by the activity of the animal spirits, which, according to Galenic theory, were subtle vapors engendered by the brain and distributed through the nervous system to the various parts of the body. In comic theory of the late eighteenth century, an excess of animal spirits came to be specifically associated with a "robust type of good humor," the kind possessed by Rabelais, for example, who "had tremendous animal spirits and was 'the king of good fellows.'"[15] It was a sudden welling of the animal spirits in all humorists of a volatile or mercurial stamp that provided the energy for whimsy, and this in turn produced a complementary burst of spontaneous laughter in the reader. The animal spirits "transfused from father to son" are the cause of "nine parts in ten" of Tristram's whimsy; for, as he tells the reader in the first paragraph, "when they are once set a-going, whether right or wrong, 'tis not a halfpenny matter, — away they go cluttering like hey-go-mad" (*TS*, 4-5).

During the moral recovery of the eighteenth century, honest laughter became an index of good nature and unrestrained laughter, of sympathy. For the Hobbesian notion of laughter as the sudden realization of superiority, there was substituted a sense of laughter in intimate relationship with childish innocence, psychological and bodily health, and innate wisdom. The relationship between wisdom and laughter was crystallized in the figure of Democritus, the laughing philosopher. It was a common touchstone for writers of burlesque comedy and had been familiarized in England by Robert Burton as the narrator of *The Anatomy of Melancholy*.[16] It was one of the many editorial masks worn by the authors of *Salmagundi*:

While we continue to go on, we will go on merrily: if we moralize, it shall be but seldom; and, on all occasions, we shall be more solicitous to make our readers laugh than cry; for we are laughing philosophers, and clearly of opinion that wisdom, true wisdom, is a plump, jolly dame, who sits in her arm-chair, [and] laughs right merrily at the farce of life (33).

Like whimsy, laughter ultimately became identified with what is valuable in human nature;

. . . not that we wish to restrict our readers in the article of laughing, which we consider as one of the dearest prerogatives of man, and the distinguishing characteristic which raises him above all other animals (329);

and it becomes one of the mysteries of burlesque comedy which so often anticipate, given a change of mode, the mysteries of Romanticism: "Everything in this world," says Walter Shandy, "is big with jest" (*TS*, 393).

Within the network of comic ideas that provide the aesthetics of *Salmagundi,* the operation of the animal spirits as whim and laughter lay in close physiological balance with the ill effects of *spleen.*[17] The relationship between laughter and the spleen was twofold; while good-natured laughter was a defense against the spleen, melancholia, and lunacy, ill-natured laughter was just the opposite; it proceeded most often from an overflowing of the spleen [18] — it was a symptom of illness. Jestbooks advertised this effect of laughter in their titles, and both *Tristram Shandy* and *Salmagundi* are in this tradition of therapeutic literature.

The health of the reader is one of Tristram's literary motives as he announces in the dedication of the first volume:"Every time a man smiles, — but much more so, when he laughs . . . it adds something to this Fragment of Life" (*TS,* 3). This provides a kind of halfway test for the efficiency of the work:

And now that you have just got to the end of these four volumes — the thing I have to *ask* is, how you feel your heads? my own akes dismally — as for your healths,I know they are much better — True *Shandeism,* think what you will against it, opens the heart and lungs, and . . . makes the wheel of life run long and chearfully round.

Was I left like Sancho Pança, to chuse my kingdom, it should not be a maritime — or a kingdom of blacks to make a penny of — no, it should be a kingdom of hearty laughing subjects . . . as WISE as they were MERRY; and then should I be the happiest monarch, and they the happiest people under heaven (*TS,* 337-78).

Whimsy is a specific against the spleen. Tristram, denying that his work has any real object of attack, says, "If 'tis wrote against any thing, — 'tis wrote, an' please your worships, against the spleen" (*TS,* 301). Langstaff recommends Wizard's explosive laugh "as a sovereign remedy for the spleen," and adds: "if any of our readers are troubled with that villainous complaint — which can hardly be, if they make good use of our works — I advise them earnestly to get introduced to him forthwith" (418).[19]

The physiology of spleen became an aesthetic formula for Sterne and his followers. It provided a structural metaphor for a work of art which could now be completely free of all didactic overtones. The narrator or fictitious author could be a character potentially splenetic and melancholic who wrote to ease himself and return to health. The value of the production would be in the spirit and manner of writing, particularly as these were whimsical or hobby-horsical; insofar, that is, as they addressed themselves directly to the disease of spleen. *Tristram Shandy* is Tristram Shandy's hobby-horse (*TS,* 584), and it is in this sense, rather than the superficial, ill-natured sense, that one must read the repeated announcement in *Salmagundi* that the authors "write for no other earthly purpose but to please ourselves" (32) or to ease themselves — and in so doing ease others.

On the other hand, satire, sarcasm, ridicule, railing — the entire range of corrective comedy — are merely ill effects of the spleen, the product of a diseased nature. Matthew Bramble becomes satirical when he is splenetic. His nephew writes of him: "Respectable as he is, upon the whole, I can't help being sometimes diverted by his little distresses; which provoke him to let fly the shafts of his satire, keen and penetrating as the arrows of Teucer."[20] Satire is the involuntary act of a man temporarily but deeply disturbed in mind and body; but such bursts of ill nature also ease the spleen,[21] and the sufferer returns to a balanced condition. In the introduction to the essay "On Greatness," one of the few pieces of invective and abuse in *Salmagundi,* Wizard claims that it was written "by my friend Langstaff, in one of the paroxysms of his splenetic complaint; and, for aught I know, may have been effectual in restoring him to good humor. A mental discharge of the kind has a remarkable tendency toward sweetening the temper — and Launcelot is, at this moment, one of the best-natured men in existence" (375–76).

While satire is still ill-natured in substance, it is no longer ill-natured in its intention, insofar as it is an involuntary gesture of the painfully sensitive and volatile humorist:

With the kindest heart under heaven, and the most benevolent disposition under heaven toward every being around him . . . [Yorick] has been continually betrayed . . . into satirical sallies which have been treasured up by the invidious, and retailed out with the bitter sneer of malevolence (*TS,* 191).

One source of the spleen was the sudden changes of the English weather. Since Irving had adopted an English theory of comedy, he tended to adopt its principles, and the weather is a prominent context for the spleen and its associated activities in *Salmagundi:*

I do not recollect, in the whole course of my life, to have seen the month of March indulge in such untoward capers, caprices, and coquetries, as it has done this year; I might have forgiven these vagaries, had they not completely knocked up my friend Langstaff; whose feelings are ever at the mercy of a weathercock, whose spirits sink and rise with the mercury of a barometer, and to whom an east wind is as obnoxious as a Sicilian *sirocco*. He was tempted some time since, by the fineness of the weather, to . . . take his morning stroll; but before he had half finished his peregrination, he was utterly discomfited, and driven home by a tremendous squall of wind, hail, rain, and snow, or, as he testily termed it, "a most villainous congregation of vapors" (187-88).

Pindar Cockloft, who is one of the most good-natured men imaginable, will "when the wind is easterly . . . become a little splenetic" (63-64). The weather is a cause of spleen and a host of associated distempers — gall, gout, "hyp," vapors, blue devils, and the "blues"; and the whimsical humorist is keenly susceptible to the effects of dismal or capricious weather.

The characterization of the humorist as a periodically infirm creature is significant on several levels of British comic theory. For one thing, it is a complement to the whimsical humorist's volatile or mercurial nature — his psychological type is that of the manic-depressive. Secondly, it is an emblem of his essentially good nature; his extreme sensitivity to external conditions like the weather is the equivalent of his often painful sensibility to the condition of others. This connection is quite explicit in Sterne's *A Sentimental Journey:*

Except the interest, said I, which men of a certain turn of mind take . . . in their own sensations — I'm persuaded, to a man who feels for others as well as for himself, every rainy night, disguise it as you will, must cast a damp upon your spirits.[22]

It is best exemplified, however, in the character of Matthew Bramble, whose "peevishness arises partly from bodily pain, and partly from a natural excess of mental sensibility." Bramble "affects misanthropy, in order to conceal the sensibility of a heart, which is tender, even to a degree of weakness"; "he is as tender as a man without a skin; who cannot bear the slightest touch without flinching."[23] Although the transition to Romanticism is not a subject of investigation in this book, I have, from time to time, ventured to suggest how closely elements of the comic aesthetic being described here parallel the aesthetic principles of Romanticism — the impulse is hard to resist. Matthew Bramble's extreme sensitivity of mind and body is clearly an early version of that imaginative pain that characterizes Keats's poet.

Extreme sensitivity to the weather was also a characteristic of the comic misanthrope. Matthew Bramble "affects misanthropy," and well he should, since the greatest triumph of the moral recovery of eighteenth-century comedy was the redemption of the misanthrope or curmudgeon of earlier comedy. The prominent examples of the *amiable misanthrope* are Bramble and Goldsmith's "man in black." But Walter Shandy also possesses characteristics belonging to this comic type, and so do many of the characters in *Salmagundi.*[24]

To attempt to explain this translation would take us deep into a tangle of eighteenth-century moral attitudes. Nevertheless, comic aesthetics effectively transformed vice into virtue and almost totally subverted an earlier version of the moral nature of man.

From a superficial point of view the change merely involved the incorporation of ill nature, as an unfortunate mental or physical moment, into a larger, good-natured, sense of humanity. Given such a moral basis for human nature, character could be nominally ugly or vicious: in winter, for example, Pindar Cockloft "is one of the most crusty old bachelors under heaven," and

When Langstaff invests himself with the spleen, and gives audience to the blue devils from his elbow-chair, I would not advise any of his friends to come within gun-shot of his citadel . . . for he is then as crusty and crabbed as that famous coiner of false money, Diogenes himself (188).

Ill nature even wells up in Christopher Cockloft, the most benevolent humorist in the serial:

I remember a few months ago the old gentleman came home in quite a squall; kicked poor Caesar the mastiff, out of his way, as he came through the hall, threw his hat on the table with most violent emphasis, and pulling out his box, took three huge pinches of snuff, and threw a fourth into the cat's eyes as he sat purring his astonishment at the fireside (158).

The amiable misanthrope was a reincarnation of that glum and sour personality who appeared most often in satirical literature as *the old bachelor.* The following sketch from the *New York Magazine* of 1797 is fairly representative of the earlier comic value of the type:

An old bachelor is a being which Nature never intended. He is a creature formed out of all those odds and ends which remained after the great work of creation was concluded: when all the finer materials were used for the composition of such as were intended for social enjoyments, what remained was hardly enough to rub round the sides of the crusty mould in which he was formed. But that he should not be insupportable to himself and the world, Dame Nature gave him self-love in abundance, a kind of illigitimate [sic] understanding, and a judgement so mixed with acidity, that it turns sour every thing within comprehension. Thus formed and thus qualified, a bachelor breathes without the possibility of enjoying happiness himself, or essentially contributing to the happiness of others. . . . Such is a bachelor! Such the existance of a bachelor! But what becomes of him after this life, God only knows![25]

In 1788, Philip Freneau had devoted an essay to "the most selfish of all human beings, the OLD BACHELOR": ". . . We may safely conclude and determine, that an Old Bachelor is, in most instances, wholly destitute of that benevolence, generosity, sympathy, and expansion of soul, which we may constantly observe in married men."[26] But in *Salmagundi*, which in less than a decade had updated comic aesthetics in America by a half century, there is no higher benevolence than that of the old bachelor:

I hold that next to a fine lady, the *ne plus ultra,* an old bachelor to be the next most charming being upon earth; inasmuch as by living in "single blessedness," he of course does just as he pleases; and if he has any genius, must acquire a plentiful stock of whims, and oddities, and whalebone habits; without which I esteem a man to be a mere beef without mustard— good for nothing at all but to run on errands for ladies, take boxes at the theatre, and act the part of a screen at tea-parties, or a walking-stick in the streets (156).

The bachelor in *Salmagundi* has the same comic weight as the whimsical humorist. They are often identified: "The Cockloft family . . . has been fruitful in old bachelors and humorists" (61); Langstaff's character is "fertile in whimwhams and bachelorisms" (189). This old bachelor is a good-natured creation; his ill-natured traits are still a part of his personality, but they are rendered amiable through the same structure of biases and impulses that expresses his richness and value as humors and whims.[27]

The *antipathy* is the misanthropic equivalent of the whim, and it ranges from an instinctive response, like an allergy, to a mental bias. There can be no doubt of its harmlessness, for it is a synonym for whim-wham (210, 274-75). All of the Cocklofts have an absurd antipathy to the French (63, 210); Langstaff, like Diedrich Knickerbocker, has antipathies to cold weather, noise, and brooms, "a household implement which he abominates above all others" (195, 477); Uncle John Cockloft had an antipathy to doing things in a hurry (274); and the Salmagundians in concert have "an invincible antipathy to making apologies" (208).

II

Whimsy is also the principle of the authorial and editorial structure of *Salmagundi*. As a structural principle, it carries the element of *self-consciousness* in writing to a capricious and unstable extreme. The self-conscious narrator is an expanded and more or less fully dramatized writer, or narrator, who appears to take his chosen task so seriously that he is continually calling the reader's attention to what he is doing. The whimsical narrator goes far beyond this: he is so mad and muddleheaded that he cannot distinguish between his life and his narrative, and *Tristram Shandy* and *Salmagundi* are respectively subtitled "Life and Opinions" and "Whim-whams and Opinions." Whimsical self-consciousness dominates Irving's *History,* where Diedrich Knickerbocker's total confusion between the past of history and the present of the writing of history and his sighing for the past keep the book in a state of burlesque animation.

The self-conscious element in literature is *a second fiction:* a fiction of the internal and external history of the creation of *the primary fiction,* the story, narrative, etc. It may also include any thought, feeling, or event in the narrator's life that occurs to him in the act of writing.

In *Tristram Shandy* and *The History of New York,* the self-conscious fiction tends, in differing degrees, to obscure or replace the primary fiction. But, at one pole of narrative fiction, the two cannot be distinguished: for example, in Part I, chapter 22, of *Don Quixote,* Quixote, discovering that one of the galley slaves, Gines de Pasamonte, is also an author, asks him what the title of his book is:

> *"The Life of Gines de Pasamonte,"* replied that hero.
> "Is it finished?" asked Don Quixote.
> "How can it be finished," replied the other, "if my life isn't? What is written begins with my birth and goes down to the point when I was sent to the galleys last time."

Tristram also bewails the fact that his great work can never be finished; and, at the end of chapter 32 of *Moby Dick*, Ishmael prays: "God keep me from ever completing anything. This whole book is but a draught – nay, but the draught of a draught. Oh, Time, Strength, Cash, and Patience."

In self-conscious literature the "realities" of artistic composition and book production are expanded and dramatized into what I have called a second fiction, and this is set in active tension with the primary fiction or narrative illusion. Any element of the second fiction may be enhanced: the character of the author; his preparation and qualifications; the manner in which he writes best, or the interferences he encounters while writing; the act of revision; the various aspects of book publication; the relationship between the author and the reader; and the reception of the work by critics and the anxiety or anger that that intolerable situation provokes:

Here then I cut my bark adrift, and launch it forth to float upon the waters. And oh! ye mighty Whales, ye Grampuses and Sharks of criticism, who delight in shipwrecking unfortunate adventurers upon the sea of letters, have mercy upon this my crazy vessel. Ye may toss it about in your sport; or spout your dirty waters upon it in showers; but do not, for the sake of the unlucky mariner within — do not stave it with your tails and send it to the bottom. And you, oh ye great little fish! ye tadpoles, ye sprats, ye minnows, ye chubbs, ye grubs, ye barnacles, and all you small fry of literature, be cautious how you insult my new launched vessel, or swim within my view; lest in a moment of mingled sportiveness and scorn, I sweep you up in a scoop net, and roast half a hundred of you for my breakfast (*HNY*, 13-14).

The best example of self-consciousness in fiction, which fuses play and an almost serious narrative complexity, is again to be found in *Don Quixote*. In Part I, chapter 8, the Don is engaged in desperate contest with a Basque. Don Quixote "rushed at the wary Basque with sword aloft, determined to cleave him to the waist; and the Basque watched, with his sword also raised and well guarded . . . while all the by-standers trembled in terrified suspense":

But the unfortunate thing is that the author of this history left the battle in suspense at this critical point, with the excuse that he could find no more records of Don Quixote's exploits.

The "second author of this work" refused to believe "that such a curious history could have been consigned to oblivion," and never despaired of finding the missing document. One day, this author-editor, Cide Hamet Benengali, was in the Alcana at Toledo, "when a lad came to sell some parchments and old papers to a silk merchant." The editor, prompted by his love of reading, which extends to old torn papers lying in the streets, takes up one of the parchment books. Unfortunately it is in Arabic, which he cannot read, and he seeks out an interpreter, who, reading a little way into the book, begins to laugh at a marginal note which claimed that "'Dulcinea del Toboso, so often mentioned in this history, was the best hand at salting pork of any woman in all La Mancha.'" The narrative is then allowed to continue: "The trenchant sword of the two valorous and furious combatants, brandished aloft, seemed to threaten the heavens . . ."

Self-consciousness in literature always tends to produce a burlesque effect, and this effect is the greater the more play the second fiction is allowed in the work. When Swift, for example, is most self-conscious, as in the digressive chapters of "A Tale of a Tub," he is least satirical. There is a good case to be made for the contention that self-consciousness and satire are incompatible modes.

There is a difference, however, between the formal self-consciousness of Aristophanes, Cervantes, Swift, and Fielding, and the fluid self-consciousness of Sterne and Irving. The full-blown whimsical humorist lacks all discrimination; in his madness, he welcomes and heaps together all possibilities of self-conscious play that can be used to enrich through vital confusion the work of art.

The self-conscious plot alternates between extreme egotism and pathos: A wise author has written a book of deep truth and erudition; the book may be well received or not but it will be misunderstood in either case; and the author both defies and challenges reader and critic, and also resigns himself, which is often difficult, to the hope that posterity will bestow upon him his due measure of fame.

It was made clear to the reader of *Salmagundi* at the beginning of the work that the act of writing conferred both dignity and prerogative upon a writer, and that these writers, "reverend, grave, and potent essayists," would rule over their work with a supreme authority, ever considering it "as beneath persons of our dignity to account for our movements and caprices" (482):

Like all true and able editors, we consider ourselves infallible; and therefore, with the customary diffidence of our brethren of the quill, we shall take the liberty of interfering in all matters either of a public or a private nature . . . we know "by the pricking of our thumbs," that every opinion which we may advance in either of those . . . will be correct, [and] we are determined, though it may be questioned, contradicted, or even contraverted, yet it shall never be revoked" (28).

This smugness is the editorial characteristic that controls much of the self-conscious play in *Salmagundi;* it corresponds to the triumphant and vindictive sense of modernity which obsesses the narrator of "A Tale of a Tub." All self-conscious narrators tend to be profound egotists, and this is another instance of the parallelism between the whimsical humorist of the eighteenth century and the Romantic genius or hero. Eighteenth-century burlesque comedy was preparing the world view that the next century would embrace with such seriousness.

The self-conscious writer lays claim to an almost prophetic (or solipsistic) authority:

Let it not be supposed, however, that we think ourselves a whit the wiser or better since we have finished our volume than we were before; on the contrary, we seriously assure our readers that we were fully possessed of all the wisdom and morality it contains at the moment we commenced writing. (323–24).

Tristram's wisdom and excellence are not matters of assurance, but of necessity: "You see as plain as can be, that I write as a man of erudition; — that even my similes, my allusions, my illustrations, my metaphors, are erudite . . . else what would become of me? Why, Sir, I should be undone" (*TS*, 85).[28]

No matter how slight, ordinary, or facetious a passage of writing may appear to be, there are sure to be deep meanings lurking beneath the surface. The narrator of "A Tale of a Tub" complains of a "superficial Vein among many Readers of the present Age, who will by no means be persuaded to inspect beyond the Surface and the Rind of Things."[29] Tristram punishes a reader "to rebuke a vicious taste which has crept into thousands besides herself, — of reading straight forwards, more in quest of the adventures, than of the deep erudition and knowledge which a book of this cast, if read over as it should be, would infallibly impart with them" (*TS*, 56). And Langstaff pities those readers who are "too stupid to look beyond the mere surface of our invaluable writings; and often pass over the knowing allusions, and poignant meaning, that is slyly couching beneath" (378).

The most common motif in self-conscious narrative involves the animation of the implicit relationship between author and reader, which interrupts, possibly determines, and, in Sterne, often alters the course of the narrative. When a narrator is also whimsical, this play becomes dizzying. The announced motives for such play were usually contempt or frustration at the reader's inability to understand the work:

— How could you, Madam, be so inattentive in reading the last chapter? I told you in it, *That my mother was not a papist.* — Papist! You told me no such thing, Sir. Madam, I beg leave to repeat it over again, That I told you as plain, at least, as words, by direct inference, could tell you such a thing. — Then, Sir, I must have miss'd a page. — No, Madam, — you have not miss'd a word. — Then I was asleep, Sir. — My pride, Madam, cannot allow you that refuge. — Then I declare, I know nothing at all about the matter. — That, Madam, is the very fault I lay to your charge; and as a punishment for it, I do insist upon it, that you immediately turn back, that is, as soon as you get to the next full stop, and read the whole chapter over again (*TS*, 56);

and the contradictory delight in trifling with the reader's commitment:

What these perplexities of my uncle *Toby* were, — 'tis impossible for you to guess; — if you could, — I should blush; not as a relation, — not as a man, — nor even as a woman, — but I should blush as an author; inasmuch as I set no small store by myself upon this very account, that my reader has never yet been able to guess at any thing. And in this, Sir, I am of so nice and singular a humour, that if I thought you was able to form the least judgment or probable conjecture to yourself, of what was to come in the next page, — I would tear it out of my book (*TS*, 80);

Langstaff informs the readers of *Salmagundi* in the opening number of the work: "We *care* not what the public think of us, and we suspect, before we reach the tenth number, they will not *know* what to think of us" (32).

Capriciousness was often carried to the extreme of a welcome entertainment of contradictions, sometimes in different parts of the work, and sometimes in the same passage:

The result of . . . [our] midnight studies is now offered to the public; and little as we care for the opinion of this exceedingly stupid world, we shall take care, as far as lies in our careless natures, to fulfill the promises made in this introduction; if we do not, we shall have so many examples to justify us, that we feel little solicitude on that account (40).

I told the reader, this time two years, that my uncle *Toby* was not eloquent; and in the very same page gave an instance to the contrary: — I repeat the observation, and a fact which contradicts it again (*TS*, 458).[30]

The largest contention of this book, which will be sketched in the last chapter, is that there is a significant relationship between Irving's *History* and certain major American works of the later nineteenth century, works whose sprawling, often inchoate, form seems to defy generic classification. To a far greater extent than the work of the English romantics, works like *Walden,* "Song of Myself," *Moby Dick,* and even *Nature* preserve elements of burlesque comedy, Shandean aesthetics, and self-conscious play in a marked and recognizable form. The effect may not always be comic but it usually is.

A capriciousness that extends to a delight in contradictions can be found in all these works. It may be announced as a ponderous truth, in Emerson's journals, for example:

Suppose you should contradict yourself, what then? With consistency a great soul has simply nothing to do.

Or it may be thrown out gaily, as in the well-known "yawp" of Whitman, which Harriet Monroe, over the protest of Ezra Pound, chose as a motto for twentieth-century poetry:

Do I contradict myself? / Very well, then, I contradict myself.

CHAPTER FOUR

POLITE SATIRE

When the first issue of *Salmagundi* appeared on January 24, 1807, its New York readers were intended to recognize it as a parody of a local periodical, *The Town,* which had put out its first number on January 1. It is very likely that the "plan of a work . . . mainly characterized by a spirit of fun," which Irving is said to have proposed to Paulding, was quite simply a projected parody of that and other local periodicals.[1] Fortunately, *The Town* died after its fifth number on January 12. The few remaining items based on *The Town* were quietly used up in the third number of *Salmagundi,* and it was then transformed into a general burlesque periodical which continued to amuse New Yorkers for a year. So quickly had the parody been vitiated that its reference to *The Town* was unknown or overlooked by the time of *Salmagundi*'s first reviews.

The three following chapters describe the place of *Salmagundi* within certain comic traditions: polite satire, political satire, and domestic humor. The studies are primarily intended to measure, through the variations and distortions imposed upon relatively settled comic traditions, the emergence of Washington Irving as a writer of burlesque comedy.

Irving was comfortable working within the tradition of domestic humor as he had found it in the Roger de Coverley sections of *The Spectator,* Goldsmith's *Vicar of Wakefield,* and his reading in Fielding and Smollett; as a result, he was able to write in this vein with some warmth and imagination. Since humor and burlesque comedy share a common border, there is no sense of him straining at transformation as he did with satire. Eventually he would settle into this comic mode. When he later acknowledged the great comic influence on his work, it would be Oliver

Goldsmith and not Laurence Sterne, whose hold upon him he had by then thrown off.

Irving had already experimented with polite and political satire in his two first works and the results were limp and colorless comedy. The satiric vision had no real meaning for him, and the singleness of vision and the irony it demanded were not his gifts. The notion of norms in man or society might have compelled a formal assent from him; but it could never have penetrated his simple and frivolous nature. Yet, if Irving was childish, so are all writers of burlesque comedy. And the American writer generally, with his new eyes and unstable vision of reality, tends to rehearse a perpetual adolescence in his works. Irving's attempt to animate satire (which, if successful, destroys it as satire), corresponds in small to the concept of morality as metamorphosis which one finds in Emerson, Thoreau, and Whitman.

Nonetheless, he persisted in devoting whole stretches of both *Salmagundi* and *The History* to satire, and, having done so, he attempted to inform them with the attitudes, concepts, and techniques of burlesque comedy. This chapter and the one following, then, deal with comic failure.

As stated in Chapter 2, the development of *Salmagundi,* rough and unconscious as it was, parallels that of Irving's early period as a whole — from forms traditionally associated with satire to forms more appropriate to humor and burlesque comedy. Irving's next work would finally break with the tradition of polite satire, within which he had hidden his real talents for so long. Like his own Rip Van Winkle, he also had timidly evaded the responsibility of creating a comic vision appropriate to America. The comic freedom achieved in *The History* was, however, short-lived; it must have been too heady and threatening a triumph. By the time of *The Sketch Book* he was back at work within the traces of a modified serial essay tradition.

Like most serials, *Salmagundi* was initially presented as the production of a group of associates. The conventional group was either a club or a family, and *Salmagundi* used both as a means of wider comic mobility. On the model of *The Spectator,* there was an editor-in-chief, Launcelot Langstaff, and two associates, Anthony Evergreen and Will Wizard. Langstaff had a general range of subject matter, while Evergreen and Wizard were restricted to areas in which they were expert, either through character or experience: in this case, fashions and the theater. This conventional appropriation of subject matter was announced in the first number and more or less adhered to during the run of the periodical. Early in the run, the Cockloft family was introduced, and they provided the subject matter for a domestic serial. Langstaff turned out to be a relative of theirs, and Evergreen and Wizard old friends of the family.

Even though the attitude of the Salmagundians toward satire is unstable and ambivalent, to say the least, the work still affords us all the evidence we need to settle the question of Irving's wide knowledge and specific use of the English serial tradition, particularly *The Spectator*. Writing almost a century later, Irving plays with *The Spectator* more than he imitates it: yet *Salmagundi* testifies, as do almost all of the earlier American serials, to the tremendous vogue of Addison and Steele in America.

In the late 1930's and in the 1940's, an effort was made to reclaim Irving as a "native" American writer by relating *Salmagundi* to a clumsy and lifeless American serial tradition. But these arguments are unjustifiable; there is no evidence for the connection, and, even if there were, it would be a hollow victory for the forces of Americanism, considering how slavishly conventional these early serials were themselves. On the contrary, allusions in *Salmagundi* are to *The Spectator* primarily, and it can be shown that Irving reread that serial while writing his own and modelled several sections of his work upon it.

It seems necessary to face this issue: for this reason the first part of the chapter deals with the stunted growth of Anthony Evergreen. Since he came out of *The Spectator* as narrowly as he did, the authors found themselves unable to use him as a comic mask. The Tripolitan Mustapha was also deeply embedded in eighteenth-century satire, but he, unfortunately, was used extensively in the sections of political satire. The remainder of the chapter consists of a series of test runs which should give a satisfactory measure of the relationship of *Salmagundi* to the tradition of polite satire and also indicate the kind of burlesque transformations that occur spontaneously throughout *Salmagundi* whenever a particular fit of model and comic energy arises. The topics I have chosen to treat are tea and scandal, French humors, and modern dancing.

Each of the editors of *Salmagundi* was initially an amalgam of various conventional traits of editors and characters in the serial tradition. Langstaff and Wizard, however, soon assumed considerable shape as humorists and self-conscious narrators. No attempt was made to transform Evergreen; instead, his humorous potentialities were transferred, in the sixth number, to Christopher Cockloft, the American "squire." Evergreen is the most conventional and purely functional of the major characters in *Salmagundi*. Articles over his name appear mostly in the first five and last two numbers, the places where the serial format and its traditional elements were most conscientiously adhered to.

Evergreen is the only editor specifically associated with the Spectator club; he tells us that he holds "poor Will Honeycomb's" memory in special consideration (44). The parallels between the introduction of

Honeycomb (*Spec.*, No. 2) and of Evergreen indicate that Irving went back to *The Spectator* for this character. If one compares the two introductions, the order of topics will be seen to be exactly the same, with the exception of a few topics which Irving did not choose to adapt to Evergreen. Honeycomb is acquainted "with the Gallantries and Pleasures of the Age," and Evergreen is experienced "in the routine of balls, tea-parties, and assemblies"; Honeycomb "should be in the Decline of his Life, but . . . Time has made but very little Impression, . . . by Wrinkles on his Forehead," and Evergreen "is a kind of patriarch in the fashionable world, and has seen generation after generation pass away . . . while he remains unchangeably the same"; Honeycomb "can inform you from which of the *French* King's Wenches our Wives and Daughters had this Manner of curling their Hair, that Way of placing their Hoods," and Evergreen can "recount the amours and courtships of the fathers, mothers, uncles, and aunts . . . of all the belles of the present day" (34); Honeycomb will tell you that "when the Duke of *Monmouth* danced at Court such a Woman was then smitten, another was taken with him at the Head of his Troops in the *Park,*" and Evergreen "can relate a thousand pleasant stories about Kissing-bridge" (34-5) and other sites of the New York of his youth. Although Evergreen's name is emblematic of his essential youthfulness, it also has traditional connections. Anthony Evergreen was the name of a correspondent in *The Guardian*,[2] whose letter was on the subject of the scantiness of female apparel, one of the themes in the polite satire of *Salmagundi.*

Because of his close ties with the tradition of polite satire, Evergreen is almost wholly unrealized as an editorial personage and as a character. His failure is an indication of how close *Salmagundi* came to being a "Letters of Jonathan Oldstyle" on a more extensive scale; for Evergreen can be considered a remnant of that earlier work, and further proof that nominal adherence to the serial essay tradition was incompatible with burlesque intentions.

As an editorial personage, Evergreen is the traditional censor of manners. This had originally been a moral role, and the language in which it is announced in *Salmagundi* still carries the original moral overtones, even though the tone is mocking: the editors announced as one of their intentions a desire to "correct the town" (28), and Evergreen stated that he intended to "keep more than a Cerberus watch over the guardian rules of female delicacy and decorum" (33).

Evergreen was intially presented as a bachelor, an elderly man — "a patriarch in the fashionable world" — and he looks with disfavor on the degeneracy of contemporary manners; however, none of these traits are present as narrative characteristics in his essays. Evergreen was also presented as a "chronicle" of amours in New York state, but not once does he provide the reader with examples from his well-stocked memory; the theme of old New York, when it does appear later in *Salmagundi*, is assigned to Langstaff. Evergreen's traits were transferred to Christopher Cockloft because he could be developed as a humorist. Of all the characters in *Salmagundi* who were nominally fashioned by reference to the serial tradition, Evergreen was the only one who could not be so developed. No attempt was made to transform him into a more sympathetic comic type, as Will Wizard was transformed from a theatrical commentator into an antiquarian.

Subsequent references to Evergreen and the functions he performs also indicate his awkward position in *Salmagundi*. He appears seldom, although, as fashion editor, he should have had the lion's share of authorship according to the original design. His designated subject matter is avoided, or it appears in random paragraphs in essays by the other editors. The extent of the dilemma posed by Evergreen — on the one hand, empty of humorous traits, and, on the other hand, committed to certain areas of subject matter — can be seen in the essay, "Style at Ballston" (387-95). The follies of behavior at this spa were in Evergreen's domain, and, in fact, it was he who had visited the place the summer before. Editorial twists are used, however, to take the essay away from Evergreen. Evergreen privately narrated the amusing incidents of his stay at the springs to Langstaff and Wizard "in several late conversations at Cockloft Hall" (387), and as a result Wizard writes an essay containing a summary of what he had heard from Evergreen.

The address of the periodical essayist to the female portion of his audience was implicit in the title of *The Tatler*, and Mr. Spectator announced that he would "dedicate a considerable Share of these my Speculations to . . . [the ladies'] Service" (No. 4), alleging that he had "Nothing more at Heart than the Honour and Improvement of the fair Sex" (No. 265). There is little difference between these announcements of policy in regard to feminine folly and its repetition in *Salmagundi* almost a century later: "The valuable Part of the Sex will easily pardon me, if from Time to Time I laugh at those little Vanities and Follies which appear in the Behavior of some of them, and which are more proper for Ridicule than a serious Censure" (*Spec.*, No. 92); and "the ladies of New York are the fairest . . . beings that walk. . . they only want to be cured of certain whims, eccentricities, and unseemly conceits, by our superintending cares, to render them absolutely perfect" (33-34). In another sense, there is a vast difference between the two statements: the faults of the New York ladies, if they be faults, have no moral reference, and the policy statement was not meant to be taken seriously — it was a quotation from the tradition. Apart from two Mustapha letters, that portion of *Salmagundi* devoted to women does not aim at moral reformation at all. Although certain conventional feminine foibles — scantiness of apparel, corseting, etc. — are raised as subjects, their treatment is grotesque and exaggerated, in the burlesque rather than in the rational or moral sphere. Nonetheless, the reference to traditional attitudes is maintained throughout, and the Salmagundians make the same claims of having successfully reformed the female sex that had appeared in the serials.

In his earlier works, Irving's indifference to the moral heritage of traditional literary forms was a negative quality, merely a hollowness on the page. In *Salmagundi,* Irving gradually learned how to use humor and burlesque comedy to compensate for his inability to believe in the efficacy of normative satire. In this instance he used both to some extent. His attitude toward women, he admits, will not be critical or satirical, but will be "governed by . . . that liberal toleration which actuates every man of fashion" (33). Irving soon substituted for this colorless attitude one of greater literary weight borrowed from the amiable eccentric of humorous literature:

I feel at this moment a chivalric spark of gallantry playing around my heart, and one of those dulcet emotions of cordiality, which an old bachelor will sometimes entertain toward the divine sex. . . . I would not, however, have our fair readers imagine that we wish to flatter ourselves into their good graces, devoutly as we adore them! — and what true cavalier does not? — and heartily as we desire to flourish in the mild sunshine of their smiles. . . . (449)

As the editors moved closer to humorous and burlesque roles, the conventional type of the polite satirist was identified with the pedant of burlesque comedy. Those who actually dare to criticize feminine eccentricity are "governed by that carping spirit with which narrow-minded bookworm cynics squint at the little extravagances of the ton" (33); they are "the grumbling smellfungi of this world, who cultivate taste among books, cobwebs, and spiders, [and who] rail at the extravagance of the age" (45). "Extravagance" is almost a celebratory term.

The dedication of a good part of the major serials to feminine interests and the ridicule of women was represented in the serials by the structural and fictional antithesis between *tea-table* and *coffee-house.* Mr. Spectator had announced that he should "take it for the greatest Glory of my Work, if among reasonable Women this Paper may furnish *Tea-Table Talk*" (No. 4), and a correspondent reported that the paper was so much a part of her "Tea-Equipage," that her servant would not serve her tea until *The*

Spectator had arrived.

Another correspondent recommended that the ladies be persuaded to substitute needlework for the hours lost at the tea-table; it would be of "advantage to themselves, and their posterity. . . [and] to the Reputation of many of their good neighbours" (No. 632). This theme is introduced in the opening number of *Salmagundi,* when Evergreen "remembers the time when ladies paid tea-visits, at three in the afternoon, and returned before dark to see that the house was shut up and the servants on duty" (35). New York is referred to as a "most sarcastic, satirical, and tea-drinking city" (209); while "the Philadelphians conduct [their tea parties] . . . with as much gravity and decorum as they would a funeral, and very properly too, for they celebrate the obsequies of many a departed reputation."[3] The appearance of the mysterious little man in black satisfies the anxiety of the neighborhood gossips for a "new tea-table topic" (429). And in a mock survey of the moral effect of *Salmagundi* on the people of New York, Langstaff ruefully admits that "they are just as much abandoned to dancing and tea-drinking" (325) as ever. The normal practice in *Salmagundi* was to run a comic topic through a series of variations and then make it the basis of an entire piece. In the second-to-last issue, Irving contributed the only extended example of mock-heroic in the serial, a poem entitled "Tea."

The topics of *tea* and *slander* had been treated with mock inflation before, for example, in Edward Young's *Love of Fame* (1725–28):

> Tea! how I tremble at thy fatal stream!
> As Lethe, dreadful to the love of fame.
> What devastations on thy banks are seen!
> What shades of mighty names which once have been!
> An hecatomb of characters supplies
> Thy painted altars' daily sacrifice . . .
> But this inhuman triumph shall decline,
> And thy revolting naiads call for wine;
> Spirits no longer shall serve under thee;
> But reign in thy own cup, exploded tea![4]

The mock-heroic political satire, *Criticisms on the Rolliad*, had included a Homeric catalogue of teas:

> What tongue can tell the various kinds of tea?
> Of blacks and Greens, of Hyson and Bohea!
> With Singlo, Congou, Pekoe, and Souchong;
> Cowslip the fragrant, Gun-powder the strong:
> And more, all heathenish alike in name,
> Of humbler some, and some of nobler fame.[5]

In America the theme was generally attached to the Boston Tea Party. In the ninth number of "The Echo," a facetious political serial by the Connecticut Wits, the following example occurs which retains a touch of the mock-epic treatment and makes the traditional polite effects of tea the cause of political degeneration:

> I who most nobly burst the *chests* of *tea,*
> And with those wicked cargoes strew'd the sea
> Till Boston's dock might rival in its store
> Kaingsi's plains, or Canton's busy shore —
> That drink Circean, whose bewitching charm,
> Had tied our tongue, unnerv'd our sinewy arm,
> Chill'd the warm breast, transform'd the man to ape,
> And given to Freedom Slavery's brutish shape.[6]

Irving's poem resembles these earlier passages, although it is considerably more sprightly. It was based, however, on Pope's "Rape of the Lock." Tea and scandal are only briefly treated there, but the references occur in the descent to the Cave of Spleen, the section of that poem which approaches burlesque comedy. Irving had probably reread Pope for his piece. Several of his lines seem to be frank imitations of the juxtapositions in Pope's poem:

> And serve up a friend as they serve up a toast; . . .
> Our young ladies nibble a good name in play
> As for pastime they nibble a biscuit away (473).

Irving's poem is actually less mock-epic than mock Gothic. In it, the ladies around the tea-table are like a meeting of witches in "solemn divan," and the gossip and slander are "an *auto da fe,* / At the gloomy cabals — the dark orgies of tea!" Both of the "epic" similes in the poem are taken from the witches' scenes in Macbeth, e.g.:

> While with shrugs and surmises, the toothless old dame,
> As she mumbles a crust she will mumble a name;
> And as the fell sisters astonished the Scot,
> In predicting of Banquo's descendants the lot,
> Making shadows of kings, amid flashes of light
> To appear in array and to frown in his sight,
> So they conjure up spectres all hideous in hue,
> Which, as shades of their neighbors, are passed in review.

Also, the metamorphosis in Irving's poem is more extravagant than Pope's women who become teapots: "the sweet tempered dames are converted by tea into . . . Gunaikophagi [women-eaters] ."[7]

In a previous reference to the theme of tea, Irving had hit upon an appropriate burlesque figure which was not without precedent in late eighteenth-century comic writing; it involved a pun on gunpowder tea:

As to scandal, Will Wizard informs me that, by a rough computation, since the last cargo of gunpowder-tea from Canton, no less than eighteen characters have been blown up, besides a number of others that have been wofully shattered (325).

This figure is expanded in the poem, and, in one of the mock apostrophes, the effect of tea is likened to the poisonous breath of the bohan upas of Java, which figures, along with its dissertator, Erasmus Darwin, in the virtuoso burlesques of the late eighteenth century. Among other burlesque touches there is a catalogue of the types of tea and the specific variety of slander that each produces. Finally, the original version of the poem contained a mock footnote by Will Wizard complaining that, despite his objections, Pindar had an antiquarian affection for the learned word "Gunaiko-phagi," "swore it was the finest point in his whole poem," and "absolutely refused to give it up."

The humors of the European nations and the types that were constructed around them are treated more frequently in humor and burlesque comedy than in satire; the differences among nations will not sustain a moral interpretation for long, but there is a great satisfaction at being free to play with the differences in themselves. In satire, national humors are identified as folly in order to justify the laughter: the Dutch lubber eats too much; the gay Frenchman talks, laughs, dances too much, thinks too little, and corrupts the fashions of the English and the palates of the Americans. But generally the moral translation does not allow the satirist to do more than construct an analogy or some other figure around the alien; when he treats him at length some eccentric levity arises to obscure the satirical point.

One common figure in eighteenth-century comic writing was the national catalogue, originally, perhaps, a play on conventional passages in Herodotus and Tacitus; the following figure from *Salmagundi* is quite representative of the type:

The infidel nations have each a separate chacteristic trait, by which they may be distinguished from each other; the Spaniards, for instance, may be said to sleep upon every affair of importance; the Italians to fiddle upon everything; the French to dance upon everything; the Germans to smoke upon everything; and the windy subjects of American logocracy to talk upon everything (180).[8]

National humor in *Salmagundi* quickly reduced itself to comic play with certain humors associated with the French. The prominence of French humor in *Salmagundi* has almost nothing to do with Irving's Federalism; in fact it is remarkable, given the incidence of *antidemocratic comedy* and French burlesque in the serial, that they are combined as seldom as they are.

The ridicule of the French was a prominent motif in *The Tatler* and *The Spectator* for historical reasons, and this element of polite satire found a corresponding historical dimension in Irving's New York, which abounded in artisans and professionals who had emigrated from revolutionary France. In the first number, Langstaff denies that the authors of the serial are "those outlandish geniuses who swarm in New York, who live by their wits, or rather by the little wit of their neighbors, and who spoil the genuine honest American tastes of their daughters with French slops and fricaseed sentiment" (32).

French humor in *Salmagundi,* however, is free of moral weight, and the authors frequently disclaimed any satirical intentions: "When, therefore, I choose to hunt a Monsieur *for my own particular amusement,* I beg it may not be asserted that I intend him as a representative of his countrymen at large" (73; italics mine).

Disclaimers such as this should also be seen as a half-serious attempt by Irving to explain the kind of comic commitment he was making. He was rejecting any essential affiliation with satire and locating himself in the wider freedom of humor and burlesque comedy, and the disclaimers hint at this in a confused way. Irving continued the explanation given above, to try and explain exactly what he was doing when he "hunted a Monsieur." "I mean," he wrote, "only to tune up those little thingimys . . . who have no national trait about them but their language, and who hop about our town in swarms, like little toads after a shower." Without some theory of representation to link the character with a class there can be no satire; yet these characters have no "national trait about them but their language"; in fact, they "represent nobody but themselves." Furthermore, consider the vitiation of the satirical that has taken place, when the felt equivalent of the traditional verbs, to censure, to ridicule, etc., is the verb "to tune up," and the object of attack is clothed in the attributes of a hoptoad and referred to as a "thingimy."

The technique of incorporating French humors into the serial is the basic structural device for all comic elements in *Salmagundi.* The "bit" will be casually brought into a number of early essays, briefly, unexpectedly often, and in combination with a different comic context or motif each time; a pattern of repetition and accumulation. One essay will eventually be devoted to many of the comic possibilities generated thus far. After that, it returns to the earlier sporadic incorporation, this time in combination with other elements that have also received their climactic treatment. This is merely the technical model; there are many deviations. The effect is somewhat like the running gag of farce, but, more importantly, it anticipates the floating present of the burlesque narrator's sensibility where an observation or idea that enters the mad mind of the whimsical humorist never fixes itself in a temporal past, but continues to make circling reappearances in his mind, often upsetting whatever direct train of thought the narrator is desperately trying to focus upon at the moment. This technique, which might be called "comic overlap or weaving," also dominates much modern comedy, particularly works by Samuel Beckett, Günter Grass, William Burroughs, and John Hawkes, where it is also associated with madness.

The comic Frenchman was incorporated into *Salmagundi* in three ways, and these correspond well enough to the three modes of the comic differentiated in this study. A standard theme of traditional polite satire, France as the source of fashions, is used early in *Salmagundi,* and then drops out of the serial.[9] The whimsical antipathy to the French on the part of the Cockloft family receives a humorous fictional treatment in the middle numbers. And the theme of dancing, one of the most pervasive associations to the French in comedy, is treated throughout the serial in a burlesque mode. Its climax in the "chapter" from "The Chronicles of Gotham" is the best example of burlesque comedy to be found in *Salmagundi.*

It is often possible in the polite sections of *Salmagundi* to assign specific sources in the serial tradition. In the case of the French and fashions, the treatment in *Salmagundi* is explicitly based on certain fancies and structures in *Spectator* No. 265. Irving was not trying to hide his source:

Poor Will Honeycomb . . . would have been puzzled to point out the humors of a lady by her prevailing colors; for the "rival queens" of fashion, Mrs. Toole and Madame Bouchard, appeared to have exhausted their wonderful inventions in the different dispostion, variation, and combination of tints and shades (44).

Mrs. Toole and Madame Bouchard were New York milliners; and the variety of tints and shades may have been a fact of the New York assemblies of 1807, although even that seems to be a little colored by the fiction of the *Spectator* essay: Will Honeycomb at the back of a box at the opera, notices "a little Cluster of Women sitting together in the prettiest coloured Hoods," and looks "with as much Pleasure upon this little party-coloured Assembly, as upon a Bed of Tulips."

The essay "Fashions" combines the theme of fashions with the structure of the burlesque combat. The rivalry between Mrs. Toole and Madame Bouchard is treated as a significant battle in the conflict between England and France. The Spectator was also responsible for this aspect of Irving's piece; for in No. 265 he had made the following fanciful application of the rage for colored hoods: "I am informed that this Fashion spreads daily, insomuch that the Whig and Tory Ladies begin already to hang out different Colours, and to shew their Principles in their Head-dress." Madam Bouchard "has burst like a second Bonaparte upon the fashion world," and Mrs. Toole "seems determined to dispute her ground bravely for the honor of old England," "The ladies have begun to arrange themselves under the banner of one or other of these heroines of the needle, and everything portends open war" (81). As in the poem "Tea," Irving uses *Macbeth* as a supplementary frame: "Madame Bouchard marches gallantly to the field flourishing a flaming red robe for a standard, 'flouting the skies;' and Mrs. Toole, nowise dismayed, sallies out under cover of a forest or artificial flowers, like Malcolm's host."

A more extended use of Frenchmen in *Salmagundi* is as comic grotesques who exist in whimsical altercation with the Cocklofts. A number of Cocklofts are made to share this whimsical antipathy, each one blowing it up to more absurd proportions. Pindar Cockloft is the first to be given this "genuine Cockloft prejudice": he had once been brought to death's door by a *ragout;* "he groaned at Ça Ira, and the Marseilles Hymn . . . set his teeth chattering." The "introduction of French cockades on the hats of our citizens absolutely" threw him into a fever and led to his abrupt retirement from town (63). Christopher Cockloft has "a profound contempt for Frenchmen" as well, and he "firmly believes that they eat nothing but frogs and soup-maigre" (153–54):

The Cocklofts . . . carry their absurd antipathy to the French so far, that they will not suffer à clove of garlic in the house; and my good old friend Christopher was once on the point of abandoning his paternal country mansion of Cockloft Hall, merely because a colony of frogs had settled in a neighbouring swamp (210).

Christopher's aversion is not political; it is said to stem from his great-aunt Pamela's "having . . . run away with a . . . French count, who turned out to be the son of a generation of barbers."

The "tale" of Charity Cockloft weaves together the variations on French humors which had been sporadically thrown out in the preceding numbers of the serial. Charity is an old maid, and her dominant humor is prying into her neighbors' affairs. When the boardinghouse of Frenchmen directly opposite proves unfathomable, Charity becomes "the seventh Cockloft that has died of a whimwham!"

The trait most often associated with the French in British comic writing was caprice, which obviously lends itself to burlesque treatment. In *The Spectator,* they are a "Fantastick" and a "ludicrous" nation (Nos. 15, 45); in *Salmagundi,* they are still "a nation of right merry fellows, possessing the true secret of being happy; which is nothing more than thinking of nothing, talking about anything, and laughing at everything" (73). In the evolution of the comic Frenchman this humor soon travelled to his feet; France had in fact been the home of most of the modern dances of the eighteenth century, and the French dancing master was a familiar type in British farce. Irving carried this humor to an exteme; the absurd possibilities of animating his grotesque hoptoad in various combinations with modern dancing strongly appealed to him.

The figure of the dancing Frenchman received an extensive rehearsal before its culminating treatment in "The Chronicles of Gotham." The dancing Frenchman appeared in the first assembly piece, and, in the second, Wizard triumphs over the French by running over half a score of them as he "thundered down the dance like a coach and six" (139). The dancing Frenchman had a place in all of the national catalogues in *Salmagundi:* in a catalogue of theatrical modes of dying, for example, the French prefer to die throwing a "somerset" (166), and in a catalogue of *great men,* the French candidate is "he who can most dextrously flourish his heels above his head" (377). "The Chronicles of Gotham" is a burlesque allegory which presents the conquest of New York by the dancing Frenchman.

The theme of modern dancing, whether attached to, or apart from, the Frenchman, was also a theme of polite satire. The comedy of the cotillion was the gymnastic extravagance expended upon it,[10] that of the waltz was its lasciviousness. The treatment of the cotillion in *Salmagundi* affords the best example of the techniques to which elements of polite satire were submitted which, when successful, translated these elements into the world of burlesque comedy.

The source of Irving's initial treatment of the cotillion was a passage on modern dancing in *The Town.* Both the original and Irving's versions follow:

[The dancers had] not a quarter room enough to do their latest Parisian steps in, without grievously annoying their lovely partners, by the extended leg and foot, before, and behind, and sideways, and round about, as the case happened to be; for it is to be observed, that this new style of dancing consists in having the legs any where but under the body, and this is thought to be very fine; though, for ourselves, we confess that we think it more calculated for the stage than the ballroom.

> I never dance cotillions, holding them to be monstrous distorters of the human frame, and tantamount in their operations to being broken and dislocated on the wheel. . . . In the course of these observations I was struck with the energy and eloquence of sundry limbs, which seemed to be flourishing about without appertaining to anybody. After much investigation and difficulty, I at length traced them to their respective owners, whom I found to be all Frenchmen to a man. . . . I have since been considerably employed in calculations on this subject; and by the most accurate computation I have determined that a Frenchman passes at least three-fifths of his time between the heavens and the earth, and partakes eminently of the nature of a gossamer or soap-bubble. One of these jack-o'-lantern heroes, in taking a figure, which neither Euclid nor Pythagoras himself could demonstrate, unfortunately wound himself — I mean his feet — his better part — into a lady's cobweb muslin robe; but perceiving it at the instant, he set himself a-spinning the other way, like a top, unravelled his step, without omitting one angle or curve, and extricated himself without breaking a thread of the lady's dress! he then sprung up, like a sturgeon, crossed his feet four times, and finished this wonderful evolution by quivering his left leg, as a cat does her paw when she has accidently dipped it in water (47-48).

Although one passage is the source of the other, their qualities could hardly be more distinct. The former passage contains one witty conceit, which is used for purposes of ridicule. Irving's version has nothing whatsoever to do with ridicule; as a matter of fact the extent of his comic elaboration has the contrary effect of softening the ludicrous aspects of the cotillion and Frenchmen. Part of the transformation is due to the presence of a narrator with traditional characteristics that either are, or verge on, burlesque traits. There are traces in him of certain stock humorists: the meddler, the testy eccentric, the pedantic scientist, and, most importantly, a type of humorist that resembles the *quiz* of polite serials and *the lying traveller* of burlesque comedy — a precursor of the deadpan humorist of native American humor. The narrator's tone is neutral as he presents the reader with absurd hyperboles, and the anecdote itself is a lie, a hoax, or a tall tale. Finally, the reality referred to is the world of burlesque comedy, a topsy-turvy place of grotesque characters and events, capable of sustaining unbelievable animation.

The theme of dancing was extended in terms of various feminine characteristics and male types. It was associated with the polite satire theme of female corseting, which runs through *Salmagundi* and was about the closest approach that Irving made to bawdy in the serial. The corseted female first appears as Wizard's partner in a cotillion (139-40). This is reprised later in a letter from a correspondent, Julian Cognous, who reports on another assembly:

In the middle of one of the cotillons, the company was suddenly alarmed by a tremendous crash at the lower end of the room; and on crowding to the place, discovered that it was a fine figure which had unfortunately broken down from too great exertion in a pigeon wing (468).

Dancing was combined with the fashionable theme of cobweb muslin, a fragile fabric in which both the Frenchman and Will Wizard become enmeshed. The theme was also combined with several of the comic frameworks in *Salmagundi*. The Haitian equivalent of Billy Dimple, who is "famous at the *pirouette* and the pigeon-wing" (137), is Tucky Squash, who scientifically shuffles "'double trouble'"'and "'hoe corn and dig potatoes,'" while playing "on a three-stringed fiddle like Apollo" (138-39). Under the mistaken apprehension that he is in a place of worship, Mustapha presents his version of the modern dance:

. . . to my utter astonishment and dismay, they were all seized with what I concluded to be a paroxysm of religious phrenzy, tossing about their heads in a ludicrous style from side to side, and indulging in extravagant contortions of figure; now throwing their heels into the air, and anon whirling round with the velocity of eastern idolaters, who think they pay a grateful homage to the sun by imitating his motions. I expected every moment to see them fall down in convulsions, foam at the mouth, and shriek with fancied inspiration (455-56).[11]

These are several of the casual experiments to which the theme of modern dancing was subjected. Other comic directions for this theme are merely hinted at and never even attain the tangential treatment of a paragraph or two. For example, one of Wizard's initial qualifications was his "intimate knowledge of the buffalo, and war-dances of the northern Indians" (37). The dances are alluded to in the middle of the periodical (291), and recur again as part of Mustapha's loutish expectations prior to witnessing his first assembly; "I had heard of the war dances of the natives, which are a kind of religious institution, and had little doubt but that this must be a solemnity of the [same] kind" (451-52). It is probable that Irving had been considering introducing Indian dances as a burlesque frame for modern dancing. There is also a series of references which indicate that Irving had been thinking of presenting modern dancing as a mock system of universal communication (328-29).

These comic drafts were rejected, and Irving chose the comic Frenchman again for "The Chronicles of Gotham." There, the whimsical fancies which had earlier been associated with the Frenchman and the dance are projected as a total fiction of a nation of Hoppingtots engaged in burlesque warfare with a besieged New York. The strategy upon which the piece is based had appeared earlier in the serial: "I am under serious apprehensions that the period is not far distant when . . . the heels, by an antipodean maneuver, [will] obtain entire pre-eminence over the head" (328-29).

There is no discursive argument for comic success, or failure, although in attempting it one may be driven to quote and summarize at too great length. This judgment resides in the "feel" of a piece of writing. But the fact is that *Salmagundi* is primarily a polite serial closely associated with the tradition – *The Spectator* particularly – in a clear, albeit nominal, sense. Many other polite themes could have been chosen for this chapter, and roughly the same case could have been made for them: that there was a determined attempt made by Irving to transform this material by animation and exaggeration – treating it in a spirit of pure fun and celebratory ebullience, which, when successful, set satirical elements dancing or exploding, and continually trying to bring them into association with comic devices that belong to burlesque comedy.

CHAPTER FIVE

POLITICAL SATIRE

The major vehicle for political satire in *Salmagundi* was a letter serial from a captured Tripolitan captain held hostage in America. The letters of Mustapha Rub-A-Dub Keli Khan are naked imitations of Goldsmith's *The Citizen of the World* (1760-61) and are perhaps the dullest pieces in *Salmagundi*. They alone deserve the harsh and generally unfair judgments passed on Irving in 1825 by the American novelist John Neal: "essays, after the manner of Goldsmith – a downright, secret, laboured, continual imitation of him – abounding, too, in plagiarisms."[1]

There was no fixed nationality for the foreign visitor of satire. Among the earliest were a Persian and a Turk; Mr. Spectator had used four American Indian kings, Goldsmith a Chinese, and Philip Freneau a Tahitian.[2] The Mahometan stereotype and his oriental style had entered English literature soon after the translation of *The Arabian Nights* (1706-8).

The failure of this letter serial is partly due to an uncreative dependence upon Goldsmith, but it is also another failure in attempted satire, a comic mode in which Irving invariably failed, for the simple reason that his response to folly and vice was not moral. It was a matter of comic delight or disgust, a matter of burlesque comedy or invective and abuse, but never adequate satire. "The Letters of Jonathan Oldstyle" shows Irving strangled by a corrective voice that he simply cannot make his own.

Mustapha is limited, by weight of tradition, to the voices of the rational lout and the conscious moralist, and it was beyond Irving's power to render him whimsical. In the serial, burlesque elements, particularly the vision of America as a world of words, are continually depressed by the limitations of the narrator, and they become tiresome and repetitious because there is no opportunity for combination and amplification through the mind of this foreign narrator. As a result, the best political satire in *Salmagundi* is found elsewhere in the serial.

Irving had a deep personal revulsion to politics, and he tended to express or exorcise his disgust through invective or burlesque comedy. The following excerpt from a letter of May 2, 1807, to Mary Fairlie, is a good example of Irving's successful treatment of politics. Although the tone is one of self-conscious mockery, it begins with a statement of Irving's serious aversion to politics, which is associated with foulness and dirt. Its climax is an apostrophic rejection of civic virtue as "nauseous" and "dirty," and there immediately follows a transformation of the world of politics, the animus, into a pigmy world of absurd proportions:

We have toiled through the purgatory of an election, . . . I got fairly drawn into the vortex, and before the third day was expired, I was as deep in mud and politics as ever a moderate gentleman would wish to be; and I drank beer with the multitude; and I talked handbill-fashion with the demagogues, and I shook hands with the mob — whom my heart abhorreth. . . . The first day I merely hunted for whim, character, and absurdity, according to my usual custom. . . . But the third day — Ah! then came the tug of war. My patriotism all at once blazed forth, and I determined to save my country! Oh, my friend, I have been in such holes and corners; such filthy nooks and filthy corners, sweep offices and oyster cellars! . . . faugh! I shall not be able to bear the smell of small beer or tobacco for a month to come!

Truly this saving one's country is a nauseous piece of business, and if patriotism is such a dirty virtue — prythee, no more of it. I was almost the whole time at the Seventh Ward — as you know, that is the most fertile ward in mob, riot, and incident, and I do assure you the scene was exquisitely ludicrous. Such haranguing and puffing and strutting among all the little great men of the day. Such shoals of unfledged heroes from the lower wards, who had broke away from their mammas, and run to electioneer with a slice of bread and butter in their hands. Every carriage that drove up disgorged a whole nursery of these pigmy wonders, who all seemed to put on the brow of thought, the air of bustle and business, and the big talk of general committee men (*PMI*, I, 151-52).

Of all the editorial statements mocked in the opening essays of *Salmagundi*, one that was conspicuously absent was a statement regarding the political neutrality of the editor. A little further in the number, however, the contemporary reader would have encountered the following allusion: "I was, however, much pleased to see that red maintained its ground against all other colors, because red is the color of Mr. Jefferson's *******, Tom Paine's nose, and my slippers" (44); and he would immediately have recognized that *Salmagundi* was to be, among other things, representative

of a contemporary tradition of *antidemocratic satire.* This comic movement represented conservative political opinion in both England and
America and was devoted to attacking the new ideas in science, religion,
and government, ridiculing their social effects, and abusing the principals
involved. Its English champion was William Gifford, editor of *The Anti-
Jacobin Review;* its champions in America were Joseph Dennie and
Thomas Green Fessenden. The latter, ironically, was to become the object
of scurrilous attacks by the Salmagundians in the months to come.

A distinction should be made between antidemocratic or Georgian
and rational or Queen Anne political satire. The difference in the vision of
politics and political evil which generated the two traditions was great, and
this led to a similarly large difference in tone, style, and the choice and
treatment of theme.

In rational satire, political evil or corruption was usually the result of
narrowness, whether the private ends of party or personal interest. The
antidemocratic satirists, however, were united by the ideal of a Christian
community under attack rather than any ideal of rational governance. For
them, political evil was the result of ideational tides of democracy, infidelity, and scientific impersonality set abroad by perverse agents to undermine Christian society. Corruption was a plague rather than a human flaw,
and any new development in any area of civilization and culture was
immediately suspected of being a carrier in disguise.

While this distinction is a matter of emphasis in the sense that the
Queen Anne satirists often made their political and religious prejudices sufficient grounds for levelling abuse, the later satirists, on the other hand,
were almost never reasonable. There is a stridency in their satire that may
be a result of the revolutionary pressures that they felt on all sides, in
science, politics, and religion. Both traditions of political satire are to be
found in *Salmagundi,* and they are theoretically separable.

The primary references in the rational satire of *Salmagundi* are to
elements of political satire in the works of Addison and Steele, Swift,
Goldsmith, and Fielding. To a lesser extent American satirists — Francis
Hopkinson, Philip Freneau, and Hugh Henry Brackenridge — will also
enter this discussion. Except in rare instances, however, there can be no
determination of influence in this portion of *Salmagundi.* For one thing,
elements of political satire were treated as common property by pam-
phleteers and writers for periodicals; it is generally impossible to point to
the source of political themes and figures of speech when so many sources
in addition to the original were usually available; the aim of much political
satire was to follow a model as closely as possible, so that the full force of
the new application could be appreciated. A good example of this would
be the successive imitations of Arbuthnot's *John Bull* through Paulding's

own *John Bull and Brother Jonathan* (1812).

As usual with satire, Irving began by borrowing elements, not to apply and direct them according to their traditional weight and meaning, but with the hope of breeding them in new and fertile connections.

Two of the political characters in *Salmagundi* came from rational satire: the *quidnunc* and the *great man*. Initially the *quidnunc* [one who asks "what now?"] was an inquisitive meddler who avidly sought out and retailed political intelligence:[3] The entire population of Laputa, Gulliver finds, have a "strong Disposition . . . towards News and Politicks; perpetually enquiring into publick Affairs, giving their Judgments in Matters of State; and passionately disputing every Inch of a Party Opinion."[4] This species of character was often combined with the *wiseacre* or *almanac*, who knows everything that is happening. The foolish humor of the *quidnunc* was prominent in *The Tatler;* one of its first stated intentions was to furnish foreign intelligence for "the use of politic persons, who are so public spirited as to neglect their own affairs to look into the transactions of State" (No. 1). This humor persists in *Salmagundi,* although it has shifted slightly, now associated with the American theme of "patriotism":

Every man, of whatever rank or degree — such is the wonderful patriotism of the people — disinterestedly neglects his business to devote himself to his country; and not an insignificant fellow but feels himself inspired, on this occasion, with as much warmth in favor of the cause he has espoused, as if all the comfort of his life, or even his life itself, was dependent on the issue (259).

Langstaff comes upon Ichabod Fungus — "one of those fidgeting, meddling quidnuncs with which this unhappy city is pestered" — reading the first number of *Salmagundi.* Fungus is

. . . one of our "Q in a corner fellows," who speaks volumes in a wink conveys most portentous information by laying his finger beside his nose, and is always smelling a rat in the most trifling occurrence. He listened to our work with the most frigid gravity — every now and then gave a mysterious shrug, a humph, or a screw of the mouth; and on being asked his opinion at the conclusion, said, he did not know what to think of it; he hoped it did not mean anything against the government, that no lurking treason was couched in all this talk. These were dangerous times — times of plot and conspiracy. . . . (56)

The first number of *Salmagundi* had contained an allusion to "Mr. Jefferson's *******," and Fungus tells the company that "he did not at all like those stars after Mr. Jefferson's name — they had an air of concealment." *Spectator* No. 567 is devoted to the type of the Syncopists, the political writers who "recommend their Productions" by "the secret Vertue of an Innuendo," and the author parodies this kind of writing in a passage in which random words have their vowels missing, have all but their first and last letter missing, are replaced by asterisks, etc. In the next essay, Mr. Spectator presents a scene in a coffee-house, where he, like Langstaff, overhears several readers discussing the political implications of his "Syncopy":

This Fellow, says he, *can't for his Life keep out of Politicks. Do you see how he abuses* four *great Men here?* I fix'd my Eye very attentively on the Paper, and asked him if he meant those who were represented by Asterisks. *Asterisks,* says he, *do you call them? They are all of them Stars. He might as well have put Garters to 'em . . . I have read over the whole Sentence,* says I; *but I look upon the Parenthesis in the Belly of it to be the most dangerous Part, and as full of Insinuations as it can hold.*[5]

Dick Paddle, who undertakes to answer Fungus, "is known to the world as being a most knowing genius. . . . Dick assured old Fungus that those stars merely stood for Mr. Jefferson's red *what-d'ye call-'ems,* and that, so far from a conspiracy against their peace and prosperity, the authors, whom he knew very well, were only expressing their high respect for them."[6] In later parts of *Salmagundi* and *The History,* the foreign quidnunc becomes the more American barroom and street-corner orator (178).

The great man as an object of political satire was used extensively in the eighteenth century; one thinks particularly of Gay's *Beggar's Opera* and Fielding's *Jonathan Wild.*[7] Washington Irving attempted several times to adapt the manner of Fielding's treatment to American political types, although, in place of Fielding's ironic distance, there is a barely disguised anger in Irving's adaptations.

The introduction to the sketch "Billy Luscious" in *The Corrector* — "As every movement of a *great man* is interesting, I cannot but notice the important biography of Billy Luscious" (Corr., 55) — is simply a curtailed version of the opening of *Jonathan Wild.*

Irving's next attempt in this vein was the essay "On Greatness" in *Salmagundi,* where he sketched "the rise, progress, and completion of a *little great man*" (378). The altered designation was the American equivalent of the English type. It carries behind it the sneer of the Federalist at the levelling tendency of democratic politics, and it may also allude to the controversy between Buffon and Jefferson over the diminution of species in America. Irving did not coin the phrase; Goldsmith devoted an essay to the "little great man," but Irving's type is a very free adaptation.[8]

There are several analogies between Irving's sketch of Timothy

Dabble and *Jonathan Wild.* Both authors warn the reader in advance of the error of confusing greatness with goodness; and both authors devote a section of their work to the exploits and details of their heroes' youth which prove that "nature had certainly marked him out for a great man" (380).[9] Beyond these resemblances, Irving's type is very different from Fielding's or Gay's. Their great men are cunning and powerful scoundrels in the world of politics or crime. In *Salmagundi,* Irving takes the direction he followed in *The Corrector:* his great men make up a series with "pimps, bailiffs, lottery-brokers, [and] chevaliers of industry" (376). "Our great men are those who are most expert at crawling on all fours, and have the happiest facility of dragging and winding themselves along in the dirt" (377-78). Irving expresses the difference by a familiar paradox: "To rise in this country a man must first descend" (379). The little great man is actually an adaptation of the traditional *tool, drudge,* and *toadeater;* because in the satirical view of America, as opposed to that of Augustan England, privilege is the result of popularity rather than power, and is conferred from below by the mob: Dabble achieves high office by the lucky accident of getting himself tarred and feathered (385-86). In short, Irving's little great man is the democratic politician.

The sketch of Timothy Dabble is the most savage piece of invective in *Salmagundi,* and it seems to have been a conscious exercise in the manner and spirit of Swift. It is developed largely in terms of animal abuse. Dabble's talents expand in the ward porter-houses, "like the toad, which, shrinking from balmy airs and jocund sunshine, finds his congenial home in caves and dungeons, and there nourishes his venom and bloats his deformity" (384). The sketch is introduced by a simile which is quite Swiftian in spirit, but which was borrowed from Jefferson's *Notes on Virginia:*

The aspiring politician may be compared to that indefatigable insect, called the tumbler, pronounced by a distinguished personage to be the only industrious animal in Virginia, which buries itself in filth, and works ignobly in the dirt, until it forms a little ball, which it rolls laboriously along, like Diogenes in his tub; sometimes head, sometimes tail foremost, pilfering from every rut and mud hole, and increasing its ball of greatness by the contributions of the kennel. Just so the candidate for greatness; — he buries himself in the mob; labors in dirt and oblivion, and makes unto himself the rudiments of a popular name from the admiration and praises of rogues, ignoramuses, and blackguards. His name once started, onward he goes, struggling and puffing, and pushing it before him; collecting new tribute from the dregs and offals of society as he proceeds, until having gathered together a mighty mass of popularity, he mounts it in triumph; is hoisted into office, and becomes a great man (379)[10]

The anger unleashed at democratic politics, which is evident in the preceding quotations, is not the conventional emotion of *The Corrector.* It is sincere, if a trifle unbalanced. The disgust aroused by American democracy is allayed by symbolically pelting democratic effigies with excrement, either indirectly — "some creeping insect who will prostitute himself to familiarity with the lowest of mankind; and, like the idolatrous Egyptian, worship the wallowing tenants of filth and mire" (264-65) — or directly — "by the time it is dark, every kennel in the neighborhood teems with illustrious members of the sovereign people, wallowing in their congenial element of mud and mire" (401).

Early in the run of *Salmagundi,* an occasion arose for Irving to exercise the skill in personal abuse he had acquired writing for *The Corrector. The Weekly Inspector,* a New York magazine, had contained an inoffensive notice of the first number of *Salmagundi* in its issue for February 7. On February 13 Irving replied by attacking the editor of *The Weekly Inspector,* Thomas Green Fessenden. Fessenden joined battle with him at some length on February 21. Three days later, Irving, Paulding, and William Irving ended this spurious feud with a parody of Fessenden's verse satires, entitled "Flummery." "Flummery" was unanswerable because it contained little more than personal abuse, and the Salmagundians allowed Fessenden the last word in a squib of March 6.

Thomas Green Fessenden was the most prominent American satirist of his day, a writer of frenzied invective and a staunch Federalist. The contemporary writers he most admired, and upon whose work he modeled his own, were William Gifford and John Mathias.[11] He was perhaps the chief American exponent of antidemocratic satire at the turn of the eighteenth century. The other important vehicle for this low vein of political satire in the period was *Salmagundi* itself. The grounds of the quarrel between Irving and Fessenden, whatever they may have been, were in defiance of the bonds of political sympathy; for the objects and themes of Fessenden's abuse were the same as Irving's.[12]

To my knowledge, no literary historian has grouped together the British and American writers that I have designated as antidemocratic satirists; yet, if for no other reason than that they were the organized resistance to nineteenth-century Romanticism, they deserve generic treatment. The successive shocks of the American and French Revolutions tended to polarize satire in England and America. Although there was a good deal of diversity in the liberal camp, differences among conservative satirists, whether Tory, Federalist, or Anti-Jacobin, tended to be swallowed up in the intensity of their reaction. For them this was Armageddon, the triumph of infidelity, and they lashed out at it with a more than moral fury. The object of their attack was the chaos and license which they felt threatened all standards, whether in the political principles of William Godwin and Tom Paine, the poetry of the Della Cruscans, the sentimental German drama of Schiller and Kotzebue, or the philosophy of men like Erasmus Darwin.

The stronghold of this movement was *The Anti-Jacobin,* and its opening address, written by George Canning, was a testimony to political extremism. It makes no pretense at rationality, but promises that bias, and often hysteria, will be the norm of political satire:

. . . of JACOBINISM in all its shapes, and in all its degrees, political and moral, public and private, whether as it openly threatens the subversion of States, or gradually saps the foundations of domestic happiness, we are the avowed, determined, and irreconcileable enemies. We have no desire to divest ourselves of these inveterate prejudices; but shall remain stubborn and incorrigible in resisting every attempt which may be made either by argument or (what is more in the charitable spirit of modern reformers) by force, to convert us to a different opinion.[13]

Economy as a theme of political satire originated as a term of contempt, applied by the Tory landed gentry to the mercantile Whigs. That, at least, would seem to be the sense of its use in *Spectator* No. 174, which relates an argument at the club between Sir Roger de Coverley and Sir Andrew Freeport. Sir Roger identifies economy with overreaching and parsimony; it is the merchant's morality and infinitely "below a Gentleman's Charity to the Poor, or Hospitality among his Neighbours." Sir Andrew defends "the Oeconomy of the Merchant," and concludes that "the Conduct of the Gentleman must be the same, unless by scorning to be the Steward, he resolves the Steward shall be the Gentleman." In general, Addison and Steele praised economy as a virtue, but a serial of 1793, *The Looker-On,* devoted an essay to mock-systems of economy in learning and morality which were nothing more than the glorification of selfishness. Christopher Anstey, in *The New Bath Guide,* and John Wilkes, in *The North Briton,* ridiculed the Bute administration for economy in government — the administration that Smollett, an indefatigable exponent of economy, wrote in hire for.[14]

In America, the theme of economy was a mainstay of anti-Jeffersonian satire, and the ghost of Benjamin Franklin, whose "Way to Wealth" Irving had sneered at in *The Corrector,* was raised as a scornful precedent: "There is nothing in which our democratic politicians are more profoundly absurd," Fessenden wrote, "than in their estimates of *national economy.* The penny-saving maxims of Dr. Franklin, injudiciously applied to affairs of national magnitude, are of very mischievous tendency."[15]

The Port-Folio associated economy with the upheavals of demo-cratic politics, whereby the tradesman and mechanic assume legislative control: "Economy is our tutelary saint, and this blinking beldame, with her pence table in her hand, is busied of late, in basely stooping to the ground, picking up cents, rusty nails, pointless needles and headless pins." Items of economy which took up hours of congressional debate were "suited exactly to the humour of our *haberdasher* politicans, such items are *tape, thread* and *buckram,* perfectly proper in a taylor's bill, perfectly fit to be huckstered by a pedlar."¹⁶

Economy is the first of many incomprehensible terms which Mus-tapha encounters in America:

ECONOMY, my friend, is the watchword of this nation; I have been study-ing for a month past to divine its meaning, but truly am as much perplexed as ever. It is a kind of national starvation; an experiment how many com-forts and necessaries the body politic can be deprived of before it perishes. It has already arrived to a lamentable degreee of debility, and promises to share the fate of the Arabian philosopher, who proved that he could live without food, but unfortunately died just as he had brought his experi-ment to perfection (123).

Among the items in *Salmagundi* discussed by an economic Congress were the patching up of a hole in the wall of the Senate building (225) and the replacing of Mustapha's breeches. Mustapha is startled by the insignifi-cance of the latter topic, until he is told by the officer in charge of him and his fellow prisoners that "it all proceeds from economy. If the govern-ment did not spend ten times as much money in debating whether it was proper to supply you with breeches, as the breeches themselves would cost, the people who govern the bashaw and his divan would straightway begin to complain of their liberties being infringed. . . ." (223).

Jefferson's second inaugural, as satirists immediately recorded, was devoted to talk of a peaceful and economical administration, and some of the satire on economy parodies this speech.¹⁷ However, most of the satire attached itself to the debacle of his second administration, his naval fleet of gunboats. He wrote to Paine in 1807: "I believe that gunboats are the only *water* defence which can be useful to us and protect us from the ruinous folly of a navy." "The gunboats desired by Jefferson were small, cheap craft equipped with one or two guns and kept on shore under sheds until actually needed, when they were to be launched and manned by a sort of naval militia." "In 1807, instead of stalwart frigates, the United States Navy owned sixty-nine of these horrid little two-gun scows, which at high tide loved to float up into cornfields and mud."¹⁸

Thomas Jefferson was personally stigmatized with the common anti-

Jacobin epithets, philosopher and atheist, which amounted to the same charge:

> Phlegmatic, cunning and wrong-headed,
> To visionary tenets wedded.[19]

The pursuit of economy and the consequent ill-defended state of America was as often attributed to Jefferson's philosophy as to Franklin's mercantile principles.[20]

The material for the charge of atheism levelled at Jefferson was taken from his 1787 publication, *Notes on the State of Virginia.* The well-known statement in his argument for religious tolerance — "But it does me no injury for my neighbour to say there are twenty gods, or no god. It neither picks my pocket nor breaks my leg" — was quoted by almost every Federalist writer, including Irving, at some time during Jefferson's two administrations. Jefferson had also advanced several arguments against the necessity of believing in the universal deluge of revelation, and this, Mustapha discovers, is the true reason for the Federalist conspiracy "to dethrone his highness, the present bashaw, and place another in his stead" (173).[21]

Other items of personal abuse used to ridicule Jefferson included his rusticity and lack of ceremony, his experiments and speculations in natural philosophy, his literary abilities, and his attitude toward the Indians, his neighbors' wives, and, above all, toward blacks of the female sex. Irving's opening shot at the president — "red is the color of Mr. Jefferson's *******" (44) — is an allusion to his casual attire on public occasions. Mustapha discovers that "the present bashaw" is "declining in popularity, having given great offense by wearing red breeches and tying his horse to a post" (78). In the second movement of Demy Semiquaver's modern symphony, the music represents a great body of ice passing West Point, "saluted by three or four dismounted cannon from Fort Putnam." This is followed by "Jefferson's March" to the air of "Yankee Doodle" (243).

Irving also alluded to Jefferson's virtuoso experiments while President. Mustapha tells us that Jefferson "amuses himself with impaling butterflies and pickling tadpoles" (78). This was part of most full-scale attacks on Jefferson:

> Cease, cease, old man, for soon you must,
> Your faithless cunning, pride, and lust,
> Which Death shall quickly level:
> Thy cobweb'd Bible ope again;
> Quit thy blaspheming crony, *Paine,*
> And think upon the *Devil.*

Resume thy shells and butterflies,
Thy beeetle's heads, and lizard's thighs,
The state no more controul:
Thy tricks, with *sooty Sal,* give o'er;
Indulge thy body, Tom, no more;
But try to save thy *soul.*

What suits *beau Dawson* suits not thee,
Beau Dawson's brisk as any bee,
Thou feeble art, alack!
And as thy yellow lanthorn phiz,
Was long, of each *white* maid, the quiz,
It e'en now bores the *black.*[22]

Jefferson's affair with a certain Black Sally was also included in most satiric attacks on the president. This piece of scurrility was still making the rounds in 1832, and Mrs. Trollope elaborated it to Petronian proportions: "the hospitable orgies for which his Montecielo was so celebrated, were incomplete, unless the goblet he quaffed were tendered by the trembling hand of his own slavish offspring."[23] Irving apparently could not resist making an allusion to this; in Wizard's essay on *Othello,* Desdemona is said to "have had a predilection for flat noses; like a certain philosophical great man of our day" (164).

The attack on Paine was seriously mounted after his return to America in 1802: "The *age of reason* is fully restored at Washington. Men sit calmly, without any apprehension of the roofs of new houses tumbling upon the unconscious head. Tom Paine serenely swallows his brandy at Lovell's hotel";

Moreover 'tis a proper season
To burnish up the "Age of Reason,"
Lest, peradventure, too much piety
Sap the foundations of society.
And we moreover understand, he
Supports the state — by drinking brandy,
And if he lives, will free the nation
From debt, without direct taxation.[24]

The abuse of Paine in *Salmagundi* was restricted to his supposed alcoholism. The charge of drunkenness found facetious corroboration in Paine's great carbuncled nose, and noses, general or specific, interested Washington Irving. The initial slur against Jefferson in *Salmagundi* also added that red was the color of Tom Paine's nose (44), and Mustapha tells us that Jefferson "invited a professed antediluvian from the Gallic empire, who illuminated the whole country with his principles — and his nose" (173).

Part of the second movement of Semiquaver's symphony has the North River Society applying to "Common Sense" for his lantern, to the air of "Nose, nose, jolly red nose" (244).[25]

The satirical theme which Irving found most congenial to his comic fancy was freedom of speech, which had always been a staple theme of anti-democratic satire. Mustapha is amazed to find that, in America, free speech, like its fellow slogans, liberty of conscience, freedom of suffrage, etc., is merely a shibboleth, callously applied by democrat and demagogue alike to justify a spectrum of low and licentious behavior;[26] that the freedom of the press actually means the right of unrestrained slander;[27] and that free debate in Congress either results in months of talk on totally trivial subjects or the inability to respond to an emergency until months of talk have elapsed.[28]

Behind the direct treatment of this topic, however, there is a more fundamental vision of democratic talk as tumult, chaos, and ultimately, orgiastic riot. It almost seems as if the noise of democratic politics grows consistently through the serial; Mustapha has never heard anything like it:

In the gardens of His Highness of Tripoli are fifteen thousand beehives, three hundred peacocks, and a prodigious number of parrots and baboons: and yet I declare to thee, Asem, that their buzzing, and squalling, and chattering is nothing compared to the wild uproar . . . now raging within the bosom of this mighty and distracted logocracy (341-42).

Mustapha witnesses an election, when the entire country is given over to "buzz, murmur, suspense, and sublimity!": "At length the day arrives. The storm that has been so long gathering and threatening in distant thunders, bursts forth in terrible explosion; all business is at an end; the whole city is in a tumult; the people are running helter-skelter, they know not whither, and they know not why" (262-63). Mustapha has a final vision of a democratic election, and it is here that Irving comes closest to the central traumatic figure of antidemocratic satire — the diabolical riot of French Jacobinism amidst the bloody streams of the slaughtered nobility:

O Asem! I almost shrink at the recollection of the scenes of confusion, of licentious disorganization which I have witnessed during the last three days . . . I have beheld the community convulsed with a civil war . . . individuals verbally massacred, families annihilated . . . and slangwhangers coolly bathing their pens in ink and rioting in the slaughter of their thousands. I have seen, in short, that awful despot, the People, in the moment of unlimited power, . . . scattering mud and filth about, like some desperate lunatic relieved from the restraints of his strait waistcoat. I have seen beggars on horseback, ragamuffins riding in coaches, and swine seated in places of honor; I have seen liberty; I have seen equality; I have seen fraternity (257–58).[29]

Shortly after his arrival in America, Mustapha discovers the key to American politics, which he communicates to his friend:

To let thee at once into a secret, which is unknown to these people themselves, their government is a pure unadulterated *logocracy,* or government of words. The whole nation does everything *viva voce,* or by word of mouth; and in this manner is one of the most military nations in existence. Every man who has what is here called the gift of gab, that is, a plentiful stock of verbosity, becomes a soldier outright; and is forever in a militant state. The country is entirely defended *vi et lingua;* that is to say, by force of tongues (171).

America as a logocracy was Irving's major contribution to antidemocratic satire, and it is the burlesque fiction that gives structure and energy to the political satire in *A History of New York.* The comic translation of a weak and inefficient central government into a political system propelled by words, and therefore by wind, was an appropriate fiction. This fiction had some objective basis: specifically, Jefferson's attempts to cope with British aggression by means of the embargo and the "peaceful coercion" of proclamation; and, generally, the debates in Congress, the rampant journalistic activity of post-Revolutionary America, and the overall haranguing nature of American politics with its town meetings, election meetings, holiday speeches, and tavern and street corner arguments. In *Salmagundi,* however, it becomes a burlesque fiction. As in the case of whimsy, the comic principles of wordiness and windiness are so thoroughly applied to American institutions and customs that they eventually constitute a transformation of America into a burlesque world animated by blustering verbosity.

Irving had already noted the figure in his European journal in 1804: "The quarrels among the lower classes in this country are generally settled by the *tongue* and he that has the most volubility and strongest lungs carries the day" (Wright, 96). The theme was introduced into *Salmagundi* in the first Mustapha letter which was devoted to a comic theme of great currency then and later, the inept maneuvers of a training company. Irving focuses upon the "single combat" between the training captain and the "grand bashaw of the city":

The battle was carried on entirely by words. . . . The grand bashaw made a furious attack in a speech of considerable length; the little bashaw, by no means appalled, retorted with great spirit. The grand bashaw attempted to rip him up with an argument, or stun him with a solid fact; but the little bashaw parried them both with admirable adroitness, and run him clean through and through with a syllogism (126).

He has taken the fact of talking and blithely superimposed upon it the two most frequent battle metaphors in *Salmagundi,* or in burlesque comedy for that matter: the tourney of romance and the philosophical disputation, the battle of the folios.

Analogies, and sometimes sources, can be found for many parts of the logocracy theme in *Salmagundi.* The name itself may have been taken from the following passage in Sterne: "It is ten to one . . . whether you have ever read the literary histories of past ages; — if you have, — what terrible battles, 'yclept logomachies, have they occasioned and perpetuated with so much gall and ink-shed" (*TS.,* 87). That short chapter ends with a figure often used in *Salmagundi:* "'Twas not by ideas, — by heaven! his life was put in jeopardy by words" (*TS,* 87). The following conceit from "The Battle of the Books" is a prototype of much of the figurative play in this section of *Salmagundi:*

Now, it must here be understood, that *Ink* is the great missive Weapon in all Battles of the *Learned,* which, convey'd thro' a sort of Engine, call'd a *Quill,* infinite Numbers of these are darted at the *Enemy,* by the Valiant on each side, with equal Skill and Violence, as if it were an Engagement of *Porcupines.* This malignant Liquor was compounded by the Engineer, who invented it, of two Ingredients, which are *Gall* and *Copperas;* by its Bitterness and Venom, to *Suit* in some Degree, as well as to *Foment* the Genius of the Combatants.[30]

The most important analogy to the logocracy section is the eighth chapter of "Tale of a Tub." The comic motif behind these parts of the two works is the same. Swift's chapter is devoted to the sect of Aeolists, and in it he reinterprets philosophy and religion in terms of wind, much as Irving does politics. While there is no strict parallelism, there is a strong resemblance, and it is certain that Irving was familiar with "A Tale of a Tub" in 1807.

Both Swift and Irving use a logical figure which has an interesting history in English comedy. It occurs in *Much Ado about Nothing* in the banter between Benedick and Beatrice: "Foul words is but foul wind, and foul wind is but foul breath, and foul breath is noisome, therefore I will depart unkissed" (V.ii.51-53). It seems to be echoed in *Hudibras,* in Ralpho's argument "Oaths are but words, and words but winds," and Swift translates it into a syllogism on learning: "Words are but wind; and learning is nothing but words; *ergo,* learning is nothing but wind." Irving uses the figure in an apostrophe on America:

Unhappy nation! thus torn to pieces by intestine talks! never, I fear, will it be restored to tranquility and silence. Words are but breath; breath is but air; and air put into motion is nothing but wind. This vast empire, therefore, may be compared to nothing more or less than a mighty wind-mill, and the orators, and the chatterers, and the slang-whangers, are the breezes that put it in motion (177).

The conception behind much of the logocracy burlesque is that of bluster — an inflated claim to certain powers and abilities which are immediately denied by one's situation or subsequent actions. This is the characteristic of the traditional bragging captain, like Falstaff or Bodabil. It had been ill-naturedly applied to certain great men, heads of state, generals, etc; for example, during the Revolutionary War, it had been the comic strategy of satirical attacks upon General Gage in the light of his listless campaign of 1775; he also was ridiculed for fighting his battles by proclamation.[31]

Government by proclamation and philosophy was the Federalist translation of Jefferson's conviction that the nations of the world could exist without war. Mustapha describes the president as

. . . a man of superlative ventosity, and comparable to nothing but a huge bladder of wind. He talks of vanquishing all opposition by the force of reason and philosophy; throws his gauntlet at all the nations of the earth, and defies them to meet him — on the field of argument! . . . Does an alarming insurrection break out in a distant part of the empire — his highness utters a speech! — nay, more, for here he shows his "energies" — he most intrepidly despatches a courier on horseback, and orders him to ride one hundred and twenty miles a day, with a most formidable army of proclamations, *i.e.* a collection of words, packed up in his saddle-bags. He is instructed to show no favor nor affection; but to charge the thickest ranks of the enemy, and to speechify and batter by words the conspiracy and the conspirators out of existence (178-79).[32]

The democratic town meeting was the scene of the first book of John Trumbull's "M'Fingal," and he presented this institution in the following wordy shape:

> They met, made speeches full long-winded,
> Resolv'd, protested and rescinded;
> Addresses sign'd; then chose committees. . . .
> With every tongue in either faction
> Prepared like minute-men for action. . . .
> With equal uproar scarcely rave

Opposing Winds in Aeolus' cave;
Such dialogues with earnest face
Held never Balaam with his ass.[33]

Irving had used Balaam's ass in a similar manner in the Mustapha letter
which also described a town meeting.[34] Irving should have been familiar
with Trumbull's mock epic; on the other hand, the similarities of his
description may very well have been due to the realities of this American
institution:

Everything partakes of the windy nature of the government. In case of any
domestic grievance, or an insult from a foreign foe, the people are all in a
buzz; town-meetings are immediately held where the quidnuncs of the city
repair . . . each swelling and strutting like a turkey-cock; puffed up with
words, and wind, and nonsense. After bustling, and buzzing, and bawling
for some time, and after each man has shown himself to be indubitably the
greatest personage in the meeting, they pass a string of resolutions, *i.e.*
words, which . . . are whimsically denominated the sense of the meeting
(178).

The most extensive political burlesque in *Salmagundi* was devoted to
democratic editors, or slang-whangers; Irving tended to treat the theme
almost wholly in terms of the battle metaphor. The editor is introduced by
Mustapha as a kind of crusader: "They [the people] have accommodated
themselves by appointing knights, or constant warriors, incessant brawlers,
similar to those who, in former ages, swore eternal enmity to the followers
of our divine prophet" (172).

Slang-whangers, Mustapha reports, "are appointed in every town,
village, or district, to carry on both foreign and internal warfare, and may
be said to keep up a constant firing 'in words'" (172). Irving likened
editors and their abuse to cannons firing into a besieged town, thundering
"away their combustible sentiments at the heads of the audience" (260).
In his most ambitious application of this metaphor, the opprobrious epithets become the cannonballs pouring out of the cannon's mouth: "Every
day have these slang-whangers made furious attacks on each other and
upon their respective adherents; discharging their heavy artillery, consist-
ing of large sheets, loaded with scoundrel! villain! liar! rascal!
nincompoop! dunderhead! wiseacre! blockhead! jackass!" (173-74).[35]

The fiction of language as artillery is a common one in burlesque
comedy. Irving's use of it, however, was adapted from Sterne, who himself
adapted it from Rabelais: "And here, without staying for my reply, shall I
be call'd as many blockheads, numsculs, doddypoles, dunderheads, ninny-
hammers, goosecaps, joltheads, nicompoops [*sic*], and sh—t-a-beds — and

other unsavory appellations, as ever the cake-bakers of *Lerné,* cast in the teeth of King *Gargantua's* shepherds" (*TS,* 632). In Rabelais the strings of insults lead to fighting and eventually to war.[36]

Irving also applied other reductive figures to politics, namely eating and drinking; and these were also conventional strategies of English and American political satire. In *The Citizen of the World,* Goldsmith fancies an election at which one candidate treats with gin, the other with brandy. Lien Chi visits the village "in company with three fidlers, nine dozen of hams, and a corporation poet, which were designed as reinforcements to the gin-drinking party." He is asked by an angry mob whether he is for the distillery or brewery, but they are luckily "called off to a skirmish between a Brandy-drinker's cow, and a Gin-drinker's mastiff." One of the candidates harangues the mob on the subject of his liquor, and one of the voters, "excessively drunk . . . being asked the Candidate's name for whom he voted, could be prevailed upon to make no other answer but Tobacco and Brandy." Mustapha at an election sees the people kindled by that "patriotic and argumentative beverage," beer: "These beer-barrels, indeed, seem to be most able logicians, well stored with that kind of sound argument best suited to the comprehension and most relished by the mob . . . [it] seems to be imbued with the very spirit of a logocracy" (265).

Irving is probably indebted to Goldsmith also for the notion of eating as a substitute for politics. Lien Chi had noticed that in England, "When a Church is to be built, or an Hospital endowed, the Directors assemble, and instead of consulting upon it, they eat upon it. . . . But in the election of Magistrates the people seem to exceed all bounds."[37] "The people of the American logocracy," Mustapha wrote, "who pride themselves upon improving on every precept or example of ancient or modern governments, have discovered a new mode of exciting [the] love of glory . . . they honor their great men by eating, and . . . the only trophy erected to their exploits, is a public dinner" (398-99).

In *The History* Irving correctly decided to use the world of food and drink as a festive and celebratory fiction to characterize the golden age of New Amsterdam. The world of words is traditionally sterile; it is the chilling mantle which the pedant, whether doctor or politician, tries to cast over the living world. In *The History,* the world of words becomes the fiction for the second reign, which represents the fall of Irving's true America into history under William the Testy (Thomas Jefferson). Yet the political satire to which this section of *The History* is devoted is as limited in Irving's best work as it is in *Salmagundi.* For Irving was potentially a festive comedian in the line of Rabelais and Sterne, and politics could never be for him, however much he tried and however much he wanted to treat it as a pressing concern, more than an area of blind revulsion. The traditional elements out of which his fiction of America as a logocracy came offered him the possibility of transforming that deep anger into burlesque comedy. We can see him working on this possibility in sections of *Salmagundi*, but the achievement, which should have been the second reign in *The History*, never occurred.

CHAPTER SIX

DOMESTIC HUMOR

"The spirit and manner of domestic-social fiction, as Fielding was to provide it in *Joseph Andrews,* Goldsmith in *The Vicar of Wakefield,* and Austen in all her novels, begins to arise from the criss-cross of relationships and events in the affairs of the Bickerstaffs."[1] Much more influential was *The Spectator*'s treatment of Sir Roger de Coverley, particularly in the summer essays, which sketched in some detail a locale and a neighborhood of humorists. *The Guardian* was wholly domestic in format; Nestor Ironsides, the editor, was an aged tutor to the Lizard family and most of the essays begin among the inhabitants of Lizard-Hall. *Salmagundi* is also a domestic serial: most of the major characters are members and associates of the Cockloft family, and much of the rudimentary fictional play in the serial takes place at the town residence of the Cocklofts and Cockloft Hall.

Launcelot Langstaff is an American relation of Bickerstaff's. His surname is derived from *The Tatler* and refers to the well-known eleventh number wherein the genealogy of Isaac Bickerstaff is given. The family descended from "one Jacobstaff, a famous and renowned astrologer, who by Dorothy his wife, had issue seven sons," all staffs. The first son was Bickerstaff, and the second was Longstaff. "The descendants from Longstaff," we are told, "were a disorderly, rakish sort of people . . . [who] rambled from one place to another." This wandering disposition, soon to become an essential characteristic of the American in literature — like Natty Bumppo, Ishmael, Whitman's "I," and Huck Finn — is withheld from Langstaff but given to the Yankee in *The History* as one of his distinguishing traits.

Langstaff's kinship to the long line of editors modelled on the Spectator is suggested by the following statements of attitude: "he ... mingles freely with the world, though more as a spectator than an actor" (195); "I can sit in a corner, indulge in my favorite amusement of observation, and retreat to my elbow-chair like a bee to his hive, whenever I have collected sufficient food for meditation" (280); and "I love to open the great volume of human character; to me the examination of a beau is more interesting than that of a daffodil or narcissus, and I feel a thousand times more pleasure in catching a new view of human nature, than in kidnapping the most gorgeous butterfly" (279).

The last quotation, however, is a paraphrase from Goldsmith's *Vicar of Wakefield,* with only a little shading from *The Spectator.*[2] Langstaff and the other editors owe part of their modelling to the editorial personae of the eighteenth-century serials, but they owe more to the amiable humorists of eighteenth-century comic fiction.

The early British serials served as a kind of commonplace book for the writers of comic fiction. The serials contained a large and various stock of types, already attached to briefly sketched settings, relationships, and even plots. The most memorable of these was certainly the type of *the Tory squire* as represented by Sir Roger de Coverley, among whose descendents were Mr. Allworthy of *Tom Jones* and Sir William Thornhill of *The Vicar of Wakefield.* Another of Sir Roger's progeny, Christopher Cockloft, dominates the domestic portion of *Salmagundi.* Paulding and Irving located their Tory squire on the banks of the Hudson, and, along with him, a variety of traits, properties, anecdotal structures, and the first phase of an enduring theme, the *good old days.*

Launcelot and Christopher are literally squires: "Mr. Christopher Cockloft, or, to do him justice, Mr. Christopher Cockloft, Esq." (146); and the male Cocklofts are frequently referred to as "honest" or "true old cavaliers" (313, 355). The form that Christopher's good nature takes — paternalistic benevolence to tenants, retainers, and dependents, and a cordial hospitality — comes out of English country fiction. Visiting in the country with Sir Roger, Mr. Spectator is "extremely pleased . . . to observe the general Benevolence of all the Neighbourhood toward my Friend. The Farmers Sons thought themselves happy if they could open a Gate for the good old Knight as he passed by; which he generally requited with a Nod or a Smile, and a kind Inquiry after their Fathers and Uncles" (*Spec.,* No. 116). Christopher is also "looked up to with love and reverence" by "the honest farmers round his country-seat"; "they never pass him by without his inquiring after the welfare of their families, and receiving a cordial shake of his liberal hand" (153). To Sir Roger's servants, "The Knight is the best Master in the World . . . and as he is beloved by all about him, his Servants never care for leaving him. . . . By this Means his Domesticks are all in Years, and grown old with their Master. You would take his Valet de Chambre for his Brother. . . . You see the Goodness of the Master even in the old House-dog, and in a grey Pad that is kept in the Stable with great Care and Tenderness out of Regard to his past Services" (*Spec.*, No. 106). It was to this essay that Irving undoubtedly turned in his initial sketch of the Cockloft establishment, adapting it from memory to his own style of humor:

The domestics are all grown gray in the service of our house. We have a little, old, crusty, gray-headed negro, who has lived through two or three generations of the Cocklofts, and of course has become a personage of no little importance in the household. He calls all the family by their Christian names; tells long stories about how he dandled them on his knee when they were children. . . . The family carriage was made in the last French war, and the old horses were most indubitably foaled in Noah's ark (150).

In the matter of religion, the Cocklofts are staunch supporters of the Church of England (147). Christopher is not, as one might expect, a Federalist; a quarter-century after American Independence he is still a Tory (153-54).

The appurtenances and attitudes of the Cockloft family identify them as British aristocrats, who live in nineteenth-century America as if it were ancestral England. "The Cockloft family . . . is of great antiquity," tracing "their descent from a celebrated Roman knight, cousin to the progenitor of his majesty of Britain" (145). Christopher's "veneration for antique trumpery" is his outstanding humor; he carries it so far that "he can scarcely see the dust brushed from its resting-place on the old-fashioned testers, or a gray-bearded spider dislodged from its ancient inheritance, without groaning: and I once saw him in a transport of passion on Jeremy's knocking down a mouldering martin-coop with his tennis-ball, which had been set up in the latter days of my grandfather" (358-59).

The first letter of Jonathan Oldstyle had been devoted to the theme of the degeneracy of the present, and a nostalgia for a past which stood for richness, simplicity, and order; and this became a prominent theme in *Salmagundi*. Although Irving was generally bored with the actual antiquities of Europe and England when he visited there in 1804 and 1805, they served him in America as a context for this nostalgia, which was soon to grow very serious indeed. It remained with Irving throughout his literary career, and is often the only meaning a given work contains. It is not surprising that *The Sketch Book* became in part an American's testimony to his sense of the moral and aesthetic richness of the English countryside. The English countryside, now back where it belonged, became the ideal civilization for Irving in 1822. *Bracebridge Hall*, published in that year, is the only volume Irving wrote after 1809 that has any artistic validity of conception and execution. To safeguard himself from reality he writes of the squirearchy at the point of its disappearance in history. It is a mythic golden mean, between an historical London and America, a setting which many American writers, in their own way, tried to establish.

Roger de Coverley's story is that of a man who had been a London buck in his youth – "Supped with my Lord *Rochester* and Sir *George Etherege,* fought a Duel upon his first coming to Town, and kick'd Bully *Dawson* in a publick Coffee-house for calling him Youngster" (*Spec.,* No. 2). After he was crossed in love by a perverse widow, he had lost interest in the female sex in general, contented himself with remaining a bachelor, and "grew careless of himself," continuing "to wear a Coat and Doublet of the same Cut that were in Fashion at the Time of his Repulse" (*Spec.,* No. 2). This is a rather common plot in English comic fiction; it can even be found in the story of Uncle Toby and the Widow Wadman. Its parts are distributed among the originals of *Salmagundi:* Pindar, during his youth, "figured as a dashing blade in the great world; and no young fellow of the town wore a longer pig-tail, or carried more buckram in his skirts" (62). Wizard, preparing to meet an old flame, "had been at unusual pains in decorating his person, and broke upon my sight arrayed in the true style that prevailed among our beaux some years ago" (135). Sir Roger's widow is the cause of the old knight's whimsicality, but Pindar, Langstaff, and Uncle John Cockloft all lose their ladies as a result of their own whim-whams.

The humors of a benevolent, love-crossed old aristocrat in amiable relationship with a countryside of doting originals may be called the humors comedy of high life, in order to distinguish it from that comedy of middle life found in much of Fielding's and Smollett's fiction. Here the perspective of English life alters considerably. The corresponding comic situations are those of a bachelor plagued by meddling females, who usually wish to trap him into marriage, and a husband henpecked by a sour-tempered (or extravagant, or pretentious) wife. The theme of this comedy is the *battle of the sexes,* and, in it, the female emerges as the dominant comic type, whether as *old maid* or *termagant wife.* It is a very late phase of the love comedy of Western Europe, and bears about the same relationship to its tradition as the Punch and Judy show to the harlequinade.

Next to the old bachelor, the old maid was one of the most frequently sketched characters in eighteenth-century periodicals.[3] Among the editorial promises made in *Salmagundi* is that it will teach old maids how to get along without husbands. The cause of the old maid's misfortunes is usually her ugliness. Natural ugliness as a source of laughter was solemnly abjured by satirical theory; however, it could be treated as a source of good-natured laughter. Tabitha Bramble, for example,

. . . is tall, raw-boned, aukward, flat-chested, and stooping; her complexion is sallow and freckled; her eyes are not gray, but greenish, like those of a cat, and generally inflamed; her hair is of a sandy, or rather dusty hue; her forehead low; her nose long, sharp, and, towards the extremity, always red in cool weather; her lips skinny, her mouth extensive, her teeth straggling and loose, of various colours and conformation; and her long neck shrivelled into a thousand wrinkles.[4]

Charity Cockloft was "according to her own account, a celebrated beauty" in her teens, "though I never could meet with anybody that remembered when she was handsome; on the contrary, Evergreen's father . . . says she was as knotty a little piece of humanity as he ever saw; and that, if she had been possessed of the least sensibility, she would, like poor old *Acco,* have most certainly run mad at her own figure and face the first time she contemplated herself in a looking-glass" (211).

Since they have been rejected by the male sex, old maids tend to become censorious prudes, finding wantonness and other matter for disapproval in the most ordinary conduct of women younger than themselves. This is the case of Tabitha Bramble, Mrs. Slipslop in *Joseph Andrews,* and Mrs. Deborah Wilkins in *Tom Jones.* The editor of the facetious serial *Literary Leisure* put an old maid in charge of the female department, since, as a soured misanthrope, she is "qualified for judging of the conduct of others."[5] One of Christopher Cockloft's daughters, Margery, "seemed disposed to maintain her post as a belle, until a few months since; when accidentally hearing a gentleman observe that she broke very fast, she suddenly left off going to the assembly, took a cat into high favor, and began to rail at the forward pertness of young misses. From that moment I set her down for an old maid" (155).

As a consequence of her sexual frustration, the old maid tends to become a religious enthusiast. Tabitha Bramble is a violent Methodist, and Charity takes "a considerable lean toward Methodism, was frequent in her attendance at love feasts, read Whitefield and Wesley, and even went so far as once to travel the distance of five-and-twenty miles to be present at a camp-meeting" (212).

Of course, the old maid secretly desires sexual encounters, although she pretends to be insulted or horrified by male advances. One of the finest comic strains in *Humphry Clinker* comes out of situations in which Tabita protests male behavior while engaging frantically in some gesture of pursuit.[6] The following anecdote has the quality of these comic scenes in Smollett:

My good aunt prided herself on keeping up this buckram delicacy; and if she happened to be playing at the old-fashioned game of forfeits, and was fined a kiss, it was always more trouble to get it than it was worth; for she made a most gallant defense, and never surrendered until she saw her adversary inclined to give over his attack. Evergreen's father says he remembers once to have been on a sleighing party with her, and when they came to Kissing-bridge, it fell to his lot to levy contributions on Miss Charity Cockloft, who, after squalling at a hideous rate, at length jumped out of the sleigh plump into a snow-bank, where she stuck fast like an icicle, until he came to her rescue. This Latonian feat cost her a rheumatism, from which she never thoroughly recovered (211–12).

The humors plot that Irving was often drawn to in his later work — the battle of the sexes between the termagant wife and the henpecked husband — is not dramatized in *Salmagundi,* although it enters the serial in several oblique forms. Most of the humorists are bachelors who retain enough of their traditional ill nature to thoroughly abhor meddling housewives; Langstaff, like Diedrich Knickerbocker after him, has an intense antipathy to brooms. Will Wizard shares this humor, and it infects the theatrical criticism which is given to him as a pedant and antiquarian. At the theater, Wizard is asked to settle a dispute over a controversial speech in *Othello* — "the celebrated wish of Desdemona, that heaven had made her such a man as Othello":

It was a very foolish, and therefore very natural, wish for a young lady to make before a man she wished to marry. It was, moreover, an indication of the violent inclination she felt to wear the breeches, which was afterwards, in all probability, gratified, if we may judge from the title of "our captain's captain," given her by Cassio — a phrase, which in my opinion, indicates that Othello was, at that time, most ignominiously henpecked (165).

There seem to be two reasons for the absence of any direct treatment of this complex so common to domestic fiction: the first is that Irving never faced the problem of fiction in more than a rudimentary way; his essayist-narrators are never able to release their stories from the commentary or sensibility to which the piece is devoted, and this theme, more than others, demands the objective illumination of the fiction through narrative and dialogue. Secondly, Irving's fiction, like that of most of the major American writers who followed him, is devoted to an essentially male world. His most American work, *A History of New York,* is also the work most free of female intrusion. Domestic humor and polite satire deal with worlds in which women have some place; but burlesque comedy, which is set in a comic paradise, will not, unlike its edenic counterpart, accommodate females easily. One has the sense in reading Rabelais that there are no females in the work; and in *Tristram Shandy* neither Mrs. Shandy nor the Widow Wadman is effectively present. Burlesque comedy attempts to deny that its infantile paradise contains the seeds of its own destruction.

The History, however, is a work written in the present, and its framing fiction is a version of the plot of the battle of the sexes. It has a sharp edge, as it would have again in "Rip Van Winkle." Knickerbocker is a penniless author, frantically racing against time and his landlady's inevitable discovery that he is penniless. Eventually, she tells her husband that he must order the lodger out, and, although Seth Handaside sympathizes with Knickerbocker, he will not stand up against his wife's anger. This all has a familiar ring to it; similar episodes occur repeatedly in *Tom Jones* and *Joseph Andrews*, can be found in *The Vicar of Wakefield*, and had been used earlier in America — by Philip Freneau in several of his humorous essays and by H. H. Brackenridge in *Modern Chivalry*.

This fiction pushes its way into the history itself. It preys upon Knickerbocker's mind and shapes his narrative in ways that anticipate the extremely self-conscious contemporary fiction of Vladimir Nabokov: "I would give half my fortune (which at this moment is not enough to pay the bill of my landlord) to have seen him [Stuyvesant] accoutred cap-a-pie" (*HNY*, 28-29):

Willingly would I, like the impetuous Peter, draw my trusty weapon and defend it through another volume; but truth, unalterable truth forbids the rash attempt, and what is more imperious still, a phantom, hideous, huge and black, forever haunts my mind, the direful spectrum of my landlord's bill — which like a carrion crow hovers around my slow expiring history, impatient of its death, to gorge upon its carcass (*HNY*, 444-45);

If we could but get a peep at the tally of dame Fortune, where, like a notable landlady, she regularly chalks up the debtor and creditor accounts of mankind, we should find that . . . though we may for a long while revel in the very lap of prosperity, the time will at length come, when we must ruefully pay off the reckoning. Fortune, in fact, is a pestilent shrew, and withal a most inexorable creditor; for though she may indulge her favourites in long credits, and overwhelm them with her favours; yet sooner or later, she brings up her arrears with the rigour of an experienced publican, and washes out her scores with their tears (*HNY*, 202).

The largest domestic element in *Salmagundi* was the topic of modern style and the type of *the upstart*, the "new man." Although it is sometimes treated in the mode of genial humor and burlesque comedy, it is the one relatively serious strain in the work. This concern attests to Irving's deep social conservatism and his intense dislike of the course that American civilization was taking. It is Irving's only social theme; but in his later works it would appear as less a critique of modernity than a static nostalgia for the past or a fictional quest for an age of lost values. In *Salmagundi,* the ideal alternative to the negative values of modern style, which are mostly associated with the American merchant class, is an Americanized version of ancestral England. In a few instances, however, Langstaff chooses to locate his nostalgia in the old Dutch culture of New York. Langstaff relishes the customs "handed down to us from our worthy Dutch ancestors" (478):

> It is with great regret, however, I observe that the simplicity of this venerable usage has been much violated by modern pretenders to style, and our respectable new-year-cookies and cherry-bounce elbowed aside by plum-cake and outlandish liqueurs, in the same way that our worthy old Dutch families are out-dazzled by modern upstarts and mushroom cockneys (479).[7]

In *The History,* desire for a ceremonial (and creative) past grows to substantial proportions; in that work, Irving chose old New Amsterdam to represent that past:

> Thrice happy, and never to be forgotten age! when every thing was better than it has ever been since, or will be again — when Buttermilk channel was quite dry at low water — when the shad in the Hudson were all salmon, and when the moon shone with a pure and resplendent whiteness, instead of that melancholy yellow light, which is the consequence of her sickening at the abominations she every night witnesses in this degenerate city! (*HNY,* 147).

The opposition of Old New York and the English countryside is symbolic of the duality of Irving's career. The first led him to burlesque comedy, and the second to a muted humor; the first led to myth and the second to a sentimentalized sociology of manners.

Modern style and the upstart are introduced toward the end of an essay devoted to the Cocklofts, as illustrations of the rubs and frustrations of modern life that often make Christopher so testy:

> It turned out that my cousin, in crossing the street, had got his silk stockings bespattered with mud by a coach, which, it seems, belonged to a dashing gentleman who had formerly supplied the family with hot rolls and muffins! . . . it would have edified a whole congregation to hear the conversation which took place concerning the insolence of upstarts, and the vulgarity of would-be gentlemen and ladies, who strive to emerge from low life by dashing about in carriages to pay a visit two doors off; giving parties to people who laugh at them, and cutting off all their old friends (158).

A full treatment of the theme appeared two issues later in an essay entitled "On Style," a title associated with the graver moral essays in the periodical tradition. At its center is the story of the Giblet family, which illustrates "the gradation of a family aspiring to style, and the devious windings they pursue in order to attain it" (200). Old Giblet is a vicious character, and, it may be, a version of Irving's father:

He was the most surly curmudgeon I ever knew. He was a perfect scare-crow to the small-fry of the day, and inherited the hatred of all these un-lucky little shavers: for never could we assemble about his door of an evening to play, and make a little hubbub, but out he sallied from his nest like a spider, flourished his formidable horsewhip, and dispersed the whole crew in the twinkling of a lamp (201-2).

Giblet is the only miser in Salmagundi:

The only rules of right and wrong he cared a button for, were the rules of multiplication and addition, which he practiced much more successfully than he did any of the rules of religion or morality. He used to declare they were the true golden rules; and he took special care to put Cocker's arithmetic in the hands of his children, before they had read ten pages in the Bible or the Prayerbook (202).

Irving was the son of a successful merchant, and he had a deep psycholog-ical antipathy to business. He suffered a breakdown in 1817 as a result of his forced involvement in his family's business.

As early as *The Corrector,* Irving had indirectly expressed his deep, personal aversion to the materialism and practical morality to which Amer-ican civilization had devoted itself, and, there, it was expressly associated with Benjamin Franklin. But, unlike the theme of democratic politics, this was a theme that Irving chose to avoid. The treatment of Giblet in *Salma-gundi* is the one exception; it contains the strongest personal note struck in that work. After this, Irving's hatred of American materialism and mer-cantilism seems to have been unconsciously repressed in his writing, although it was stimulated whenever an American (like Ichabod Crane) entered a work.

With this one exception, Irving was able to treat the upstart and style genially. The word *style* itself, Wizard writes, is essentially a whim-sical word:

This same word Style, though but a diminutive word, assumes to itself more contradictions, and significations, and eccentricities, than any mono-syllable in the language is legitimately entitled to. It is an arrant little humorist of a word, and full of whimwhams, which occasion me to like it hugely (197).

87

Among the whimsical antipathies of the humorists in *Salmagundi,* there is a common aversion to modern style and upstarts, although each manifests his humor in a different area of life. Christopher's whim, however, extends to the appurtenances of domestic life: to furniture — "the fragile appendages of modern style [which] seemed to be emblems of mushroom gentility" (358) — trees, and houses; he stigmatizes poplars "as mere upstarts, just fit to ornament the shingle palaces of modern gentry" (358).

The ability to regain a mode of genial humor in this connection was the result of an act of displacement from a real father or Franklin to a familiar literary type. The comic type that was ultimately chosen to represent the new man and his vulgar pretensions to fashion was a safely hedged English species, the *mushroom cockney.* Like the French *émigrés,* the cockneys are also seen as an invading army attempting to conquer New York by their exhibitions of style. The cockney is introduced by Irving about halfway through *Salmagundi,* displaying "his horsemanship along Broadway . . . worried by all those little yelping curs that infest our city" (206-7), and he stays in the serial, while the American merchant drops out. In the twelfth number, Irving and Paulding collaborated on a playful sketch of Tom Straddle of *"Brummagem,"* who came to America to *"astonish the natives a few"* (281-84).

The cockney was a happy choice; he could be treated humorously or whimsically, without engaging Irving's anger, since his origin was purely literary: he was a combination of the *nouveau-riche* merchant and the servant who attempts to live up to his master's style and falls horribly in debt. Both types were repeated endlessly in English farces of the period which played in the New York theaters that Irving attended so frequently. The many allusions to these plays in *Salmagundi* establish this low comic form as yet another of the many traditional contexts that bear upon Irving's work and give it breadth of comic reference and thus comic meaning.

Charles Brummagem, a character in Prince Hoare's *Lock and Key,* may be explicitly alluded to in the Stradddle sketch. The particulars of his fashionable aspirations find their echo in that essay and many other parts of the work. Brummagem is "a fellow full of lies and ignorance, who values you only for the number of quarters in your scutcheon, tells you long stories of tables and chairs having been in his family for one hundred years, which in reality he bought second-hand yesterday," and he claims to be "descended from the Brummys, who came over with the Conqueror."[8]

Other farce characters were adapted by Irving to serve as models for the parvenu. Caleb Quotem, for example, has "more trades than hairs in his wig: and more tongues than trades." There are echoes of this play (*The

Review [1808] by George Colman the Younger) throughout *Salmagundi.*
A cockney theatrical critic, "'Sbidlikensflash" (the name is probably taken
from Fielding's farce *Don Quixote in England* [1773]), who gave his
nationality and some of his traits to the cockney upstart when he appeared
later in the serial, is described at a New York assembly as "'up to everything' . . . like Caleb Quotem" (46). The situation of this play is a desire
on everyone's part to have a place at the review; and the Giblets, rebuffed
despite the great style in which they have arrayed themselves, "like Caleb
Quotem, determined to have 'a place at the review'" (204).[9]

    Colman's *The Heir at Law* deals with a common farce situation, that,
for example, of Molière's *Georges Dandin* and *Le Bourgeois Gentilhomme.*
Lord Duberly is a wealthy merchant, recently become nobility, whose wife
tries to retailor him in the pattern of fashionable society, while he, like
Dandin, would much prefer to sit in the kitchen, smoking his pipe, with
his feet up on the stove. He defends his old trade and cannot see the difference between drinking his tea from a cup and drinking it from a saucer,
but "he must learn to dance and jabber french . . . I know what's ele-
gance." The formula for becoming a fine gentleman in that play has many
similarities to the recipe in *Salmagundi:* "sport a curricle — walk Bond
street — play at Faro — get drunk — dance reels — go to the opera — cut
off your tail — pull on your pantaloons — and there's a *buck* of the first
fashion for you."[10] The wealthy merchant of *The Review* is more like
Brummagem than Duberly. Deputy Bull exclaims in the play, "Suppose I
did sell a few figs, upon Ludgate Hill. . . . . An't I now, Mr. Deputy Bull . . .
with my carriage, — and country house, here, at Windsor, — all in taste?"[11]
Sylvester Daggerwood, in Colman's play of that name (1795), is the son of
an eminent button-maker at Birmingham, which was also Straddle's
occupation. Other farce characters that Irving knew and drew upon for his
type of the cockney upstart were Sir Pertinax Macsycophant and Abel
Handy from Charles Macklin's *Man of the World* (1754), and Major
Sturgeon, the fishmonger of Brentford, from Samuel Foote's *The Mayor
of Garrett* (1763).

    Smollett's *Humphry Clinker,* however, seems to have provided Irving
with the greatest number of hints and models for his treatment of the
cockney and style. The vulgarity of the rising classes is a major theme of
that work and often produces a physical relapse in the sensitive Matthew
Bramble. Smollett was used most extensively in the third *Salmagundi* essay
on these themes, "Style at Ballston," which is the freest of all and often
approaches burlesque comedy. There are many resemblances between the
observations of Evergreen at Ballston Springs and Bramble at Bath, which
may be the result of a common stock of comic elements or even a common treatment of the realities of resort life. The climax of both pieces is

an explosion of violence at dinner time, because the fashionable pretender is unused to the starvation that attends the discipline of spa life. Here are Smollett's and Irving's respective versions of the scene:

". . . every table is to be furnished with sweet-meats . . . which, however, are not to be touched till notice is given by the ringing of a bell. . . . This will be no bad way of trying the company's breeding – "
. . . the bell beginning to ring, they flew with eagerness to the desert, and the whole place was instantly in commotion. There was nothing but justling, scrambling, pulling, snatching, struggling, scolding, and screaming. The nosegays were torn from one another's hands and bosoms; the glasses and china went to wreck; the tables and floors were strewed with comfits. Some cried; some swore; and the tropes and figures of Billingsgate were used without reserve in all their native zest and flavour; nor were those flowers of rhetoric unattended with significant gesticulation. Some snapped their fingers; some forked them out; some clapped their hands, and some their back-sides . . . and everything seemed to presage a general battle.

[Evergreen] relates a number of "moving accidents," which befell many of the polite company in their zeal to get a good seat at dinner; on which occasion a kind of scrub-race always took place, wherein a vast deal of jockeying and unfair play was shown. . . . But when arrived at the scene of action, it was truly an awful sight to behold, . . . the tumultuous uproar of voices crying some for one thing, and some for another. . . . The feast of the Centaurs and Lapithae was nothing when compared with a dinner at the great house . . . (391-92).

The substitution of the Cockney for the self-made American gave Irving the distance necessary for genial comedy and burlesque play, but the choice of an English mercantile equivalent of the American, who is mistaken in America *for the real thing*, also allowed Irving to express indirectly a complex of feelings that were probably not yet clear in his own mind – his adulation of the English and his repugnance toward his own civilization:

I should never have taken the trouble to delineate . . . [Straddle's] character had he not been a genuine cockney. . . . Perhaps my simple countrymen may hereafter be able to distinguish between the real English gentleman, and individuals of the cast I have heretofore spoken of, as mere mongrels, springing at one bound from contemptible obscurity at home to daylight and splendor in this good-natured land. The true-born and true-bred English gentleman is a character I hold in great respect; and I love to look back to the period when our forefathers . . . hailed each other as brothers (289).

The attempt to take on the American businessman had threatened to tap deep feelings in Irving. Perhaps it also threatened to take Irving into a vein of American literature which would not be comic, and would involve his confronting the American scene as it had historically defined itself. The substitution of the English Cockney not only relieved him of that necessity, it also cleared the path symbolically for the transition to his middle period, by exorcising his sentimental England of possible American values.

CHAPTER SEVEN

BURLESQUE COMEDY

The various and increasing shifts in modality from satire to burlesque comedy during the run of *Salmagundi* were both spontaneous and fluid, but they correspond to a shift from *the town* as the setting of the serial to a burlesque *Gotham*. The town, that concentrated patch of urban spectacles, was the setting of polite satire. Gotham, on the other hand, hailed from the distant world of English folk humor and jest: to discourage King John from establishing his court in their city, so the story goes, the inhabitants of Gotham feigned imbecility, and during his visit, worked at the absurdest tasks. For this, legend distinguished them by the appellation of *the wise men of Gotham*. The association of absurdity and wisdom made Gotham an appropriate topsy-turvy setting for burlesque comedy.

The town is the setting for the first numbers of *Salmagundi*, although the initial use of the term was also another of Irving's puns — a disguised proclamation of his parody. There is a high incidence of associated terms, such as the "ton," the "beau-monde," and the "fashionable world," all of which had ironic force in the early serials. The editorial statements at the beginning of *Salmagundi* all refer to this conventional setting: The Salmagundians intend to "correct the town," "to present a striking picture of the town" (28), "particularly to notice the conduct of the fashionable world" (33).

The use of Gotham as a setting for comedy has a regular though infrequent history in seventeenth- and eighteenth-century English literature. It was most often used in connection with minor burlesque forms — the jest and the nonsense rhyme: most of the titles alluding to "the wise men of Gotham" were collections of jests rather than extended works.[1] In time the rational intention of the Gothamites was buried, and they became associated with absurdity alone, as well as a grotesquery which often verged on the obscene:

> Thence to Gotham, where no zany,
> Though not all fools, I saw many;
> Here I found a harlot prancing,
> And in the moon-shine nimbly dancing:
> There another full of gig
> Sat astride a filthy pig.[2]

Although Paulding was the first to allude to Gotham in *Salmagundi,* it was Irving who used it most frequently and made it a burlesque metaphor for New York. Irving is also the only one of the three collaborators who shows any familiarity with the legends of Gotham. His American Gothamites are "descended from three wise men, so renowned of yore for having most venturesomely voyaged over sea in a bowl" (423),[3] and Diedrich Knickerbocker classes prior historians "with those notorious wise men of Gotham, who milked a bull, twisted a rope of sand, and wove a velvet purse from a sow's ear" (*HNY,* 49).

The fusion of the burlesque Gotham with New York was perhaps the richest and deepest example of comic synthesis, the bringing together of independent serial threads, which soon established itself as the method for developing the periodical. Even in *Salmagundi,* it moved the city back into the past and associated it with an older New York, which was a realm of pure comedy. For Irving, it constituted an act of freedom that eventually generated the comic vision of *The History.* Gotham was eventually put in the charge of Linkum Fidelius, an antiquarian author of rare and obscure folios, who prefigures Diedrich Knickerbocker in a superficial way:

Wisely was it said by the sage Linkum Fidelius, "howbeit, moreover, nevertheless, this thrice-wicked towne is charged up to the muzzle with all manner of ill-natures and uncharitablenesses, and is, moreover, exceedinglie naughte." This passage of the erudite Linkum was applied to the city of Gotham, of which he was once Lord Mayor, as appears by his picture hung up in the hall of that ancient city; but his observation fits this best of all possible cities "to a hair" (207).

The piece in *Salmagundi* that resembles most closely the world of *The History* is presented as chapter 109 of Linkum's monumental "Chronicles of Gotham."

In that essay and the earlier "Plans for Defending Our Harbor," Irving's treatment of New York broke into an area of comic freedom rarely found in *Salmagundi.* The latter essay is set at a time when madness prevails, when the city is under the spell of "midsummer fancies and dog-day whimwhams," when "everybody's head is in a vertigo, and his brain in a ferment." New York takes on the absurd simplicity of Rabelais' burgher Cockaigne and Sterne's Strasbourg, and deliberately so, for Irving introduces his two masters into the essay, for the purpose of modal direction:

A day was appointed for the occasion, when all the good citizens of the wonder-loving city of Gotham were invited to the blowing-up; like the fat innkeeper in Rabelais, who requested all his customers to come on a certain day and see him burst (313);

The dinners were cold, and the puddings were overboiled throughout the renowned city of Gotham; and its sapient inhabitants, like the honest Strasburghers, from whom most of them are doubtless descended, who went out to see the courteous stranger and his nose, all returned home after having threatened to pull down the flagstaff by way of taking satisfaction for their disappointment (314).[4]

The burlesque reconstruction of America was tentatively extended to other cities — cities because *Salmagundi* could not transcend the cosmopolitanism of the serial format. But any attempt to create a comic America was bound to fail without a spectrum of specific regional humors. Irving was familiar with the incipient stereotypes of the Southerner and Yankee but was apparently not yet disposed to put them in altercation with his Gothamites. The most that Irving would do in *Salmagundi* was to contrast New Yorkers and Philadelphians in terms of a conceptual opposition — whimsy as against rigidity, the nineteenth as against the eighteenth century:

"They [the Philadelphians] are an honest, worthy, square, good-looking, well-meaning, regular, uniform, straight-forward, clock-work, clear-headed, one-like-another, salubrious, upright, kind of people, who always go to work methodically, never put the cart before the horse, talk like a book, walk mathematically, never turn but in right angles, think syllogistically, and pun theoretically, according to the genuine rules of Cicero and Dean Swift; — whereas the people of New York — God help them — tossed about over hills and dales, through lanes and alleys, and crooked streets — continually mounting and descending, turning and twisting — whisking off at tangents, and left-angle-triangles, just like their own queer, odd, topsy-turvy, rantipole city, are the most irregular, crazy-headed, quicksilver, eccentric, whimwhamsical set of mortals that ever were jumbled together in this uneven, villainous, revolving globe, and are the very antipodeans to the Philadelphians" (251).

Irving did not realize the implications of Gotham and its topsy-turvy laws until *The History of New York*. The topics that follow are exercises in the traditional elements of burlesque, purged finally of all satirical or rational control.

In a discussion with Mrs. Scriblerus about the bringing up of their son, Cornelius describes a necessary phase of Martin's education:

. . . to perambulate this terraqueous Globe is too small a Range; were it permitted, he should at least make the tour of the whole System of the Sun. Let other Mortals pore upon Maps, and swallow the legends of lying travellers; the son of Cornelius shall make his own Legs his Compasses; with those he shall measure Continents, Islands, Capes, Bays, Streights and Isthmus's [*sic*] : He shall himself take the altitude of the highest mountains. . . . When he has div'd into the bowels of the earth, and survey'd the works of Nature under ground . . . I hope he will bless the world with a more exact survey of the deserts of Arabia and Tartary, than as yet we are able to obtain.[5]

These travels were made and published, and, so runs the Scriblerian hoax, were known to the world as *Gulliver's Travels.*

The lying traveller is not completely separable from the Gothamite or fool, particularly in his comic figuration as man upside down. One of the earliest lying travellers, Othello, describes himself as voyaging to the heights of white, cultured Venice from the extremes – the black and savage undersides of the world. In the deepest comedy, the "lies" which the traveller tells are those fantasy-truths of the underworld in ourselves. Gulliver makes the opposite voyage, into a world of animals, and returns to civilization bringing with him intolerable but salutary truths about man. These deeper myths must at least be mentioned, even though Irving is unwilling or unable to play with them.

The identification of an editor or narrator as a world traveller and dispenser of marvelous tales was a popular one, and it can be found in many comic works that have no actual travel fictions in them. The Spectator described himself as an insatiable traveller, who had once made a "Voyage to *Grand Cairo,* on purpose to take the Measure of a Pyramid" (No. 1), but he does not travel in the serial. Many other serial editors included this as part of their initial autobiography to their readers. In his "Pindariana," Peter Pindar warns his readers to "expect no wonders, as I am neither a MANDEVILLE, a PSALMANAZAR, nor an ABYSSINIAN BRUCE. Unfortunately I have met with no 'Anthropophagi and men whose heads do grow beneath their shoulders.'"[6] The idea of converting beggars' children into a source of national wealth in Swift's "A Modest Proposal . . ." was also "inspired" by a story of Psalmanazar's.

Salmagundi is begun under the inspiration and authority of Psalmanazar, a famous impostor who achieved much notoriety in early eighteenth-century London by passing himself off as a Formosan; this would be the appropriate mock interpretation of the three lines of macaronic verse attributed to the imposter on the title page. And we are told that Will Wizard, *Salmagundi*'s lying traveller, "understands all languages, not excepting that manufactured by Psalmanazar" (74).[7]

Wizard's adventures in his travels had been more diplomatic and sentimental than physical. Among his lies are the common claims of intimacy with foreign great men and the love of their beautiful daughters. Wizard and Dessalines, emperor of Haiti, had been "great cronies — hand and glove — one of the most condescending great men I ever knew" (138); and news of "the late *fracas* at Canton" alarms Will "for the safety of his friends, Kinglun, Chinqua, and Consequa" (307).

The only use to which Wizard's travels are put in the serial is his propensity to launch into a long and boring traveller's tale at any opportunity. This humor was the property of the squire or old gentleman of domestic humor, but in *Salmagundi* it began to approach the long-winded madness of the burlesque dissertator: "thundering long stories they are, let me tell you; set Will once a-going about China or Crim Tartary, or the Hottentots, and Heaven help the poor victim who has to endure his prolixity; he might better be tied to the tail of a jack-o'-lantern. In one word — Will talks like a traveller" (134). Evergreen introduces Wizard to Miss Sophy Sparkle — "a young lady unrivaled for playful wit and innocent vivacity" — at a ball:

To add to my distress, the first word he spoke was to tell Miss Sparkle that something she had said reminded him of a circumstance that happened to him in China; and at it he went in the true traveller style; described the Chinese mode of eating rice with chopsticks; entered into a long eulogium on the succulent qualities of boiled birds' nests; and I made my escape at the very moment when he was on the point of squatting down on the floor, to show how the little Chinese *Joshes* sit crosslegged (140).

In *The History*, rich and exotic travel lore is the result of Knickerbocker's insatiable reading rather than his travels. He is, however, identified as a lying historian, and his comic role, although it is inferior in execution and conception to that of the best of his eighteenth-century forebears, is enriched by a positive identification between lies and the products of the creative fancy. In this and in other ways, *The History* is a seminal work which regularly translates the terms of Shandean or burlesque comedy into the new world of American romanticism, and it should someday be studied exclusively from this point of view.

The lying traveller can be regarded as a special type of the universal butt of comedy. The most prominent masks in Old Comedy, those of the learned doctor and the bragging soldier, are masks for liars.[8] We have been told time and time again that one of the primary functions of comedy is to expose the abuse of learning, of false knowledge; but it would be more proper to argue that what comedy exposes is the sterility of thought itself.

Considering Plato's elevation of the false doctor to preeminence over the many other enemies of order and civilization, and the persistence with which this type has been chosen as the object of comic attack, we might expect that here if anywhere the negative vision presented would be unambiguously satirical — tempered with a more or less direct anger and clearly to be read in terms of an argument or set of beliefs, in the validity and nobility of the mind and learning. Yet the opposite is the case. From Aristophanes' presentation of an absurd Socrates in his *Clouds* — a high priest of the wind and a spouter of airy nonsense — this figure seems to demand of the comic artist burlesque mockery, play, and the inconsequential and absurd tropes and frames of nonsatiric comedy. Aristophanes' Socrates, however much he may have been hated as a revolutionary, is involved in fictions that are far from the truly disturbing aspects of scientific blindness and infidelity. The works of later satirists which treat the abuse of learning most directly — *The Memoirs of Scriblerus,* "A Tale of a Tub," the third book of *Gulliver's Travels, The Dunciad,* the one-act plays of Molière — are remarkable within the context of their authors' work for self-consciousness, comic indirection, and an indulgence in almost pure play and nonsense.

In *Salmagundi* and *The History,* Irving acknowledges through a substantial series of allusions and recognizable structures his deep involvement in this area and this tradition of comedy — The philosopher, in *Salmagundi,* "who maintained that black was white, and that, of course there was no such color as white" (44) is Aristophanes' Socrates.

Although the type of the learned doctor appeared more often as the *pedant* in the middle ages and Renaissance, he originated as the *philosopher,* and of the two standard variants, the philosopher was the more congenial butt for American satire in the eighteenth century, because the "American" had always distrusted abstract speculation, at least from the time of the Revolution. The inadequacy and the inefficiency of logic and metaphysics are the respective themes of Paine's *Common Sense* and Franklin's *Autobiography.*

The comic philosopher was usually either a logician or a metaphysician or both; either a man capable of demonstrating absurd truths that were incompatible with common sense, or a builder of intricately abstract castles in the air.

Hudibras is such a philosopher, and in the following passage, he is identified with the mad Gothamite of folk tradition:

Could twist as tough a rope of sand;
And weave fine cobwebs, fit for scull
That's empty when the moon is full. . . .
He could raise scruples dark and nice,
And after solve 'em in a trice. . . .
He knew the seat of Paradise,
Could tell in what degree it lies;
And, as he was disposed, could prove it,
Below the moon, or else above it:
What Adam dreamt of when his bride
Came from her closet in his side:
Whether the devil tempted her
By a High-Dutch interpreter:
If either of them had a navel . . . (I, i, 158–81)

Tristram is a philosopher; so are Master Alcofribas and the narrator of "A Tale of a Tub." It seems possible that there was an initial intention in *Salmagundi* to cast Langstaff as a philosopher to complement Wizard, who was very early given the attributes of a pedant and antiquarian. Langstaff is compared to Lucian's Diogenes: "He is then as crusty and crabbed as that famous coiner of false money, Diogenes himself" (188).[9] Toward the end of the serial, there occurs the following passage of whimsical bragging, which foreshadows Diedrich Knickerbocker:

I could here amuse myself, and stultify my readers, with a most elaborate and ingenious parallel between authors and travellers; but in this balmy season . . . it would be cruel to saddle them with the formidable difficulty of putting two ideas together and drawing a conclusion, or, in the learned phrase, forging *syllogisms in Baroco* (321).

Other than Langstaff, the only philosopher in *Salmagundi* is Jeremy Cockloft, who is both a logician and a natural philosopher. Jeremy has just graduated from Columbia University, and he values himself above all "upon his logic, has the old college conundrum of the cat with three tails at his fingers' ends, and often hampers his father with his syllogisms, to the great delight of the old gentleman; who considers the major, minor, and conclusion, as almost equal in argument to the pulley, the wedge, and the lever, in mechanics" (97). The device of clothing the syllogism by analogy is also found in the *"Treatise of Syllogisms"* of Crambe, Martin's tutor in *Scriblerus:*

He suppos'd that a Philosopher's brain was like a great Forest, where Ideas rang'd like animals of several kinds; that those Ideas copulated and engender'd Conclusions; that when those of different Species copulate, they bring forth monsters of absurdities; that the *Major* is the male, the *Minor* is the female, which copulate by the Middle Term, and engender the Conclusion.[10]

Walter Shandy is a natural logician:

Persuasion hung upon his lips, and the elements of Logick and Rhetorick were so blended up in him . . . that NATURE might have stood up and said, — "This man is eloquent" . . . what is more astonishing . . . he knew not so much as in what the difference of an argument *ad ignorantium,* and an argument *ad hominem* consisted (*TS,* 52).

Walter is addicted to syllogizing: on the trip back from London after Mrs. Shandy's false pregnancy, she happens to mention the word weakness, and "sure as ever the word *weakness* was uttered, and struck full upon his brain, — so sure it set him upon running divisions upon how many kinds of weaknesses there were . . . and then he would do nothing but syllogize within himself for a stage or two together" (*TS,* 42).

Comic play with the syllogism and Aristotle's treatises on logic may have originated in the antischolastic burlesque of the Renaissance; there is still a high incidence of it in the eighteenth century, particularly among the Scriblerians and Sterne. In *Tristram Shandy,* for example, Sterne adjusts syllogizing to the great chain of being and points out that angels and spirits syllogize "by INTUITION; — and beings inferior, as your worships all know, — syllogize by their noses" (*TS,* 237).[11]

In Irving, the syllogism takes on substance and becomes a literal weapon in philosophical warfare. He describes a syllogistic tournament:

The battle was carried on entirely by words, according to the universal custom of this country. . . . The grand bashaw attempted to rip him up with an argument, or stun him with a solid fact, but the little bashaw parried them both with admirable adroitness, and run him clean through with a syllogism. The grand bashaw was overthrown . . . (126),

which resembles an earlier use of this figure in *The Memoirs of Scriblerus:*

METAPHYSICKS were a large field in which to exercise the Weapons *Logick* had put into their hands. Here Martin and Crambe us'd to engage like any prize-fighters, before their Father, and his other learned companions of the Symposiacks. And as Prize-fighters will agree to lay aside a buckler or some such defensive weapon, so would Crambe promise not to use *simpliciter & secundum quid,* provided Martin would part with *materialiter & formaliter:* But it was found, that without the help of the defensive armour of those Distinctions, the arguments cut so deep, that they fetch'd blood at every stroke.[12]

Comic artists also played with the formal names of syllogisms, often reducing them in effect to musical babble. Sterne loved to compose in this way. The reference to the *"Argumentum Bacalinum"* [*sic*] in *The Corrector* (27) is borrowed from Tristram's dissertation on arguments, particularly the following passage from it:

I do therefore, by these presents, strictly order and command, That it be known and distinguished by the name and title of the *Argumentum Fistulatorium* [the argument of one who plays on the shepherd's pipe] , and no other; — and that it rank hereafter with the *Argumentum Baculinum* [argument of a stick] (*TS,* 71).[13]

Jeremy Cockloft is a *natural philosopher,* an *experimental philosopher,* and their practical counterpart, a *projector.* The substance of his knowledge was taken from Swift's treatment of natural philosophy in *Gulliver's Travels.* Jeremy is a prodigy of natural philosophy:

He lately frightened a simple old uncle almost out of his wits, by giving it as his opinion that the earth would one day be scorched to ashes by the eccentric gambols of the famous comet, so much talked of; and positively asserted that this world revolved round the sun, and that the moon was certainly inhabited (149).

The inhabitants of Laputa are continually disturbed by fears relating to the celestial bodies. Among them is an allusion to Haley's comet, borrowed by Irving: "That, the Earth very narrowly escaped a Brush from the Tail of the last Comet, which would have infallibly reduced it to Ashes; and that the next, which they have calculated for One and Thirty Years hence, will probably destroy us." The other Laputan fears have to do with the sun, and Irving incorporated them in a modified form into *The History.*[14]

Jeremy's projects and experiments all have a common motif; they are concerned with explosions. At college, "No student made better squibs and crackers to blow up the chemical professor" (96); "He once shook down the ash-house, by an artificial earthquake"; he "nearly blew his sister Barbara and her cat out of the window with the thundering powder"; he once made a pot of black broth which "actually threw the cook-maid into convulsions" (97); he knocked down the gardener in an experiment "to try Archimedes' plan of burning-glasses" ("It became dangerous to walk through the court-yard for fear of an explosion"); and he blew up "a favorite Chinese gander" of Mrs. Cockloft's (319–20). The metaphors of the *explosion* and those of *birth* and *fever* are fictions for structuring burlesque experience. The source of these metaphors is the essential fiction of burlesque comedy where the festive rehearsal of the explosion of order and the return to chaos is repeated endlessly and where the celebration of gastric and excremental processes is often punctuated by harmless explosions.

The essay, "Plans for Defending Our Harbor," is organized in terms of fever and explosion metaphors. It begins:

Surely never was a town more subject to midsummer fancies . . . our notions, like our diseases, seem all epidemic; and no sooner does a new disorder or a new freak seize one individual but it is sure to run through all the community. This is particularly the case when the summer is at the hottest, and everybody's head is in a vertigo, and his brain in a ferment (310-11):

and it concludes:

Everybody seems charged to the muzzle with gunpowder − every eye flashes fire-works and torpedoes − and every corner is occupied by knots of inflammatory projectors, not one of whom but has some preposterous mode of destruction, which he has proved to be infallible by a previous experiment in a tub of water! (319).

This essay contains an allusion to Rabelais and three explicit allusions to *Tristram Shandy,* two of them to the Rabelaisian "Hafen Slawkenbergius' Tale." The essay also contains a fictitious anecdote, which, as far as I can discover, is not taken from Rabelais, but is certainly invented in the spirit of that author: an anecdote about the blowing up by sneezing of the army of the great king Bigstaff by Captain Trenchement (316).

This essay is Irving's version of the traditional *academy of philosophers and projectors* which may be found in the *Clouds,* Lucian, Rabelais, "A Tale of a Tub," and Book III of *Gulliver's Travels.* It is usually presented spatially, through the survey of an institute, each room of which is occupied by a different learned madman. Irving has a crowd of projectors gathered for a specific occasion, but these are parallel grouping principles. One of the projects for frustrating the English is to "let Governor's Island be raised by levers and pulleys − floated with empty casks, etc., towed down to the Narrows, and dropped plump in the very mouth of the harbor!" (316). This is certainly Irving's bow to the flying island of Laputa.

Another trait of the burlesque philosopher is given to Jeremy Cockloft:

Jeremy Cockloft the younger, who, like a true modern philosopher, delights in experiments that are of no kind of use, took the trouble to measure one of Will's risible explosions, and declared to me that, according to accurate measurement, it contained thirty feet square of solid laughter (310).

The act of *measurement* carried to an absurd degree of precision or applied to incongruous, often immeasurable objects and the act of suffocating categorization, which have always been prominent comic figures associated with the philosopher or pedant, must be seen as critiques of the mind itself rather than attacks against scientific excesses. In the late nineteenth and the twentieth centuries, these would be among the charges seriously levelled at the reign of analytic philosophy, and they would be seen not as transparent methods of arriving at truths but as psychic attempts to inhibit participation in experience.

In the *Clouds,* Aristophanes has his Socrates engaged in an ingenious experiment for measuring the jump of a flea.[15] That devoted philosopher, Mr. Walter Shandy, saw all of science as a matter of precise measurement:

. . . he would weigh nothing in common scales; − no − he was too refined a researcher to lay open to so gross an imposition. − To come at the exact weight of things in the scientific steel-yard, the fulcrum, he would say, should be almost invisible, to avoid all friction from popular tenets; − without this the minutiae of philosophy, which should always turn the balance, will have no weight at all. − Knowledge, like matter, he would affirm, was divisible *in infinitum;* − that the grains and scruples were as much a part of it, as the gravitation of the whole world. − In a word, he would say, error was error, − no matter where it fell, − whether in a fraction, − or a pound, − 'twas alike fatal to truth, and she was kept down at the bottom of her well as inevitably by a mistake in the dust of a butterfly's wing, − as in the disk of the sun, and moon, and all the stars of the heaven put together (*TS*, 145).

The comic philosopher, whether Hudibras, the narrator of a "A Tale of a Tub," or Will Wizard, is often presented as measuring trifles:

> For he, by geometric scale,
> Could take the size of pots of ale;
> Resolve, by sines and tangents straight,
> If bread or butter wanted weight;
> And wisely tell what hour o' th' day
> The clock does strike, by Algebra.[16]

Precise measurement was a trait also associated with the *connoisseur* or *cognoscente*. This type and the *virtuoso* and *dilettante* were three species of the learned fool especially singled out for burlesque or satirical treatment in the eighteenth century. The connoisseur was a type of critic who pretended to scientific exactitude in matters of taste; less frequently in comic writing, he was a critic with intuitive but absolute taste.[17] The virtuoso was a man of little or no knowledge, but one who claimed scientific status by virtue of collecting natural curiosities or antiquities; less frequently the term was synonymous with the term *projector*. The dilettante was a critical or scientific amateur. Comic writers used these terms flexibly, at times interchangeably, but the meanings given above have the greatest frequency.

In the initial tag of his Shandean novel, *Flim-Flams*, Isaac D'Israeli singles out as the object of his burlesque, "LITERATI, DILETTANTI, AND COGNOSCENTI . . . [who are] big with jest . . . but wisdom not."[18] And in the first essay in *Salmagundi*, the editors, playing with the principle of burlesque equivalence between the comic writer and his subject matter, proclaim "We are critics, amateurs, dilettanti, and cognoscenti and . . . we know by the pricking of our thumbs, that every opinion which we may advance in either of those characters will be correct" (28).

The connoisseur is usually presented as absurdly sensitive to fine distinctions and the necessity of precision. Tristram, for example, describes Trim "bent forwards just so far, as to make an angle of 85 degrees and a half upon the plain of the horizon," and adds: "The necessity of this precise angle of 85 degrees and a half to a mathematical exactness, – does it not shew us, by the way, – how the arts and sciences mutually befriend each other" (*TS*, 122). Tristram is a connoisseur; he measures his father's blush, who "redden'd, pictorically and scientintically speaking, six whole tints and a half, if not a full octave above his natural colour" (*TS*, 162), and, at the beginning of the book, he measures his dedication in order to prove that "it is far from being a gross piece of daubing, as some dedications are" (*TS*, 16).[19]

Yet, in terms of the principle of burlesque equivalence, connoisseurs, as a class, are also Tristram's adversaries, and he lashes out whimsically at them:

I'll undertake this moment to prove it to any man in the world, except to a connoisseur; – though I declare I object only to a connoisseur in swearing, – as I would do to a connoisseur in painting, &c. &c. the whole set of 'em are so hung round and *befetish'd* with bobs and trinkets of criticism, – or to drop my metaphor, which bye the bye is a pity, – for I have fetch'd it as far as from the coast of *Guinea;* – their heads, sir, are stuck so full of rules and compasses, and have that eternal propensity to apply them upon all occasions, that a work of genius had better go to the devil at once, than stand to be prick'd and tortured to death by 'em (*TS*, 180).

None of the major characters in *Salmagundi* were developed as connoisseurs. Wizard was introduced as "a great connoisseur in mandarin dresses and porcelain" (37), but nothing was made of it. 'Sbidlikens, the cockney, however, is a connoisseur of the theater and in the field of music. He is prepared to censure Mrs. Darley if she "offers to dare to look less than the 'daughter of a senator of Venice,' — the standard of a senator's daughter being exactly six feet" (37). When Evergreen finds 'Sbidlikens at Mr. Wilson's concert, he "had put on his cognoscenti phiz" (58). 'Sbidlikens is a critic whose taste "has attained to . . . an exquisite pitch of refinement" (37), and he has reduced the principles of art to mathematical order: he has a system which equates different kinds of theatrical slaps with different degrees of passion (163), and finds fault with Cooper's manner of dying: "'It was not natural,' he said; for it had lately been demonstrated by a learned doctor of physic, that when a man is mortally stabbed, he ought to take a flying leap at least five feet, and drop down [dead] '" (165).

The *virtuoso* was a favorite object of Scriblerian comedy. Scriblerus' father, Cornelius, is one: "He had already determin'd to set apart several annual Sums, for the recovery of *Manuscripts,* the effosion of *Coins,* the procuring of *Mummies;* and for all those curious discoveries by which he hoped to become . . . a second *Peireskius.*" Dr. Fossile, the butt of the Scriblerian farce, *Three Hours after Marriage,* is also a virtuoso; he is a collector of shells and has a museum of which the prize curiosities are a stuffed alligator and an Egyptian mummy.[20]

Julian Cognous is the only virtuoso in *Salmagundi.* At the conclusion of his letter to the editor quoted earlier, he announced that he had "hung up the skeleton of the corset in the museum beside a dissected weasel and a stuffed alligator" (469). Cognous is the type of the English virtuoso, and, the year before, in presenting a sketch of the type, *The Port-Folio* had explained that this was "a character, however uncommon in America, which frequently excites the wonder or provokes the ridicule of the European satirist." This was not quite the case; the virtuoso is frequently treated in Brackenridge's *Modern Chivalry,* and this is not surprising considering the demand in America for museums filled with natural curiosities.[21]

The other major type of learned fool of burlesque tradition was the *antiquarian* or *pedant,* and during the run of *Salmagundi,* Will Wizard was steadily developed in that direction; this was in effect a rehearsal for Diedrich Knickerbocker. Almost all of the well-known eighteenth-century humorists had a hobby-horse of an antiquarian or pedantic flavor: Parson Adams and Euripides, Doctor Primrose and monogamy, Matthew Bramble and health, and of course Walter Shandy and names and noses. Wizard's penchant is much more general, for his hobby-horse is simply ancient manuscripts and black letter texts.[22]

One of the earliest antiquarian references in *Salmagundi* is a mock threat that the authors will burn their essays if they are not bought, "and, like the books of the sibyls and the Alexandrian Library, they will be lost forever to posterity" (32).[23] The other more common side of this theme, the recovery of texts from oblivion — and civilizations too, according to Knickerbocker — was given to Wizard:

An old book printed three hundred years ago is a treasure; and a ragged scroll, about one-half unintelligible, fills him with rapture. O! with what enthusiasm will he dwell on the discovery of the Pandects of Justinian, and Livy's history; and when he relates the pious exertions of the Medici, in recovering the lost treasures of Greek and Roman literature, his eye brightens (417).

The learned text as an image of history — destroyed or recovered to the irreparable loss or gain of mankind — was to become a permanent theme of Irving's, and a serious one in his later work. While in Italy, Irving had met John Hayter, an English antiquarian sent out by the Prince of Wales to transcribe the papyri of the Herculaneum library, unearthed the year before. Irving had visited that site, and also that of Pompeii, and Hayter had shown him the method used to unroll the papyrus scrolls, which Irving had found very ingenious. The references to Herculaneum in *Salmagundi* are trifling, but in *The History* this figure becomes a major metaphor for the historian and history:

By this time my readers must fully perceive, what an arduous task I have undertaken . . . raking in a little kind of Herculaneum of history, which had lain nearly for ages, buried under the rubbish of years, and almost totally forgotten — raking up the limbs and fragments of disjointed facts, and endeavouring to put them scrupulously together, so as to restore them to their original form and connection — now lugging forth the character of an almost forgotten hero, like a mutilated statue — now decyphering a half defaced inscription, and now lighting upon a mouldering manuscript, which after painful study, scarce repays the trouble of perusal (*HNY*, 166-67).

Cockloft Hall contains a burlesque library comparable to the library on the Island of St. Victor in Rabelais, and "in point of usefulness and eccentricity, with the motley collection of the renowned hero of La Mancha" (414). Irving, however, barely renders the library; there was no intellectual tradition to which he felt drawn. The library contains "specimens of the oldest, most quaint, and insufferable books in the whole compass of English, Scotch, and Irish literature" (414), but the only example of its contents that he gives seems to allude to scholasticism: "A phillippic, by Archbishop Anselm, against the unseemly luxury of long-toed shoes, as worn by the courtiers in the time of William Rufus, which he purchased of an honest brickmaker in the neighborhood, for a little less than forty times its value" (414).[24]

The antiquarian is the possessor of quaint and invaluable manuscripts, which he deciphers, translates, edits, and prepares glosses for. This was not only part of the traditional subject matter of burlesque comedy; in the Renaissance and after it was often the fiction for the burlesque work itself. This work is often a published manuscript or contains manuscripts, and the editing, translating, and commenting become areas of self-conscious play.

The moral satirist of the serial tradition was soon transformed into the ill-natured pedant, a variant of the snarling critic attacked by Swift in "A Tale of a Tub" and Pope in *The Dunciad*. Opposed to this type, there existed the amiable and whimsical pedant, who probably came from romance rather than Scholastic or Renaissance scholarship, where he was usually the hero's tutor; and this original relationship is retained in the characters of Crambe, Holofernes, and Walter Shandy, who insists on undertaking his son's education himself. In *The Memoirs of Scriblerus, Gargantua*, and *Tristram Shandy*, the education of the hero is a major unit of the burlesque work.

This pedant has usually studied at the great Dutch, German, or Polish universities. He may, however, be without formal education, like Walter Shandy (*TS*, 52-53), Will Wizard — "Will has not had the advantage of an education at Oxford or Cambridge, or even at Edinburgh or Aberdeen" (36) — or Parson Adams, who "had applied many Years to the most severe Study, and had treasured up a Fund of Learning rarely to be met within a University."[25] The first trait usually mentioned in connection with the pedant was his mastery of languages, particularly those of an exotic flavor, usually Hebrew[26] or the Oriental tongues.[27]

The literary form associated with the pedant is the *dissertation.* While few burlesque works take the form of a dissertation, they usually abound in specific dissertations, threatened or begun, or sometimes unfolded with formal completeness.[28] The digressions in "A Tale of a Tub" are dissertations; *Flim-Flams* contains almost a dissertation a chapter, and the fifth chapter of *Scriblerus* is "A Dissertation upon Play-Things." For obvious aesthetic reasons, the dissertation cannot be suffered to assume its own length; the usual method of handling it is to have the pedant, withdrawn in his intellectual labyrinth, interrupted by something in the scene that sets him off on one of his obsessive intellectual interests or abruptly ends it. In most instances, the author will provide some connection — the more absurd and outrageous the better — between the dissertation and the narrative fiction. Cornelius Scriblerus, for example, had compiled a dissertation on Hercules' shield "proving from the several properties, and particularly the colour of the Rust, the exact chronology thereof." He plans to entertain a company of guests with it on the evening of his son's christening. At the point in the dissertation where the shield is to be uncovered and used in the demonstration: ". . . his cheeks grew paler, his hand trembled, his nerves failed, till on sight of the whole the Tremor became universal: The Shield and the Infant both dropt to the ground, and he had only strength enough to cry out, 'O God! my Shield, my Shield!'" "The Truth was, the Maid (extremely concern'd for the reputation of her own cleanliness, and her young master's honour) had scoured it as clean as her Andirons."[29] Walter Shandy thinks in terms of dissertations, begins them continuously, but is rarely allowed to get far into them before he is interrupted.

Most of the dissertations in *Salmagundi* are mentioned as having been delivered or to be given in the future; the subjects are ludicrous or absurd, but generally subjects for which there are analogies in comic writing. Jeremy Cockloft's "dissertation on the phlegmatic nature of a goose's gizzard" (104) may allude to Rabelais' often-mentioned thirteenth chapter on the goose as "Arse-wipe." The satirical dissertation "on buttons and horse flesh" given to the cockney Straddle (288), echoes both Tristram's dissertation on buttonholes (*TS,* 290) and the dissertation on horses given by Leonora's father in *Joseph Andrews.*[30]

The essays "On Style" and, to a lesser extent, "On Greatness" are intended to be complete, set dissertations. Their form is not nearly so intricate as the form of those written by the Scriblerians and Sterne; it does, however, correspond to the form of the dissertation on the nature of stink in *Humphry Clinker.*[31] That begins with a definition and includes historical precedents for such a meaning, a catalogue of national attitudes on the subject, arguments based on authorities, etc. Irving was probably not intellectually prepared to present a survey of learned opinions on style; Wizard's research on the subject was limited and futile: "Blair's Lectures on this article have not thrown a whit more light on the subject of my inquiries; they puzzled me just as much as did the learned and laborious expositions and illustrations of the worthy professor of our college, in the middle of which I generally had the ill luck to fall asleep" (197).

The nations upon whom the mantle of pedantry hung most comically were Holland and Germany. Sterne's editor states that the Dutch had long been identified with "ponderous and myopic dullness" (*TS,* 430). Other reasons why the Dutch should have been chosen from among the nations that advanced scholarship in the Renaissance, however, have to do with connecting lines of burlesque characterization: the "barbarous" sounds of the Dutch language and the portrayal of the Dutch as a fat, vacuous people, which was the basis for Irving's characterization in *The History*.

The Dutch and Germans were usually associated with commentary. Tristram tells us that it was astonishing, considering his father's intellectual ability, that he had never heard "one single lecture upon *Crackenthorp* or *Burgersdicius,* or any *Dutch* logician or commentator" (*TS,* 52); and, after discussing the condition of Yorick's manuscript sermons, Tristram turns suddenly to a Dutch commentator and asks him, "tell me then, Mynheer Vander Blonederdondergewdenstronke, why they should not be printed together?" (*TS,* 430).[32] Joseph Dennie concluded his third "Farrago" essay as follows: "The character and journal of Meander, scarcely need a commentary. There shall be none. I was not born in Holland, and only Dutchmen are qualified to write notes."[33] Wizard at his study demonstrates a "phlegmatic patience unknown in these degenerate days, except, peradventure, among the High Dutch commentators" (416). Wizard is also responsible for the following Dutch argument, which Irving probably adapted from Swift:

We were on the point of acquitting Jeremy [of plagiarism] with honor, on the ground that it was impossible, knowing as he is, to borrow from a foreign work one month before it was in existence; when Will Wizard suddenly took up the cudgels for the critics, and insisted that nothing was more probable, for he recollected reading of an ingenious Dutch author who plainly convicted the ancients of stealing his labors! — So much for criticism (334).[34]

In Demy Semiquaver's modern symphony, the effect of "Citizens quarreling in Dutch" is to be rendered by a "chorus of a tin trumpet, a cracked fiddle, and a hand-saw" (242). The stridency of the Dutch and German languages, to which Irving often alluded in *The History*,[35] was used as evidence for their great antiquity, according to the following association made by Jeremy: "quere, why do the Harsimites talk Dutch? — story of the Tower of Babel, and confusion of tongues" (100). The first languages that Gulliver tried on the Lilliputians were High and Low Dutch; the Houyhnhnms "pronounce through the nose and throat, and their language approaches nearest to the High Dutch or German."[36] One of the scholarly issues of the post-Renaissance period was which of the tongues still spoken was the most ancient language. In the last essay in *Salmagundi*, Wizard claims "that the universal language which prevails there [the moon] is high Dutch; thereby proving it to be the most ancient and original tongue, and corroborating the opinion of a celebrated poet, that it is the language in which the serpent tempted our grandmother Eve (497).[37]

Diedrich Knickerbocker is himself a Dutch commentator; in *The History* he carries on this tradition of pedantry, and in addition surrounds himself with the authority of his fellow Dutchmen: Grotius, Pufendorf, Vossius, Lavater, Lauterbach, etc.

The major authority in *Tristram Shandy* is the "great and learned" Hafen Slawkenbergius; in *Salmagundi* it is Linkum Fidelius. There are few specific parallels between these fictitious authorities, but the position they occupy in both works is very much the same. Both are High or Low Dutch commentators; Linkum "demonstrated before the whole University of Leyden, that it was possible to make bricks without straw" (64). Both are obscure: Hafen's works are "extremely scarce" (*TS*, 244) and Linkum is an "unheard of writer of folios" (29). And both are men of great genius: "Slawkenbergius his book may properly be considered, not only as a model, – but as a thorough-stitch'd DIGEST and regular institute of *noses;* comprehending in it, all that is, or can be needful to be known about them" (*TS,* 232). Linkum has applied his acumen to every conceivable subject: the ancient Scots (40), experimental philosophy (64), the ancient history of Philadelphia (102, 250-51), sturgeons (107), the underworld (117), the character of Chinese ladies (167), style (197), the original set-tlers of America (292), the bald eagle (297), the nature of man (420), and the nature of habit (427). The works of both are being prepared for publication by descendents of their discoverers: Tristram translates and publishes in the center of his work a gnomic tale by Hafen; the Salma-gundians quote excerpts from Linkum's manuscript folios, and Wizard, toward the end of the serial, is pictured as working on Linkum's manu-scripts in the library. *A History of New York* is, in a sense, a new version of Linkum's "Chronicles of Gotham."

The last essay in *Salmagundi* is wholly given over to burlesque pedantry; and it is the closest in tone and strategy to *A History of New York,* but the resemblance is not yet that close. The initial display of pedantry is facetious: a tag attributed to Virgil and its translation by Linkum, and an appeal to the authority of Confucius (495).

Wizard describes two of the essays he had prepared for eventual inclusion in *Salmagundi.* The first is a refutation of "all those wild theories respecting the first settlement of our venerable country." The second clusters several burlesque themes from *Salmagundi,* which Irving was pre-sumably thinking of in connection with his next work: antiquarian deciphering, the moon as a subject of scientific inquiry and experiment, the Yankees of Connecticut – "I had likewise written a long dissertation on certain hieroglyphics discovered on those fragments of the moon, which have lately fallen, with singular propriety, in a neighboring State, and have thrown considerable light on the state of literature and the arts in that planet" (497).

The climax of the burlesque strain in *Salmagundi* is the essay "Of the Chronicles of the Renowned and Antient City of Gotham" (419–28). It has many resemblances to the mock battles in *Tristram Shandy* and *Gargantua*. The essay is also the translation of an ancient manuscript,[38] and the elements of this format are reproduced with a self-conscious consistency. Finally, it tries to integrate as many as possible of the burlesque themes that were developed during the run of the serial.

"The Chronicles" is the recasting in antiquarian form − part epic, part romance, and part ancient treatise − of the conquest of the youths and maidens of New York by French *émigré* dancing masters. "The Chronicles" outlines the "great discomfiture" and the "perilous extremity" suffered by "the thrice renowned and delectable city of Gotham" from the "invasion and assaults of the Hoppingtots." Among the several models which this essay plays off against is Herodotus, who would also be appealed to in *The History*. Under his influence, the "swarm" of expatriated Frenchmen becomes a barbarian invasion "like the Scythians of old, overrunning divers countries and commonwealths, and committing great devastations wheresoever they do go, by their horrible and dreadful feats and prowesses" (420). And like many of the barbarian tribes in Herodotus, they are distinguished by a miraculous deformation, in this case "for being right valorous in all exercises of the leg." In keeping with the tone, which is an imitation of medieval chroniclers, Irving adds, "of them it hath been rightly affirmed that no nation in all Christendom or elsewhere, can cope with them in the adroit, dexterous, and jocund shaking of the heel."

The stimulus for the invasion is a need of food-stuffs by the Hoppingtots, who are led by "two redoubtable and renowned warriors, hight Pirouet and Rigadoon;[39] ycleped in such sort, by reason that they were two mighty, valiant, and invincible little men; utterly famous for . . . victories of the leg." Prior to the battle, a council is held among the Hoppingtots, where "the cunning Pirouet and that arch catiff Rigadoon" hotly stir up and wickedly incite the Hoppingtots by describing the feasts that await them within the walls of Gotham.

The Hoppingtots caper "Toward the devoted city of Gotham, with a most horrible and appalling chattering of voices [singing and playing *Ça Ira*]," appearing, to the horrified inhabitants, to be aided by the powers of witchcraft and necromancy. At the height of the battle, the Hoppingtots are rallied by Rigadoon, "flourishing his left leg with great expression of valor, and most magnificent carriage":

'My copesmates, for what wait we here? are not the townsmen already won to our favor? do not their women and young damsels wave to us from the walls in such sort that, albeit, there is some show of defense, yet is it manifestly converted into our interests?' So saying, he made no more ado, but leaping into the air about a flight-shot . . . after the manner of the Hoppingtots, he gave a short partridge-run, and with mighty vigor and swiftness did bolt outright over the walls with a somerset (426).

This essay, as I have said, had been anticipated by many prior strains in *Salmagundi,* particularly the themes of dancing and the French, and the grotesque animation that usually attended their conjunction. The topsy-turvy principle of the "Chronicles" had also appeared in the serial: "I am under serious apprehensions that the period is not far distant when the discipline of the dancing-master will supersede that of the grammarian; crotchets and quavers supplant the alphabet: and the heels, by an antipodean maneuver, obtain entire pre-eminence over the head" (328-29).

Toward the end of "Plans for Defending Our Harbor," when the modern Gothamites are fidgeting with schemes for defeating the British, one of the crowd recalls Gotham's heroic and Rabelaisian past: "One pathetically lamented that we had no such men among us as the famous Toujoursdort and Grossitout; who, when the celebrated Captain Trenchement made war against the city of Kalacahabalaba, utterly discomfited the great king, Bigstaff, and blew up his whole army by sneezing" (316).

In addition to the battle metaphors that abound in *Salmagundi,* there had also occurred earlier figures involving an armed conspiracy against Gotham or the authors. The Salmagundians see themselves threatened by "All the queer fish, the grubs, the flats, the noddies, and the live-oak and timber gentlemen, [who] are pointing their empty guns at us; and we are threatened with a most puissant confederacy of the 'pigmies and cranes,' and other 'light militia'" (86); just as Yorick was threatened by "a grand confederacy, with ***** and ***** at the head of it" (*TS*, 30).[40]

The Hoppingtot champion, Rigadoon, is the final transformation of the animated Frenchman in *Salmagundi.* But Irving's dancing Frenchmen came from *Tristram Shandy;* if one compares the passage already quoted with the following from Sterne, I believe that the similarity in quality as well as the specific parallels justify this claim:

Then . . . he fetched a gambol upon one foot, and turning to the left-hand, failed not to carry his body perfectly round. . . . Well, said *Gymnast* . . . I will undo this leap; then with a marvellous strength and agility, turning towards the right-hand, he fetched another frisking gambol as before; which done, he set his right-hand thumb upon the bow of the saddle, raised himself up, and sprung into the air, poising and up-holding his whole weight upon the muscle and nerve of the said thumb, and so turned and whirled himself about three times: at the fourth, reversing his body and overturning it upside-down, and foreside back, without *touching any thing.* . . .

Then . . . he incontinently turned heels over head in the air . . . then springing into the air with a summerset, he turned him about like a windmill (*TS,* 388–89).

Moreover, the manuscript from which this is read in *Tristram Shandy* is couched in the same mock diction as "The Chronicles": "'which words being heard by all the soldiers which were there, divers of them being inwardly terrified, did shrink back'" (*TS,* 387-88).

The passage which Irving adapted from Sterne was itself a close transcription of *Gargantua,* Book I, chapter 35. But there are Rabelaisian elements in "The Chronicles," which Irving could not have found in Sterne. The battle is over food and drink, and Gotham is represented to the Hoppingtots as a city crammed full of nourishment: "The antient and venerable city of Gotham was, peradventure, possessed of mighty treasures, and did, moreover, abound with all manner of fish and flesh, and eatables and drinkables" (421), "where Hoppingtots . . . might riot most merrily every day in the week on beef, pudding, and such like lusty dainties" (422). In the fourth book of Rabelais, there is recounted a similar burlesque war between Pantagruel and his followers, and a race of savages, the Chitterlings.

One strategy of the burlesque pedant as commentator was to claim that a childish or nonsense fable was actually the repository of profound but disguised mysteries. The name of Pythagoras and the context of the Orphic mysteries was usually associated with this claim. The narrator of "A Tale of a Tub," for example, claims to have glossed "Tom Thumb, whose Author was a *Pythagorean* Philosopher. This dark Treatise contains the whole Scheme of the *Metempsychosis,* deducing the Progress of the Soul thro' all her stages."[41] "The Chronicles" alludes to the format of the arcane treatise; the unknown author has not only related the event, but has included some of the commentary written upon it by Linkum Fidelius. The author paraphrases Linkum on the mythic origins of the Hoppingtots:

The learned Linkum Fidelius, in his famous and unheard of treatise on man . . . is particularly minute and elaborate in treating of the nation of the Hoppingtots, and betrays a little of the Pythagorean in his theory, inasmuch as he accounteth for their being so wonderously adroit in pedestrian exercises, by supposing that they did originally acquire this unaccountable and unparalleled aptitude for huge and unmatchable feats of the leg, by having heretofore been condemned for their numerous offenses against that harmless race of bipeds . . . the frogs, to animate their bodies for the space of one or two generations (420–21).

Finally, "The Chronicles" is also a recently discovered manuscript, and Irving surrounds it with an appropriately self-conscious framework. It is "an old rusty, musty, and dusty manuscript" (418) found in "my grand-father's mahogany chest of drawers." It is "but one sheet of a stupendous bundle which still remains uninvestigated" (419), chapter 109, to be exact. And it has been translated from Dutch black-letter by Will Wizard. Reading it, we begin to hear the pedantic editorial manner of Dietrich Knicker-bocker in comments like the following: "Be this, however, as it may, the matter, albeit it has been the subject of controversy among the learned, is but little pertinent to the subject of this history; therefore we shall treat and consider it as naughte." (421).

Irving was already projecting his next production when this essay was written, and this was presumably a rehearsal for that among other things. "The Chronicles" is not a selection from the history of Dutch America, but a note on the back of the manuscript indicates that it was presented to Langstaff's grandfather "by his particular friend, the illus-trious Rip Van Dam, formerly lieutenant-governor of the colony of New Amsterdam" (419). Like *The History,* "The Chronicles" is a mythic his-tory of New York. In Irving's next work, the archaic voice would be aban-doned, and history itself transformed into a burlesque metaphor; for the one thing that the "Chronicles of Gotham" conspicuously lacks is any ade-quate relationship to the American past.

CHAPTER EIGHT

THE HISTORY OF NEW YORK

The Annihilation of America

Diedrich Knickerbocker's *History of New York,* the final work of Irving's first period, was published in December 1809. It was an immediate success, and there has always been a sizeable minority of critics and literary historians, increasing significantly of late, who hold to the opinion that it is Irving's best work.[1]

The *History* is not merely a good comic work in the tradition of Sterne and Rabelais or interesting because of its early place in American literature. Despite its many surface flaws and sprawling contours (a fault shared with works of Melville, Thoreau, and Whitman), it is a coherent and meaningful act of the imagination. Despite its overtly derivative nature, it is a distinctively American creation.

In the previous chapters, Irving's development as a comic writer has been studied against the background of diverse comic traditions. These chapters can be regarded as a study in the development of a vocabulary and grammar appropriate to burlesque comedy. These materials and techniques are all at work in *The History,* and a survey of their incidence there would amount to a repetition of what has already been said.

If *Salmagundi* was an exercise in comic vocabulary and provided Irving with a grammar that he could finally call his own, the history of Dutch America is the corresponding comic rhetoric. Because this history was Dutch, traditional comic associations lent themselves easily to the creation in America of an essentially comic world, the mythical land of Cockaigne. The act of creating a festive and ceremonial America, where history had only been able to produce a solemn and industrious civilization, and where jollity again suffers its inevitable defeat in the face of gloom, would probably have forced even a lesser writer to explore in his fiction the content and meaning of American civilization.

Like Irving's previous work, *The History* is created out of literature, not life — although the dichotomy is a false one, for *Gargantua* possesses or is able to release forms of vitality that cannot ordinarily be found after childhood in civilized life. If *The History* is "unquestionably the most allusive of all American literary compositions written before 1825,"[2] that is because, like *Gargantua* and *Tristram Shandy,* it is not merely made out of, but is about, the process of literature. Burlesque comedy has always presumed the continuing reality and interference of the world of past art that was so obstreperously reclaimed by moderns like Pound and Eliot; in the case of Joyce, there is burlesque comedy.

The History is a book about comedy. The various shifts of comic modality that occur in the book are the appropriate expression of the shifting values that the book traces. The reigns of the three Dutch governors — the overt historical organization of the major part of *The History* — are treated in different comic modes: that of Wouter van Twiller as burlesque comedy and, to a minor extent, domestic humor; William Kieft's as political satire (the only comic mode that Irving felt could be used to treat the present); and Peter Stuyvesant's in the more conventionally known, lower forms of burlesque comedy — burlesque epic and romance.

The first book of *The History,* which treats historical, anthropological, and philosophical speculation about a series of origins, is much more than a wild parody of works of sacred history, like Thomas Prince's *Theological History of New England,* which quite logically begin their narratives with the creation of the world; or an imitation of the opening of *Tristram Shandy.* It is an attempt to annihilate the history of America and the history of the mind, through the *disorganized* and inverted play of a mind operating through more primitive and childish impulses, a mind that in its very activity undermines the ordering principles which civilization has demanded of both the inner and the outer world.

The first five chapters are devoted to the desperate efforts of Knickerbocker to fight his way through the mass of speculation that surrounds the origin of America *as thought,* and, if true thought, then *as fact,* and it has the effect of destroying the legitimacy of thought and fact. His overt intention is to separate *myth* from *history,* but his speculations are continually involved with and interrupted by the act of thinking about them which creates a comic drama of the mind struggling to free itself from the tyranny of thought.

Irving was finally able to apply the mad solipsism of the whimsical humorist to significant purpose in these chapters. Knickerbocker finds that he cannot distinguish false from true speculation, cannot prevent himself from speculating about speculation. Sober theories grow so fantastically as his mind does battle with them that they seem to spill over and remake the world in their own grotesque image, animating and totally confusing the conventional stability of the mind and the world. Ultimately, he leaves the world clear and empty, to be recreated and resettled by the comic imagination.

If *Salmagundi* depended upon a comic theory of madness and a concept of fiction as self-conscious play which was derived from *Tristram Shandy, The History* depends as much upon another feature of Sterne's work, the breakdown of the intellect and the consequent unsettling (which amounts almost to an abolition) of the world of experience, accomplished primarily through the mad deflections of Tristram's narrative course. As a philosophical historian, Diedrich Knickerbocker is an amalgam of Will Wizard, Jeremy Cockloft, and Linkum Fidelius. But all that they give us of the narrator of *The History* is an outside glimpse, like Irving's descriptions of Wizard "poring over old scrawls . . . diving into receptacles of trumpery . . . [and] prying into the quaint obscurity of musty parchments" (*Sal.,* 415–16). The best earlier model for Knickerbocker is Walter Shandy.

It is difficult to give a concise account of Walter Shandy, since reflections of him continually shine and disappear along the hectic current of Tristram's narration. Like Knickerbocker, however, he is essentially an amiable and burlesque re-creation of the traditional comic philosopher. He philosophizes constantly, and, in his zest for ratiocination, he is unable to respond to any other appeal — "What is the character of a family to an hypothesis?" he retorts to a pious objection by Toby, "Nay, if you come to that — what is the life of a family?" (*TS,* 69). And he is unable to distinguish between large and trivial issues: between "my aunt *Dinah*'s affair" and "the retrogradation of the planets to *Copernicus*" (*TS,* 68). Walter is an extremely eccentric and whimsical philosopher, as Tristram repeatedly tells us: "In truth, there was not a stage in the life of man . . . but he had some favourite notion to himself, springing out of it, as sceptical, and as far out of the high-way of thinking, as these two which have been explained" (*TS,* 145). Like Knickerbocker, he is at the mercy of his eccentricity — so "that it laid him open to some of the oddest and most whimsical distresses" (*TS,* 217).

Comic writers have always treated the philosopher as a kind of compulsive madman, a solipsist who clings to his mental image of reality, however absurd, in defiance of all experience. Walter Shandy is such a philosopher:

. . . my father stood up for all his opinions: he spared no pains in picking them up, and the more they lay out of the common way, the better still was his title. . . . he held fast by 'em, both by teeth and claws, — would fly to whatever he could lay his hands on, — and in a word, would intrench and fortify them round with as many circumvallations and breastworks, as my uncle *Toby* would a citadel (*TS*, 223). . . . My father had such a skirmishing, cutting kind of a slashing way with him in his disputations, thrusting and ripping, and giving every one a stroke to remember him by in his turn . . . (*TS*, 588).

Walter is hobby-horsical, obsessed with a few notions which he attaches to everything in life and defends with fanatical vigor. Knickerbocker, on the other hand, is unstable and capricious, ranging over a whole variety of moods, affected by some undefined inner impulse. In this respect he resembles Walter's heteroclite son. He is unable to separate fact from fancy; he moves from theory to legend and literature too easily and suffers from the tensions these shifts produce with that other world in which these distinctions are valuable and necessary. Not only can he not separate his thinking about America from the speculations devoted to that new fact, but he acts as if the act of the mind were prior, as if it created and continued to manipulate the external reality as ideas drifted and associations interfered with a straight line of reasoning. As he agonizes and battles his way through the tangle of intellectual possibilities, which he has partially created himself out of his own feverish probing, realities from the settlement of America back to the creation of the world begin to agitate, smoke, and finally explode.

The heading of Book I announces that it will contain "divers profound theories and philosophic speculations . . . very learned, sagacious, and nothing at all to the purpose" (15). As Knickerbocker rummages through theoretical opinions on a variety of subjects, he calls into being a world of words which magically exhausts its subject and itself. Whereas the satirist, standing on firm ground, might hold up a patently false theory and dispel it by pretending to take it seriously, Knickerbocker *creates the very world in which the "false" theory belongs;* it replaces his starting point, the context of speculation. Although Knickerbocker does battle with these theories, he does so in their worlds; if the theories explode, Knickerbocker is knocked over by the force of the blast.

The following quotation is an indication of how powerful the ontology of solipsism in *The History* is: Knickerbocker cannot conceive of the idea of conflict without entering into the world of his conception:

It is an evil much to be lamented, that none of the worthy writers above quoted, could ever commence his work, without immediately declaring hostilities against every writer who had treated of the same subject. . . . this literary animosity is almost unconquerable. Even I, who am of all men the most candid and liberal, when I sat down to write this authentic history, did all at once conceive an absolute, bitter and unutterable contempt, a strange and unimaginable disbelief, a wondrous and most ineffable scoffing of the spirit, for the theories of the numerous literati, who have treated before me, of this country. I called them jolter heads, numsculls, dunderpates, dom cops, bottericks, domme jordans, and a thousand other equally indignant appelations (47–48).

The world of speculative philosophy is a burlesque world, and Irving creates it largely out of the combination and animation of traditional figures of speech. Although this is still the burlesque method of *Salmagundi,* the change from a slightly eccentric to a mad narrator has produced a radical intensification in the burlesque effect of the work.

Comic writers have always shared a stock of traditional figures for the speculative philosopher or metaphysician, and the world of speculative philosophy in *The History* is built out of these earlier comic figures and structures. Two stock figures of eighteenth-century antiphilosophical satire, for example, are those of the philosopher stumbling in fog or darkness chasing a will-o'-the-wisp,[3] and a philosopher lost in a labyrinth.[4] A third figure, which appealed to Irving, was that of the philosopher spinning air castles for himself to inhabit or voyaging through the upper reaches of the atmosphere. It is perhaps the oldest comic fiction within which the philosopher was sketched, whether as Socrates suspended in a basket above his thinking factory, or Lucian voyaging to the moon. It is also a figure for madness, and this and the fact that the figure expresses what the first book does — i.e., creates a world where fanciful speculation belongs — make it a particularly congenial figure to Knickerbocker.

The narrator of "A Tale of a Tub" begins his treatise by noting that ". . . the Philosopher's Way in all Ages has been by erecting certain *Edifices in the Air."* Isaac D'Israeli's burlesque narrative, *Flim-Flams,* is a chronicle of "the sufferings of Science; the disasters of universal Curiosity; and the small profits arising from certain Experiments on air and vapour!"[5] The speculative philosophers in *The History* "weave whole systems out of nothing" (48). In differentiating these philosophers from himself, Knickerbocker poses as a solid philosopher and refers his opponents to the Lucianic voyage to the moon:

When a man once doffs the straight waistcoat of common sense, and trusts merely to his imagination, it is astonishing how rapidly he gets forward. . . . But your adventurous philosopher launches his theory like a balloon, and having inflated it with the smoke and vapours of his own heated imagination, mounts it in triumph, and soars away to his congenial regions in the moon (32).

Fortunately, there is no path of common sense in *The History;* philosophic speculation is identified with the imagination and madness. Knickerbocker shares these qualities as deeply as any of his shadow adversaries. His frequent attempts to conquer the fancies which well up in him through the force of matter of fact are never successful; in fact they are themselves exercises in madness as they eventually explode the particular sober line of investigation he wishes he could follow. Irving plays with the eighteenth-century view of the imagination as neurotic, as the faculty most opposed to getting at the actual meaning of America, but it is in fact a positive force, by which that meaning is ultimately abolished.

Instability, imagination, and madness are the laws of that world in which the basic problems of cosmogony and American history are to be settled. The burlesque animation of that world was an easy task, since it had traditionally been treated as an arena of continual disputation, of proofs disproved; and the burlesque figure for the world of learning had very commonly been that of a battle of the folios or books. Conflict is the condition of Knickerbocker's aerial voyagers:

. . . until some envious rival assails their air blown pageant, shatters its crazy texture, lets out the smoke, and tumbles the adventurer and his theory into the mud. Thus one race of philosophers demolish the works of the predecessors, and elevate more splendid fantasies in their stead, which in their turn are demolished and replaced by the air castles of a succeeding generation (32).

Eventually these and other figures for philosophy and philosophical controversy assume an existential status; they become more real for the work of burlesque comedy than the arguments that called them up. This is usually effected by means of what might be called *runaway metaphor,* but could also be called *visionary metaphor.* This effect is achieved not because of the length or animation of the metaphor, but because it is the expression of the only world in which the comic data already experienced could have coherence. In the following passage, Tristram projects a vision of the world of science, which makes the qualities of ignorance and confusion the informing realities of a burlesque vision:

I tremble to think how many thousands for it, of benighted travellers . . . must have groped and blundered on in the dark, all the nights of their lives, — running their heads against posts, and knocking out their brains without ever getting to their journies end; — some falling with their noses perpendicularly into sinks, — others horizontally with their tails into kennels. Here one half of a learned profession tilting full butt against the other half of it, and then tumbling and rolling one over the other in the dirt like hogs. — Here the brethren, of another profession, who should have run in opposition to each other, flying on the contrary like a flock of wild geese, all in a row in the same way. — What confusion! — what mistakes! (*TS*, 198).

In *The History,* Irving moves at a slower pace in the direction taken by Sterne. The climax of this movement is found on pages 30 to 32 following a survey of eighteenth- and nineteenth-century theories of the creation of the earth based on the actions of comets. Knickerbocker speculates on the ease with which philosophers could create worlds, provided an abundance of comets:

. . . my unlearned readers will perhaps be led to conclude, that the creation of a world is not so difficult a task as they at first imagined. I have shewn at least a score of ingenious methods in which a world could be constructed; and I have no doubt, that had any of the Philo's above quoted the use of a good manageable comet, and the philosophical ware-house *chaos* at his command, he would engage, by the aid of philosophy to manufacture a planet as good, or . . . better than this we inhabit.

So far this is hypothetical speculation, but as Knickerbocker continues to turn this over in his mind, he turns the thoughts which have led him on into vision or fiction:

And here I cannot help noticing the kindness of Providence, in creating comets for the great relief of bewildered philosophers. . . . Should one of our modern sages, in his theoretical flights among the stars, ever find himself lost in the clouds, and in danger of tumbling into the abyss of nonsense and absurdity, he has but to seize a comet by the beard, mount astride of its tail, and away he gallops in triumph. . . . One drives his comet at full speed against the sun, and knocks the world out of him with the mighty concussion; another more moderate, makes his comet a kind of beast of burden, carrying the sun a regular supply of food and faggots — a third, of more combustible disposition, threatens to throw his comet, like a bombshell into the world, and blow it up like a powder magazine; while a fourth . . . insinuates that some day or other, his comet . . . shall absolutely turn tail upon our world and deluge it with water!

The burlesque ontology of the world of speculative philosophy may be considered a projection of the philosopher's eccentricity or madness. Walter Shandy "would move both heaven and earth, and twist and torture every thing in nature to support his hypothesis" (*TS*, 53). The final stage of Knickerbocker's madness is one in which the solipsistic absurdities of philosophy mingle with, absorb, and finally destroy an image of the actual world.

In the burlesque of syllogistic logic, for example, Knickerbocker uses the syllogism as a lever to set the world spinning. On the one hand, he attributes absurd proofs to other philosophers (38, 40), but the absurdity of the syllogism is not laughed away; it remains as a condition of the universe. On the other hand, Knickerbocker is himself an absurd syllogizer, and his proofs generally turn topsy-turvy the relationship of proof to fact:

. . . it yet remains, if possible, to shew how this country was originally peopled — a point fruitful of incredible embarrassment, to us scrupulous historians, but absolutely indispensable to our works. For unless we prove that the Aborigines did absolutely come from some where, it will be immediately asserted in this age of scepticism, that they did not come at all; and if they did not come at all, then was this country never populated — a conclusion perfectly agreeable to the rules of logic, but wholly irreconcilable to every feeling of humanity, inasmuch as it must syllogistically prove fatal to the innumerable Aborigines of this populous region. . . . to avert so dire a sophism, and to rescue from logical annihilation so many millions of fellow creatures, how many wings of geese have been plundered! (42-43).[6]

Irving concludes Book I of *The History* with a hypothetical anecdote resembling many fictions used to satirize the persecution and extermination of the American aborigines by Western powers. A perfectly traditional satire, it involves the time-honored device of introducing a superior civilization and having them treat the Europeans as they had treated the aborigines. The civilization introduced is that of the moon, and the anecdote is an obvious adaptation of the civilization on the moon, and the battle between its inhabitants and those of the sun, invented by Lucian in "A True History." In addition, however, it is a perfectly appropriate coda for the book, insofar as it fictionalizes the conquest of the earth by the moon, the symbol of whimsy, madness, and burlesque comedy. The very terms of the fiction reinforce the burlesque meaning: the inhabitants are obviously called Lunatics; they have attempted to enlighten the inhabitants of the earth by treating "them to mouthfuls of moonshine and draughts of nitrous oxyde" (66-67); and their superior strength is due to "a profound insight into that ineffable lunar philosophy, the mere flickerings of which, have of late years, dazzled the feeble optics, and addled the shallow brains of the good people of our globe" (63).

Knickerbocker introduces this as a supposition but soon insists that it is a fact and a matter of grave concern to him: "many a time, and oft . . . have I lain awake whole nights, debating in my mind whether it was most probable we should first discover and civilize the moon, or the moon discover and civilize our globe" (64).

What Irving stumbled upon in the opening books of *The History* was the deep insight that the creation of an American work of literature involves to some extent the annihilation of historical America. This insight will be treated at some length in a final chapter. This annihilation is effected in several ways which have already been discussed: the inability to distinguish between speculation and fact; the insistence that any theory, once it has been thought, has an *a priori,* and therefore a causal, relationship to the fact that stimulated it; and the replacement of the world of fact by one of mad speculation, self-consciously, by merging it with the act of thinking and associating, and substantively, through a succession of traditional comic structures which become the realities which the philosopher-historian is committed to live within and among.

The annihilation of America is more clearly effected through the overt organization of the book and motivated by Knickerbocker's desire for solid ground in which to begin the erection of his life's work. It is a childish structure, like Stephen Dedalus' attempt to locate himself through a total return address in *Portrait of the Artist;* but American literature, perhaps more than any other literature, gives itself freely to vital infantile forms. The history of America, Knickerbocker insists, depends upon its initial discovery, and this depends upon its geographical creation. Once he is launched upon this backward path, the creation of the world becomes an even more pressing starting point. The beginning Knickerbocker is driven to is the aboriginal void. The power of this childish strategy is that it has freed the artist and made it possible for him either to retell the factual history to the best of his ability, or, like a second God, to begin history anew.

A New World

The land discovered by Henry Hudson in 1609 was a new world, and in Books II and III of *The History,* Irving re-creates America as a comic utopia out of a variety of historical and literary myths; but the richest identity given to this new world is that of the Land of Cockaigne.

The relationship between Diedrich Knickerbocker and his Dutch protagonists is a complex one. They are all participants in the great adventure of creating a civilization that could potentially support and nourish the spiritual needs of its inhabitants — a theme whose death knell is sounded over and over in increasingly hysterical accents by the writers of the early decades of this century. Diedrich participates in this re-creation within the self-conscious world of writing history, savoring the delights and suffering the difficulties of creating what his Dutch Americans are at that moment discovering and settling in fictional time. But he is also fighting for his utopia in 1809, when the need for it was far greater than in

1609. Like so many American literary artists after him, he successfully attacks the windmills of time and history — the America that is and that needs to be undone — with an imaginary lance and shield. He is able to do this, on the level of imaginative strategy, as a result of the burlesque magic of Book I, which annihilated the validity of the historical past and the physical creation of the universe, clearing the way for a new and special act of genesis in nineteenth-century America.

The free act of the imagination that Knickerbocker won for himself is an extended version of a literal movement of imaginative extravagance that America stimulated. In the sixteenth and seventeenth centuries, the new continent attracted to itself legends that had been germinating over many centuries:

> The ancients had harbored traditions of wonderful western lands: the Elysian Fields, where happy souls went after death; the Islands of the Hesperides, where golden apples grew; Atlantis, that island continent swalowed up by earthquakes long before the time of Plato . . . [7]

these were only a few of the legends attached to America by the European imagination.

Most of the legends spun around the "empty" continent were paradisal, and one of the most important mythic meanings of America has been the recovery of Paradise — if only to reenact again its inevitable loss. This is the attitude toward the New World of Irving in *The History,* and it is not compromised by the fact that its expression is comic, nor by the fact that often, when Irving becomes ashamed of it, he tends to deny it, or use it satirically, to ridicule the extravagant fancyings of earlier writers on America.[8] The land discovered by Hudson is a paradise,[9] and a paradise it remains through the reign of Wouter Van Twiller, the first governor of New Amsterdam. One of the larger structures of *The History* as a whole is a burlesque version of the fall of man.

In an essay in the last issue of *Salmagundi,* appropriately devoted to the New Year, Paulding traces the "divine origin of New-Year festivity" back to the "golden age of our city" (*Sal.,* 478–79). Paulding's material on Dutch America is contained in one long paragraph; yet it was undoubtedly the germ of a conception central to *The History* and the source of many specific strains in Irving's work. In 1832 Paulding wrote to a correspondent that William Irving had often told him that that essay "gave his Brother the first idea of Knickerbockers History." Paulding added, "Of that however I wish You to say nothing."[10] Irving had admitted his debt to Paulding, albeit obliquely and facetiously, in *The History* itself; for the "ingenious and observant philosopher, who has made great discoveries in the neighbourhood of the Utopian community of Communipaw" (84), is Paulding.[11]

For Knickerbocker, the reign of Van Twiller represented "the halcyon days of the city" (105), the "sweet days of simplicity and ease" (106), the "good days of simplicity and sunshine" (135), and "those happy days of primeval simplicity, which float before our imaginations like golden visions" (136). Concluding his discussion of this period, Knickerbocker apostrophizes it as a "Thrice happy, and never to be forgotten age! when every thing was better than it has ever been since, or ever will be again" (147).

One simply cannot ignore the biblical structure of *The History*. The second chapter of the work is a survey of creation myths; the third is a survey of deluge myths, which are generally regarded as myths of a second creation. This is followed by a survey of speculations as to the mythic discovery of America by Noah, and in Book II a secular hero, Hudson, imitates the archetype and discovers a new world. Irving's history is a burlesque myth patterned after certain strategic movements in the Old Testament; in other words, a burlesque testament.

In the second chapter, Knickerbocker settles the controversy over the creation of the world by contenting himself "with the account handed us down by the good old Moses" (33), and he begins the next chapter with a paraphrase of *Genesis, V. 32:* "Noah, who is the first seafaring man we read of, begat three sons, Shem, Ham and Japhet" (35). One of the variant legends used by Knickerbocker to legitimize his sacred world is that Noah had a son, "named Thuiscon, from whom descended . . . the Dutch nation" (35).[12] Knickerbocker eventually rejects Noah's claim, but it has already become attached to *The History, as speculation,* and the voyagers aboard the *Goede Vrouw* descend, "men, women and children, in goodly groups, as did the animals of yore from the ark" (82–83).

According to biblical chronology, the period of Van Twiller corresponds to the age of the patriarchs, Abraham, Isaac, and Jacob. Knickerbocker's opening statement announces that his work is a memorial "of the days of the Patriarchs" (7). The Yankees of New England are compared to the descendents of Ishmael, Abraham's gentile son, who was driven into the wilderness and was thereafter marked by a "certain rambling propensity" (161). Irving gives this figure little play, perhaps because he has no intention of chronicling the sturdy pioneer virtues that this parallel would entail. The fact that the patriarchal model is inconsistent with the edenic image of the New World is of little importance, because the lack of consistency everywhere manifest on the level of allusion and symbol is one of the positive meanings of the work. On the one hand, it is just the capricious and careless pastiche of learning that one would expect from a muddle-brained philosopher-historian like Diedrich, and, on the other hand, the inconsistencies generally cohere on a higher level as burlesque comedy.

Following the age of the patriarchs, the Bible records a period of bondage in Egypt, followed by what amounts to a third creation: a symbolic dying in the Red Sea and the desert, and the ultimate crossing of a sacred river into a promised land, which seems to be an embryonic Cockaigne. The promised land in Irving's America is the island of Manhattan, as he indicates when discussing the etymology of the name:

But the most venerable and indisputable authority extant, and one on which I place implicit confidence, because it confers a name at once melodious, poetical and significant, is that furnished . . . by Master Juet; who clearly and correctly calls it MANNA-HATA — that is to say, the island of Manna; or in other words — "a land flowing with milk and honey!" (96).

The expedition which discovered the island was one on which "heaven seemed to shine propitious" (92).[13]

Finally, the reign of Van Twiller is compared to the tranquil reign of Solomon, the king of Israel at the height of its national glory. The only event which history has recorded of Van Twiller's unhistorical, because tranquil and ideal, reign as governor was the settling of a lawsuit, which occurred at the "very outset of the career of this excellent magistrate, like that of Solomon" (118). The issue was one of fraud, and while Van Twiller does not divide the account books in question, he does count the leaves and weigh the books and finds that one is just as thick and heavy as the other; "therefore it was the final opinion of the court that the accounts were equally balanced" (120).

There are no biblical parallels for the reign of Wilhelm Kieft, the second governor, which recounts the spiritual degeneration of the Dutch. The reign of Stuyvesant represents the heroic but futile attempt to withstand the dissolution in history which follows that inner decline, and Irving compares it to the heroic period of the history of Israel and to its period of final dissolution as a kingdom. For a parallel to Stuyvesant's defense of New Amsterdam, he draws upon Josephus (433). Irving's work is also a sacred history in the sense that it is the story of the settlement and growth of a people in a strange land, under the tutelage of a patron saint, Saint Nicholas.[14]

In the New Year essay in *Salmagundi*, Paulding had referred to old New York as the "golden age" of the city (*Sal.*, 478). The Golden Age is an idyllic vision of a past when men lived like gods and the earth brought forth abundantly without cultivation, and it is one of the myths that control the first period of Irving's *History:* "Such was the happy reign of

Wouter Van Twiller, celebrated in many a long forgotten song as the real golden age, the rest being nothing but counterfeit copper-washed coin" (146). Irving may have been acting upon Paulding's association; but he went back to the full account of the myth in Ovid's *Metamorphoses* and got from it various details which he used to structure Van Twiller's reign. One of his summary passages on this period is a self-conscious paraphrase of Ovid:

The province of New Netherlands, destitute of wealth, possessed a sweet tranquility that wealth could never purchase. It seemed indeed as if old Saturn had again commenced his reign, and renewed the golden days of primeval simplicity. For the golden age, says Ovid, was totally destitute of gold, and for that very reason was called the golden age, that is, the happy and fortunate age — because the evils produced by the precious metals, such as avarice, covetousness, theft, rapine, usury, banking, note-shaving, lottery-insuring . . . were then unknown (129)[15]

In the early period of New World Dutch history, Irving often attempts to strike a pastoral key. His ode to spring may be clumsy, as his work so often is when it attempts to carry the force of personal emotion, but it is an attempt to move from comic to lyric celebration:

Every tufted copse and blooming grove resounded with the notes of hymeneal love; the very insects as they sipped the morning dew, that gemmed the tender grass of the meadows, lifted up their little voices to join the joyous epithalamium — the virgin bud timidly put forth its blushes, and the heart of man dissolved away in tenderness. Oh sweet Theocritus! had I thy oaten reed . . . or oh gentle Bion! thy pastoral pipe, then would I attempt to sing, in soft Bucolic or negligent Idyllium, the rural beauties of the scene (92–93)

The land that Hudson sees is such a garden paradise; in many of the descriptions of the new world, Irving's tone strives to become lyric; it is as if the appeal of the myth is beginning to undermine the burlesque mode:

"The island of Manna-hata, spread wide before them, like some sweet vision of fancy, or some fair creation of industrious magic . . . some [trees were] pointing their tapering foliage towards the clouds, which were gloriously transparent; and others loaded with a verdant burthen of clambering vines, bowing their branches to the earth, that was covered with flowers" (75).

There are almost no descriptions of nature for the period of Kieft. It is a period of inner disintegration, a spiritual moment incompatible with metaphors taken from nature; its context is accordingly thought and satire.

For the period of Stuyvesant, Irving moves to an analogous structure — the hours of the day. Nature is still beautiful in the New World, but it is the beauty of twilight and evening; for this is the twilight period of New Amsterdam:

The old burghers would repair of an afternoon to smoke their pipes under the shade of their branches, contemplating the golden sun as he gradually sunk into the west, an emblem of that tranquil end towards which themselves were hastening. . . . Such was the origin of that renowned walk, *the Battery* . . . the favorite walk of declining age (277–78).

The sun setting on the garden is also an emblem of the death of promise in America and the failure of Irving's American period. The third chapter of Book VI is an interlude explicitly devoted to the image and meaning of the fading of America's and Irving's imaginative light.

The chapter is devoted to Knickerbocker's account of Stuyvesant's voyage up the Hudson, and, although it is late in the history, Stuyvesant is moving through the virgin territory of upstate New York, and time is once more abolished on the "bosom of the lordly Hudson." Knickerbocker accompanies Stuyvesant and his crew as a narrator, but the narrative drama goes farther than this. It expresses Knickerbocker's desire to actively join this community and an eventual realization that he is permanently estranged — because he is a narrator. The chapter begins with another, but shrunken, evocation of the Golden Age, when nature is paradigmatic: although this late in the history of the world it is recoverable only through art: on Stuyvesant's ship are drawn "garlands of flowers, the like of which are not to be found in any book of botany; being the matchless flowers which flourished in the golden age, and exist no longer, unless it be in the imaginations of ingenious carvers of wood and discolourers of canvass" (316).

The implications of this sentence are those of the chapter and the book as a whole. From the beginning of *The History*, Knickerbocker has been fighting furiously to create a Golden Age in the present, to redeem America from history. On the self-conscious level of the work, Knickerbocker's mind has been torn between the factual obligations of history and the mythic defiance of art. Under a variety of names — time, history, work, money, Yankee America — the enemy cannot be successfully opposed by Irving, not merely because it is so firmly fixed outside the window of the study where he writes, but because of his essential ambivalence toward the worth and efficacy of imaginative activity. The imagination may be able to restore the Golden Age, but it must effect more than the discoloration of canvas.

At this point in *The History,* Knickerbocker has already lost his fight with time. All that is left for him to do is recount the sad tale of Peter Stuyvesant's historical and psychological defeat by the Yankees of the North. This chapter is an interlude in that story, a last, feeble attempt to begin again. Significantly, it is set very near the locale of "Rip Van Winkle," for in that tale he would make still another effort to re-create America through festive comedy and again fail, for the same reason.

Knickerbocker goes on to describe the splendors of the scene, "far other . . . from that which may be witnessed at this degenerate day." The period of the voyage is a day, and Knickerbocker moves through this magic cycle describing both the natural and inner virtues associated with each phase (318–19).

The period that Knickerbocker is now most alive to is twilight; for it is then that the mind is deceived into believing that the charms of virginal American nature can support the exercise of the imagination:

But when the fairy hour of twilight spread its magic mists around, then did the face of nature assume a thousand fugitive charms. . . . The deceived but delighted eye sought vainly to . . . distinguish the fading objects that seemed sinking into chaos. Now did the busy fancy supply the feebleness of vision, producing with industrious craft a fairy creation of her own. Under her plastic wand the barren rocks frowned upon the watery waste, in the semblance of lofty towers and high embattled castles — trees assumed the direful forms of mighty giants, and the inaccessible summits of the mountains seemed peopled with a thousand shadowy beings (319).

Knickerbocker suddenly realizes that he has drifted away from his companions and that he is *alone* in his fancyings.

But all these fair and glorious scenes were lost upon the gallant Stuyvesant; naught occupied his active mind but thoughts of iron war, and proud anticipations of hardy deeds of arms. Neither did his honest crew trouble their vacant minds with any romantic speculations of the kind. The pilot at the helm quietly smoked his pipe, thinking of nothing either past, present or to come (321).

The other crew members are listening to Anthony Van Corlear spin an all too familiar (and adult) tale about the torments of nagging wives. By allowing himself to dream, to imagine, Knickerbocker finds that he has isolated himself from the very community he was endeavoring to settle in a fertile homeland.

If Paradise is ultimately a myth of the imagination and creativity, its meaning in *The History* anticipates still another feature of Irving's future artistry. Paradise belongs to an imagined past; it cannot be sustained for long within the context of the present. Yet even in the world of business, a sense of Paradise may be fleetingly possessed in time and space. Knickerbocker finds it in "one of those rich autumnal days which heaven particularly bestows upon the beauteous island of Mannahata" (150). It may also be found "within but half an hour's sail" from New York, in Communipaw, which "is one of the numerous little villages . . . which are so many strong holds and fastnesses, whither the primitive manners of our dutch forefathers have retreated, and where they are cherished with devout and scrupulous strictness" (83–85). After *The History,* Irving's imagination could only truly function for a few pages at a time in the Hudsons and Sleepy Hollows of New York.

The Land of Cockaigne

In the thirty-second chapter of his second book, Rabelais has his narrator, Alcofribas, discover a utopia in Pantagruel's mouth. According to Erich Auerbach, this is Rabelais' burlesque variant of the theme of the discovery of a new world, "one of the great motifs of the Renaissance and of the two following centuries."[16]

Rabelais' utopia is also a spatial variant of the myth of the Golden Age, but, unlike the utopia of that other Renaissance humanist, Sir Thomas More, Rabelais' is characterized as a fools' paradise, a wonderful country entirely given over to the satisfactions of sleeping, eating, and shitting.

The fools' paradise is the essential setting of burlesque, and it was given a particular form in the Middle Ages as the Land of Cockaigne. Common to all versions of the Cockaigne myth is the notion of luxuriant abundance. Cockaigne is the land of all delights, but the delights stressed are associated primarily with eating, and they take childish or domestic forms. One account tells of rivers of wine, houses built of cake or barley sugar, streets paved with pastry, and shops supplying goods free. Roast geese and fowl wander about with knives in their sides asking to be eaten, and buttered larks fall from the skies.

The discovery or location of qualities belonging to Cockaigne in America occurs from time to time in our literature, but the fiction is never as positive or as complete as the form given to it by Irving in *The History.* In 1729, William Byrd noticed that North Carolina "approaches nearer to the description of Lubberland than any other."[17] His attitude toward the men who sleep late and smoke away the remainder of the day is one of tolerant amusement, but basically he condemns them for their aversion to work, a necessary virtue for the inhabitants of a near wilderness. In 1782

Franklin, who stood in Irving's mind for the America he was attempting to defeat, articulated the contrast between Cockaigne and labor that is implicit in Byrd's observation: "In short," he writes,"America is the Land of Labour, and by no means what the English call *Lubberland,* and the French *Pays de Cocagne,* where the streets are said to be pav'd with half-peck Loaves, the Houses til'd with Pancakes, and where the Fowls fly about ready roasted, crying, *Come eat me!"*[18]

The affirmative vision of America as a paradise of nourishment and ease comes largely from folk roots, especially the tall tales of abundance that begin to appear in printed form in the 1830's. The groups that affirm a festive America tend to be, like Irving's fictional Dutchmen, minority groups that are threatened with cultural extinction at the hands of the dominant class that controls the civilization's financial power: the blacks, Norwegian immigrants, the hobo culture that gave rise to the ballad, "Big Rock Candy Mountain." In the *high* literature of the nineteenth century, Whitman creates an American Cockaigne, although in a curiously subli-mated form. In addition to being the "yelping eagle" of the heroic tall tale, the narrator of "Song of Myself" is an American Pantagruel, eating and drinking America until he has swollen to the size of the continent and attained divinity thereby.

Irving's Cockaigne owes nothing to prior characterizations of America. It was clearly inspired by Rabelais.[19] Putting aside the question of comic genius, there is no work that stands closer in spirit to parts of Irving's *History* than *Gargantua.* Rabelais' masterpiece is certainly the highest expression of the Cockaigne myth in literature, and most of the features of Rabelais' comic universe flow into Irving's New York. The Rabelaisian universe is inhabited by tremendous eaters and drinkers, but behind those towering gluttons are equally tremendous stores of food-stuffs; and, on a higher level of the fiction, the world itself is alimentary, if not literally, then metaphorically so.

Reading Rabelais, one feels a great flow of nourishment and sensual gratification streaming in toward the giant ego at its center, and various internal processes — eating, digesting, and excreting — are continuous and gratifying. The emphasis on scatology in burlesque comedy is not special; it is a complement to the eating and drinking. For burlesque, the two ends of the process have not been separated in either fact or idea.

Obscenity might seem out of place in the infantile world of bur-lesque, but it is also present, most often in the form of pure genital cele-bration.[20] Certain objects of deep comic appeal, which might almost be considered as the basic vocabulary of burlesque comedy, may be genital in origin; but that vocabulary of pipes, breeches, noses, geese, owls, oysters, pumpkins, cabbages, etc., is not used to trace the embarrassing patterns of adult sexuality. These objects seem to be symbols of an almost primitive opacity, and, like all true symbols, tap genital energy for the creation of pure comic forms.

It is unrewarding, for example, to read Hafen Slawkenbergius' tale in terms of a key which translates statements about Hafen's nose into veiled references to the penis. What we might call the allegory of obscenity flavors the piece, but Hafen's nose has a *sui generic* meaning within the story. In the following description of Gargantua's codpiece, to take an obvious example, the tone of celebration and the mythic associations far transcend the connotations of phallic humor:

. . . its shape was that of a bowed arch, well and gallantly fastened by two fine gold buckles with two enamelled clasps, in each of which was set a huge emerald, the size of an orange. For (as Orpheus says, in his *Book of Precious Stones,* and Pliny, in his final book) this fruit has an erective virtue, and is encouraging to the natural member . . . if you had seen the fine wire-thread embroidery, and the charming plaiting in goldwork, set with rich diamonds, precious rubies, rare turquoises, magnificent emeralds, and Persian pearls, you would have compared it to one of those grand Horns of Plenty that you see on ancient monuments, one such as Rhea gave to the two nymphs Adrastea and Ida, the nurses of Jupiter. For it was always brave, sappy, and moist, always green, always flourishing, always fructifying, full of humours, full of flowers, full of fruit, full of every delight, I swear to God it was a pleasure to look at![21]

Gargantua and Pantagruel is set in a land of Cockaigne, but Rabelais has identified this world with its original context — the world in Pantagruel's mouth. Its very location is an expression of the intimate connection between life and nourishment that pertains in Cockaigne. The first person that Alcofribas meets is a man planting cabbages to be sold in Gullettown. "'Jesus!'" Alcofribas asks, "'Is there a new world here?' 'Of course,' said he. 'But it isn't in the least new.'" In one of the villages of this utopia, Alcofribas was "better entertained than ever. . . . Do you know how? By sleeping. For there they hire men by the day as sleepers, and you earn five or six halfpence a time. But those who snore very loud are paid a good seven and a half."

[Alcofribas] began to think how true the saying is that one half of the world doesn't know how the other half lives, seeing that no one had ever written about those countries, in which there are more than twenty-five inhabited kingdoms, not counting the deserts and a broad arm of the sea. But I have made up a great book entitled the *History of the Gorgians.* For that is what I have called them, since they live in my master Pantagruel's gorge (Rab., 273-75).

All this bears a close resemblance to Irving's work (and when Alco-fribas returned he was given the wardenship of Salmagundia): A learned antiquarian writing the history of a hitherto undiscovered new world of eating and sleeping. There was actual influence here, since Irving knew Rabelais well and alluded to this chapter in *The History*. But it is not necessary to assert influence at this point, and the analogies are more properly the common properties of the myth. Here is a picture of Irving's Cockaigne:

The genial days of Wouter Van Twiller therefore, may truly be termed the golden age of our city . . . every respectable citizen ate when he was not hungry, drank when he was not thirsty, and went regularly to bed, when the sun set, and the fowls went to roost, whether he was sleepy or not; all of which . . . tended so remarkably to the population of the settlement, that I am told every dutiful wife throughout New Amsterdam, made a point of always enriching her husband with at least one child a year, and very often a brace (130).

The Dutch of New Amsterdam are not as outrageously comic as the enormous eaters of Rabelais; Pantagruel, for example, had to be chained as a child, for he devoured everything that crossed his path. While Rabelais regales the reader with vast catalogues of food and drink, and the imme-diate act of feasting, Knickerbocker's usual method is to channel the world of feasting through pedantic analogies and whimsical theories. Wouter Van Twiller, at council meetings, listened instead "with great attention to the discussion that was going on in his belly; which all who knew him, de-clared to be the huge court-house or council chamber of his thoughts; forming to his head what the house of representatives does to the senate" (170). In his demonstration of the excellence of corpulent aldermen, Knickerbocker parodies Plato, proving that "good feeding" pacifies the "irritable soul," and that such legislators, therefore, are "naturally dis-posed to be lenient and indulgent in the administration of their duties" (125-26). Wouter's council was chosen by weight, "and the Schepens, or assistant aldermen, were appointed to . . . *help them eat*." Eventually these too "became very eligible candidates for the Burgomasters' chairs, having fairly eaten themselves into office." Wouter's council "would sit for hours smoking and dozing over public affairs . . . faithfully observing an excel-lent maxim, which the good old governor had caused to be written in letters of gold, on the walls of the council chamber . . . "

> "The sow that's still
> sucks all the swill" (127).

There are, however, great feasts in New Amsterdam, when "Loads of fish, flesh and fowl were devoured, oceans of liquor drank" (374), corresponding to the many times in Rabelais when "huge bonfires were lit all about the city, and fine round tables, loaded with plenty of food, were set up in the streets. It was the Golden Age renewed, such good cheer did they make in that place" (Rab., 270).

Rabelais also uses a variety of figurative devices to give the reader a sense of the nutrimental quality of his world; for example, mock legends — "he made such a horrible clatter, that I was reminded of the time when the great Butter Tower, which once crowned St. Stephen's at Bourges, melted in the sun" (Rab., 264). More often, he relies upon an essential burlesque fiction: the body as its food — "Gymnaste with one blow sliced him through the stomach, colon, and half the liver, so that he fell to the ground; and as he fell he threw up more than four pot-fulls of soup and, mingled with the soup, his soul" (Rab., 116), and part of the detailed anatomy of King Lent of Sneak's Island associates bodily functions with food: "If he spat, it was basketfuls of artichokes" (Rab., 518).

Irving creates the same sense of a world of food, but his methods again are more consistent with Knickerbocker's pedantic character. In his essay on Philadelphia in *Salmagundi,* Irving had parodied the type of account of the origin of cities that was a standard feature of the travel books he had taken with him to Europe. He gives the account to Linkum Fidelius, and his mock version reduces the notion of origins to a matter of food and eating:

According to the good old rule, I shall begin with the etymology of its name, which, according to Linkum Fidelius, Tom. LV., is clearly derived, either from the name of its first founder, viz. Philo Dripping-pan, or the singular taste of the aborigines, who flourished there on his arrival . . . [he] particularly rests his position on the known fact, that Philo Dripping-pan was remarkable for his predilection to eating, and his love of what the learned Dutch call *doup.* Our erudite author likewise observes that the citizens are to this day noted for their love of "a sop in the pan," and their portly appearance (*Sal.,* 250).

The New York State of *The History* is populated by communities distinguished in myth and legend by the close relationship they bear to food and drink. One gets the strongest sense of this in the mock-epic catalogue of Dutch tribes that assemble in New Amsterdam to wage war on the Swedes:

First of all came the Van Bummels who inhabit the pleasant borders of the Bronx — These were short fat men, wearing exceeding large trunk breeches, and are renowned for feats of the trencher — they were the first inventors of the Suppawn or Mush and milk — Close in their rear marched the Van

Vlotens of Kaats kill, most horrible quaffers of new cyder. . . . Then the Van Nests . . . to these . . . are we indebted for the invention of slapjacks. . . . Then the Van Grolls of Anthony's Nose, who carried their liquor in fair round little pottles, by reason they could not bouse it out of their canteens, having such rare long noses. – Then the Gardeniers of Hudson . . . great lovers of roasted pigs tails . . . the Van Winkles of Haerlem, potent suckers of eggs. . . . Lastly came the KNICKERBOCKERS. . . . These derive their name, as some say, from *Knicker* to shake, and *Beker* a goblet, indicating thereby that they were sturdy toss pots of yore (327-29).[22]

Knickerbocker gives a shape to the fertility and abundance of America at various times; he tells us that no sooner was New Amsterdam "once planted, than like a luxuriant vine, it took root and throve amazingly; for it would seem, that this thrice favoured island is like a munificent dung hill, where everything finds kindly nourishment, and soon shoots up and expands to greatness" (100), and that the population of even Puritan New England "multiplied to a degree, which would be incredible to any man unacquainted with the marvellous fecundity of this growing country" (159).

There are even examples of what would later be called tall tales of abundance:

It must be known then that the nose of Antony the trumpeter was of a very lusty size . . . the true regalia of a king of good fellows, which jolly Bacchus grants to all who bouse it heartily at the flaggon. Now thus it happened, that . . . the good Antony . . . was leaning over the quarter railing of the galley. . . . Just at this moment the illustrious sun . . . did dart one of his most potent beams full upon the refulgent nose of the sounder of brass – the reflection of which shot straight-way down, hissing hot, into the water, and killed a mighty sturgeon. . . . This huge monster being with infinite labour hoisted on board, furnished a luxurious repast to all the crew, being accounted of excellent flavour, excepting about the wound, where it smacked a little of brimstone – and this, on my veracity, was the first time that ever sturgeon was eaten in these parts, by christian people (322-33).

The language of this anecdote is far from the vernacular; one phrase is distinctly Rabelaisian. And there are several comparable anecdotes in *Gargantua:*

[Carpalim] noticed a fine great roebuck on the edge of the wood. . . . Carpalim immediately ran after him with such speed that he seemed like a great bolt shot from a cross-bow. He caught him in a moment and, as he ran plucked down with his hands out of the air

Four great bustards,
Seven bitterns,
Twenty-six grey partridges,
Thirty-two red ones,
Sixteen pheasants,
Nine woodcocks,
Nineteen herons,
Thirty-two wood-pigeons.

And with his feet he killed ten or twelve leverets and rabbits, which were already past their pagehood, also

Eighteen rails, running in couples,
Fifteen young boars,
Two badgers,
Three large foxes (Rab., 251).[23]

The inhabitant of Cockaigne is the *lubber,* the infant writ large, the image that was clarified in Gustave Doré's illustrations for Rabelais. Wouter Van Twiller "was exactly five feet six inches in height, and six feet five inches in circumference" (116). Van Corlear is also "a jolly fat dutch trumpeter, of a pleasant burly visage" (195). New Amsterdam itself "had been puffed, and blown up from small beginnings, to a most corpulent rotundity" (444).

In keeping with Knickerbocker's character as a pedant, fatness is often made the subject of mock disquisitions: Knickerbocker proves that for endurance, love, and justice, fatness is an essential characteristic. Van Curlet's courier, for example, "was a fat, oily little man, as being least liable to be worn out, or to lose leather on the journey" (172). And Knickerbocker explains that in the pristine days of love-making:

. . . the greatness of a lover's passion seemed to encrease in proportion to the magnitude of its object – and a voluminous damsel, arrayed in a dozen of petticoats, was declared by a low-dutch sonnetteer of the province, to be radiant as a sunflower, and luxuriant as a full blown cabbage. Certain it is, that in those days the heart of a lover could not contain more than one lady at a time (143).

The celebration of sexuality (along with scatology) is the most tenuous characteristic of burlesque comedy. While the comedy of nutrition and infantile growth is relatively durable, obscenity tends to go underground or become leeringly self-conscious with the rise of an ethic of politeness. The innocent obscenity of Rabelais and the Elizabethans embarrasses Sterne, who, in most respects, shared Rabelais' impulses and temperament remarkably, and to that extent his writing becomes salacious. The impulse toward this order of burlesque celebration was infinitely more tortured in the civilized American of Irving's era; yet Irving felt it and pursued it in his *History* as far as he dared.

There is almost no sexual comedy in *Salmagundi;* at most there is a chaste kiss bestowed by the young ladies at Kissing Bridge and one withheld by Aunt Charity, who always "made a most gallant defense, and never surrendered until she saw her adversary inclined to give over his attack" (*Sal.*, 212). *The History,* however, contains a vein of bawdy that was rare in American literature, then and later. Anthony Van Corlear, the equivalent of Rabelais' phallic demon, Panurge, bundles with the beauteous lasses of Connecticut, "whom he rejoiced exceedingly with his soul stirring instrument" (266); "he was . . . a hearty, jocund rubicond, gamesome wag, and of great capacity in the doublet" (397). Among the slogans played with in *Salmagundi* was the euphemism, "to exhibit the graces." As mockingly used by Mustapha, it refers to the "thousand grotesque and ridiculous attitudes" (*Sal.,* 459) assumed by devotees of modern dancing. As used by Knickerbocker to describe the dancing of a "young vrow . . . lately come from Holland," it has quite another signification:

> To complete the astonishment of the good folks, she undertook in the course of a jig, to describe some astonishing figures in algebra, which she had learned from a dancing master at Rotterdam. — Whether she was too animated in flourishing her feet, or whether some vagabond Zephyr took the liberty of obtruding his services, certain it is that in the course of a grand evolution . . . she made a most unexpected display . . . [Peter Stuyvesant] ordered that the ladies, and indeed the gentlemen, should use no other step in dancing, than shuffle and turn, and double trouble; and forbade, under pain of his high displeasure, any young lady thenceforth to attempt what was termed "exhibiting the graces" (384–85).

A final example is a measure of Irving's relative sexual boldness, implicitly addressed to that large body of Americans who had read and tittered over their copies of Rabelais. To protect Fort Amsterdam against assault, Stuyvesant "fortified the water edge with a formidable mud breast work, solidly faced, after the manner of the dutch ovens common in those days, with clam shells" (277). Panurge's plan for the walls of Paris was to build it out of the "thing-o'-my bobs of the ladies" (Rab., 219).[24]

Irving's sexual references are usually accompanied by a faint snicker, but sexual intercourse emerges nevertheless as an appropriate human ritual, corresponding to the fertility of the new world.[25]

Corresponding to the veins of nourishment, bawdy, and scatology in burlesque, but transcending them in a not quite explicable way, is the free and running play with such symbols as pipes, breeches, noses, geese, owls, oysters, pumpkins, cabbages, etc. It is too easy to say that these objects are basic comic symbols because of their genital reference. In the discussion of the nose which follows — and which must stand for a consideration of the others — it can be observed how freely and spontaneously the symbol generates its own contexts, and how little control its phallic association really has on it, although that association plays, as it must, through the comic situation.

In a long and very curious chapter in John Ferriar's book on Sterne headed "Mr. Shandy's hypothesis of noses explained," the author attempts seriously to account for that motif in *Tristram Shandy*. He surveys the literature of noses, beginning with "an order of sages, who reckon it the perfection of wisdom, to pass their lives in silently contemplating the point of the nose" (the priesthood of Yogi or Fohi, which is given a certain amount of burlesque play in *Salmagundi* and *The History*). He passes on to the Pythagorean doctrine of noses, and the references to noses which are built into the very structure of the Greek, Latin, French, Italian, and English languages. Ferriar concludes that Sterne involved this subject in obscurity because he "had obtained a glimpse of the physiognomic doctrines respecting the nose, but he was ignorant of the general systems which had prevailed concerning the art itself." To the reader of Sterne, this may appear to be a peculiarly blind and pompous judgment, outrageously so when we consider that almost every authority Ferriar mentions was a writer of scurrilous satire or burlesque comedy: Erasmus; Vigneul-Marville, a little-known author of Rabelais' time; Tabarin, the French charlatan who influenced Molière; and the authors of *Le Pédant Joué* and *La Rinomachie,* the battle of the noses. Ferriar quotes from a medical authority, Gaspar Tagliacozzi, "a very curious speculation . . . which the learned reader will not be displeased to see, and which, I hope, he will keep to himself."[26] Ferriar quotes in particular from the *Nasea* of Pietro Aretino, which is, in effect, a secret history of the world in terms of noses:

I will tell your majesty a great secret, which all the pedants have tried without success to discover; that Ovid (Naso), was banished for no other reason than that Augustus feared that his great nose might carry off the empire from him: and he sent Ovid into exile among the snows and ice of Russia, that his nose might be shrivelled with cold.[27]

Ferriar is unwittingly correct: the symbolism of noses is part of a mystery which finds its most congenial expression in burlesque comedy.

There are countless references to noses in *Tristram Shandy,* and Books III and IV are dominated by a plot of noses beginning with the accident of Dr. Slop's having crushed Tristram's nose in delivering him.

Walter Shandy's reaction to this is profound, for not only has the Shandy family been cursed with seven generations of short noses, but a hypothesis on the excellence of long noses is one of Walter's dearest obsessions. Tristram surveys his lengthy library of noses, which includes the works of Slawkenbergius, who has written an institute of noses. The fourth book opens with Slawkenbergius' tale of the stranger with the long nose who threw all Strasbourg into a ferment of excitement and occasioned an unparalleled battle of the folios.[28]

Behind Sterne in this is Rabelais. The name of his fictitious narrator, Alcofribas Nasier, alludes to this motif, and the work contains a number of frames and fictions that play with noses; for example, a divine genealogy which includes a race of men whose noses grew so much that they "looked like the spout of a retort, striped all over and starred with little pustules, pullulating, purpled, pimpled, enamelled, studded, and embroidered gules. . . . From them Naso and Ovid derived their origins" (Rab., 172–73).

In the voyage of Pantagruel and his companions after the Oracle of the Bottle, they stop at the Island of Ennasin, all the inhabitants of which "have noses shaped like the ace-of-clubs" (Rab., 468).[29] Here is an example of the free play on noses in this work:

"Why is it," asked Gargantua, "That Friar John has such a handsome nose?"
"Because," replied Grandgousier, "God wished it so, and he makes us in such shape and to such end as pleases his divine will, even as a potter fashions his pots."
"Because," said Ponocrates, "he was one of the first at Nose-fair. He chose one of the biggest and finest."
"Stuff and nonsense," said the monk. "According to true monastic reasoning it was because my nurse had soft breasts: when she suckled me my nose sank in, as if into butter, and there it swelled and grew like dough in the kneading-trough. Hard breasts in nurses make children snub-nosed. But come, come! *Ad formam nasi cognoscitur, ad te levavi* [By the shape of his nose he is known, I have lifted up (mine eyes) to thee.]" (Rab., 172).[30]

I have already mentioned the allusions to Tom Paine's brandy nose in *Salmagundi.* Even though it was a common charge of antidemocratic satire, Irving heightened it by allusion to *The Knight of the Burning Pestle,* which overtly associates it with the penis (*Sal.,* 244). The following example of a common conceit in phallic comedy is also heightened by the incorporation of comic structures from Shakespeare:

The person who played the French horn was very excellent in his way, but 'Sbidlikens could not relish his performance, having some time since heard a gentleman amateur in Gotham play a solo on his *proboscis,* in a style infinitely superior. Snout, the bellows-mender, never tuned his wind instrument more musically; nor did the celebrated "knight of the burning lamp" ever yield more exquisite entertainment with his nose; this gentleman had latterly ceased to exhibit this prodigious accomplishment, having, it was whispered, hired out his snout to a ferryman, who had lost his conchshell; the consequence was that he did not show his nose in company so frequently as before (*Sal.,* 60).

And the serial ends: " 'How hard it is,' exclaims the divine Confutsé, better known among the illiterate by the name of Confucius, 'for a man to bite off his own nose!' At this moment I, William Wizard, Esq., feel the full force of this remark" (*Sal.,* 495). In *The History,* the following set piece burlesques, in terms of noses, the eponymous biographies found in classical history:

This great dignitary, was called Mynheer William Beekman, or rather *Beck*man, who derived his surname, as did Ovidius Naso of yore, from the lordly dimensions of his nose, which projected from the center of his countenance, like the beak of a parrot. Indeed, it is furthermore insinuated by various ancient records, that this was not only the origin of his name, but likewise the foundation of his fortune, for, as the city was as yet unprovided with a clock, the public made use of Mynheer Beckman's face, as a sundial. Thus did this romantic, and truly picturesque feature, first thrust itself into public notice (371-72).

The major treatment of noses in *The History* concerns Peter Stuyvesant's squire and trumpeter, Anthony Van Corlear. Corlear is certainly the most vital creation in *The History,* not more human perhaps, but more alive as a comic figure than even Stuyvesant himself. Corlear's burlesque ancestors include Sancho Panza, Falstaff, Hafen Slawkenbergius, and, primarily, Pantagruel's companion Panurge. Beyond the general resemblance, there is even a case to be made for actual adaptation: Panurge "was a very proper-looking fellow, but for the fact that he was a bit of a lecher. . . . He was a mischievous rogue, a cheat, a boozer, a roysterer, and a vagabond if ever there was one in Paris, but otherwise the best fellow in the world; and he was always perpetrating some trick against the sergeants and the watch" (Rab., 222). Corlear "was a jolly, rosy faced lusty bachelor, and withal a great royster, fond of his joke and a desperate rogue among the women" (335); moreover, he had a very lusty nose, "the true regalia of a king of good fellows, which jolly Bacchus grants to all who bouse it heartily at the flaggon" (322). And neither is ever without his flask or "pottle" (363 and Rab., 218). Pantagruel's first meeting with Panurge resembles that of Stuyvesant and Corlear. In both cases, there is an immediate misunderstanding followed by a great love on the part of one for the other: " 'I've taken such a liking to it,' " swears Pantagruel, " 'that if I have my way you'll never stir from my side. Indeed you and I will make such another pair of friends as Aeneas and Achates'" (Rab., 201). Stuyvesant "straightway conceived an astonishing kindness for him; and . . . ever after retained him about his person, as his chief favourite, confidential envoy and trusty squire" (250).

Corlear in his story, like Panurge in his, is a phallic deity, and his nose is only one expression of his fecundity. He is also a local deity. As a result of the miracle of killing the sturgeon with his nose — "the first time that ever sturgeon was eaten in these parts, by christian people" — the name of *Anthony's Nose* was given "to a stout promontory in the neighbourhood" (323). Corlear is mysteriously killed toward the end of *The History;* he is pulled under the Haerlem River, "battling with the spirit of the waters": "the restless ghost of the unfortunate Antony still haunts the surrounding solitudes, and his trumpet has often been heard by the neighbours, of a stormy night, mingling with the howling of the blast" (428).

Anthony also "acquired prodigious favour in the eyes of the women [of New Amsterdam] by means of his whiskers and his trumpet" (249). He voyages with Stuyvesant through New England, "twanging his trumpet like a very devil, so that the sweet vallies and banks of the Connecticut resounded with the warlike melody" and rejoicing "the beauteous lasses of those parts . . . with his soul stirring instrument" (266). When he returns to see the girls whom he had "delighted . . . so much with his trumpet," he finds them surrounded with crowds of "little trumpeters" (402). The music of Anthony's trumpet is so potent "as to produce an effect upon all within hearing, as though ten thousand bag-pipes were singing most lustily i' the nose" (195), and it is his music that compels Stuyvesant's love (249-50).

The double play of trumpet and nose stems from a traditional conceit, described by Aretino as the resemblance between a long nose and "the *Trumpet of Fame* which is sounded and felt by every one."[31] Sterne uses this reference at the opening of Slawkenbergius' tale:

Benedicity! — What a nose! 'tis as long, said the trumpeter's wife, as a trumpet.
And of the same mettle, said the trumpeter, as you hear by its sneezing.
— 'Tis as soft as a flute, said she.
— 'Tis brass, said the trumpeter.
— 'Tis a pudding's end — said his wife (*TS,* 247).

And Corlear, as champion of New Amsterdam, blows defiance at its enemies with both his trumpet — "Antony Van Corlear sounded a trumpet of defiance . . . ending with a most horrific and nasal twang, full in the face of Captain Partridg, who almost jumped out of his skin, in an extacy of astonishment" (265-66) — and his nose — "he turned aside, took his nose between his thumb and finger, and blew a tremendous blast, not unlike the flourish of a trumpet of defiance — which it had doubtless learned from a long and intimate neighbourhood with that melodious instrument" (347–48).

There is little overt scatology in Irving's *History*, but it is remarkable, given the period and the country, that there should be any. During the "most horrible battle" between the Dutch and the Swedes, Peter Stuyvesant is badly shaken by a swordblow from the Swedish hero Risingh. He falls to the ground with "a crash that shook the surrounding hills, and would infallibly have wracked his anatomical system, had he not been received into a cushion softer than velvet, which providence, or Minerva, or St. Nicholas, or some kindly cow, had benevolently prepared for his receptions" (363). Early in *The History* Irving alluded to a ballad which the Scriblerians themselves did not choose to publish. The reference is to a "stanza as fragrant as an Edinborough nosegay . . . which the mischief-loving Swift discharged on" the heads of Whiston and Ditton (29):

> So *Ditton* and *Whiston*
> May both be bep_t on
> And *Whiston* and *Ditton*
> May both be besh_t on.[32]

For the most part, Irving treats this basic element of comedy in conventionally polite ways: through breeches comedy[33] and the comic image of man "arsy-versy" — the equivalent in small of the topsy-turvy relationship that usually exists between the world of burlesque comedy and the world of experience.[34] Explaining the origin of the Dutch surnames, Ten Breeches and Tough Breeches, Knickerbocker surveys various theories of physiognomy, ending with the system of "breechology of professor Higgenbottom, which teaches the surprizing and intimate connection between the seat of honour, and the seat of intellect" (255).

In *The History* it is the Dutch of New Amsterdam who wear Rabelaisian masks, and seventeenth-century America, as Cockaigne or Lubberland, becomes the scene of their burlesque dance. Irving had been moving toward burlesque comedy prior to his absorption in Dutch New York; nonetheless there was a fortuitous meeting here of historical occasion and tradition. The Hollander as lubber was at the center of a strain of pure burlesque comedy which received its richest expression in the art of Pieter Brueghel the Elder: in paintings like "The Land of Cockaigne" or "The Fool's Paradise." Johannes Huizinga has said that in the field of burlesque, "painting may rival literature in expressive power. Before 1400 art had already attained some mastery of this element of burlesque vision which was to reach its full growth in Pieter Brueghel in the sixteenth century."[35] This was not, however, a strong element in the British comic tradition; perhaps because the English were in rivalry and at war with Holland for so much of their post-Renaissance history. These burlesque stereotypes could be revived in America because of the presence of a Dutch colony on the banks of the Hudson.

One notable presence of Dutch burlesque in English literature is Thomas Dekker's *Shoemaker's Holiday,* a play that is outstanding for its morning freshness and its celebratory qualities.[36] In that play, the male *adolescente* disguises himself as a Dutch shoemaker, and this affords Dekker the opportunity to play with stock comic motifs, the Dutch language and the Dutchman's enormous capacity for drink and food: "You shall be drunk with," the other apprentices tell the false Hans, "wert thou Gargantua"; and *lubber* and *butterbox* were contemporary comic terms for the Dutch.[37] Two passages in the play are especially interesting. In the first, a Dutch skipper offers Hans, for his master, "a ship that is come from Candia . . . [which] is all full . . . of sugar, civet, almonds, cambric, and all things — a thousand thousand things." The play ends with a feast for the apprentices, and, as the pancake bell sounds, the apprentice, Firk, fancies that he is translated to the Land of Cockaigne.[38]

The inhabitants of the fools' paradise are of course fools, but the characterization is not a condemnation. Hudson's crew were "a patient people, much given to slumber and vacuity, and but little troubled with the disease of thinking" (72);

As to the honest dutch burghers of Communipaw, like wise men, and sound philosophers, they never look beyond their pipes, nor trouble their heads about any affairs out of their immediate neighbourhood; so that they live in profound and enviable ignorance of all the troubles, anxieties and revolutions, of this distracted planet (84-85).

With Van Twiller at its head, the New Netherlands' council "would sit for hours smoking and dozing over public affairs, without speaking a word to interrupt that perfect stillness" (127). Van Twiller's reign transcends history, and it is appropriate that his death should coincide with the first outside breath from the world of history: Van Twiller is apparently asleep at a council meeting "when of a sudden, the door flew open and the little courier straddled into the apartment. . . . But fortunately . . . [the] ill tidings came too late, to ruffle the tranquillity of this most tranquil of rulers. His venerable excellency had just breathed and smoked his last — his lungs and his pipe having been exhausted together" (173-74).

In *The History,* Irving timidly attempted to identify Dutch America as the proper ground for imaginative activity. He gave us as the first successful work of fiction in our early national literature a history of America which ends with the defeat of a mythical civilization that could not sustain itself in this brave new world. As a history of America it tells as different a story from that canonized in our official histories as one could imagine, a story in which the heroes of the latter are among the forces which destroyed America. There is a sense in which Irving's work is a history, but that is a very special one. Among many other things, it is an attempt to create a vital comic fiction and identify that with the true America. Irving also gave us as the first successful narrative voice in our early national literature, a sensibility devoted wholly to the irrational movements of the mind, and he identified this as a Dutch-American voice.

The shape of this cultural defeat is first presented in Stuyvesant's voyage up the Hudson, when Knickerbocker suddenly realizes that in attempting to give this virgin land imaginative meaning and substance he may be alienating himself from his community. It is in fact Irving's ambivalence toward the imagination that is responsible for the exhaustion of the possibility of art in America, and not the internal subversion of William Kieft, the military defeat of Stuyvesant by the Yankees, nor the facts of American history. He was, ultimately, unwilling to identify the proper uses of the imagination with his Dutch Cockaigne, although it is clear that he was tempted to. In "Sleepy Hollow" and "Rip Van Winkle," this cultural identification is finally made, but it is too late; and in the second tale, it is precisely Rip's unwillingness to dream a valid Dutch-American past into vital existence that is responsible for the Yankee conquest of his village. The conceptual poles of Irving's America may be too simple; in addition to Dutch Cockaigne, there is only modern Yankee democracy, a civilization of time and work and talk. In the American comedy that finally "took," one of the first successful comic creations would be a salesman, Sam Slick, whose product was time.

The Fall of Knickerbocker's America

Dutch America is defeated historically in the reign of the third governor, Peter Stuyvesant; but the previous reign, that of William Kieft, represents its actual fall, the inner transformation of the Dutch into the Yankee. Despite Kieft's key relationship to Thomas Jefferson, he is characterized in the terms of the only enemy principle Irving was able to evolve. There is no myth of the South in Irving's American work, barely a mention: the extravagance of the wives of Southern plantation owners is alluded to once in *Salmagundi.*

The modality of the second reign is political satire. There the logo-cracy comedy of *Salmagundi,* also attributed to a fictitious Jefferson, be-comes a much more extensive vision of an America governed by words, wind, and air, and by the spirit of political experimentation. The intensity of this mental agitation is contagious and ultimately transforms the harm-less lubber population into a race of factious democrats. The burgomasters "were no longer the fat, well fed, tranquil magistrates that presided in the peaceful days of Wouter Van Twiller" (378).

... under the administration of Wilhelmus Kieft the disposition of the inhabitants of New Amsterdam experienced an essential change, so that they became very meddlesome and factious. The constant exacerbations of temper into which the little governor was thrown . . . occasioned him to keep his council in a continual worry — and the council being to the people at large, what yeast or leaven is to a batch, they threw the whole community into a ferment — and the people at large being to the city, what the mind is to the body, the unhappy commotions they underwent operated most disastrously, upon New Amsterdam (218–19).

The spiritual decline in the reign of Kieft is both sudden and miracu-lous; Knickerbocker refers it, for example, to the legend of sudden change in the *Iliad:*

It was asserted by the wise men of ancient times, intimately acquainted with these matters, that at the gate of Jupiter's palace lay two huge tuns, the one filled with blessings, the other with misfortunes — and it verily seems as if the latter had been set a tap, and left to deluge the unlucky province of Nieuw Nederlandts (230).

A more fundamental reason for the abrupt shift from prosperity to adversity, however, is that Knickerbocker's history is governed by comic concepts and not by time. The alternation here is actually a contrast be-tween a burlesque past and a satirical present, and these, after all, under one disguise or another have been the controlling terms of all of Irving's productions up to this point.

Kieft's reign stands in the same relationship to the reign of Van Twiller as present to past. Irving has neither abandoned nor resolved the political themes which occupied so much of his early writing, nor have they gained much substance in seven years. The fiction of ragged and pre-sumptuous democrats has not developed any new forms or meanings in *The History;* his political satire is still a gesture of repudiation stemming from private fears, rather than positive comic art. In *The History,* however, Irving is at least able to dramatize, in the person of the narrator, the fact that the anger and abuse directed toward the present is a personal rather than a rational issue (105-6). Had Irving gone farther in this direction and made the abuse of the present the consequence of mad or whimsical humor, he might have salvaged some of the sections of political satire from their relative dullness.[39]

If the reign of Van Twiller is structured according to edenic concepts, the reign of his successor, William Kieft, depends equally upon a grand confusion of opposing concepts, legendary and historical: the fall of man, Hesiod's Age of Iron, the "latter days" of the Old Testament, Herodotus' fall from prosperity, the concept of the wheel of fortune in Boethius, and the resumption of the "reign of Chaos and old Night" in Milton. The jumble of lore in Knickerbocker's brain produces a jumble of parallels for the spiritual degeneracy of the new world Dutch, and, far from straining one another, the various concepts blend in an easy continuity appropriate to the historical universe born of the union of scatter-brained Diedrich and Dutch history.

The transition from Van Twiller's reign to Kieft's is embodied in an extended interlude, appropriately set in the present. It is the only section of the history proper which moves into historical America, and we almost lose the whimsical voice of Knickerbocker. In it Irving comes close to bringing the allegory of the imagination at work, implicit throughout the story, to the surface. Moreover, in this interlude, as in Knickerbocker's voyage up the Hudson, we can see that such consciousness also means the abandonment of comedy as an expressive mode.

Knickerbocker recounts an afternoon's walk on the Battery, a monument in the present to the lost Dutch past. He feels that the ground on which he walks is "hallowed by recollections of the past" (148), and as he strolls, his imagination is stimulated by his surroundings to draw "a contrast between the surrounding scenery, and what it was in the classic days of our forefathers."

For some time did I indulge in this pensive train of thought; contrasting in sober sadness, the present day, with the hallowed years behind the mountains . . . when by degrees my ideas took a different turn, and I insensibly awakened to an enjoyment of the beauties around me (149-50).

Irving is not attempting to reconcile Knickerbocker to a hard and alien present through an understanding of the continuity and endurance of natural beauty. For Irving, the exercise of the imagination, however trivial it may appear to be on the page and however apologetically he may present it, usually signals an attempt to return to that myth of the past in which the lost values of contemporary civilization may be found. It is the primary structure of "Rip Van Winkle," "Westminster Abbey," and many other works. These values may also be presented as a sequestered (and almost forgotten) nook in the present, like Sleepy Hollow or Bracebridge Hall. Here, however, the means and the mode of that return are worked through a response to nature.

This day is enchanted; it is a remnant of the magical world of pristine New York, which infrequently shines upon the degenerate present: "It was one of those rich autumnal days which heaven . . . bestows upon the beauteous island of Mannahata . . . not a floating cloud obscured the azure firmament . . . the very winds seemed to hold in their breaths in mute attention, lest they should ruffle the tranquillity of the hour — and the waveless bosom of the bay presented a polished mirror, in which nature beheld herself and smiled! . . . Every thing seemed to acquiesce in the profound repose of nature" (150).

The day stimulates Knickerbocker to hope; it is an invitation to the soul to dream; and that act which is normally dramatized in Irving as an ineffective, because ambivalent, exercise, here instead calls down the wrath of the present upon the forlorn little philosopher. "In the midst of this soothing slumber of the soul, my attention was attracted to a black speck, peering above the western horizon, just in the rear of Bergen Steeple" (151). In the reign of Van Twiller, nature was idyllic, as an appropriate expression of the universe. In the present, the "black speck" of incongruity between the life of today and man's desire obtrudes upon every fair dream that the mind can fashion; it is the desire which summons the black speck.

As the storm cloud grows it successively casts into darkness the place names of old New York. It climbs "the serene vault of heaven . . . darkening the vast expanse. . . . The earth seems agitated at the confusion of the heavens."[40] Unfortunately, Irving does not yet know how to let nature tell its tale, and he returns to burlesque pedantry and, even worse, to whimsical apology — comic modes which quite fail when the childish dream of a lost past has given way to a conscious concern for the inadequacy of the imagination in the present.

For Knickerbocker the historian, myth and history are antithetical realities; bodies of myth muddle or completely obstruct his oft-stated desire to write a valid and continuous history. The attitude of Knickerbocker the poet is quite the reverse: for him, also, myth and history are antithetical, but the values of the antithesis are totally different. On the level of metaphor, the historian sees myth as fog or shadow in contrast to the clear light of history. The poet sees the past of myth and legend glowing richly in contrast to the dull matter-of-fact gray of history.

The conflict between the two Knickerbockers runs through *The His-*

tory; it is the most prominent second fiction. As soon as Knickerbocker begins the history, history fails him. He opens Book II on a matter-of-fact note: On March 25, 1609, Henry Hudson "set sail from Holland in a stout vessel, called the Half Moon, being employed by the Dutch East India Company, to seek a north-west passage to China" (70). Knickerbocker even has the journal of the *Half Moon's* mate, Robert Juet, but, and here his agitation begins, it is uneventful and dull: "it mortifies me exceedingly that I have to admit so noted an expedition into my work, without making any more of it" (71). Of course, Knickerbocker is not even trying to write history, but struggling with it, trying mentally to wrestle it into myth and romance. On another level, Knickerbocker's dilemma stems directly from the self-conscious narrative of Book I. Among the mock roles assumed there by Knickerbocker were those of the historian as a recorder of sober truth and the historian as a recorder of great events. The transformation of idea into motive, discussed earlier, repeatedly has the effect of destroying any settled idea of history throughout the book: Knickerbocker becomes the victim of an internal drama created by the active implications of his own ideas of the historian. This whimsical conflict, for example, forces the following lament from Knickerbocker:

Oh! that I had the advantages of that most authentic writer of yore, Apollonius Rhodius, who in his account of the famous Argonautic expedition, has the whole mythology at his disposal, and elevates Jason and his compeers into heroes and demigods; though all the world knows them to have been a meer gang of sheep stealers, on a marauding expedition . . . alas! the good old times have long gone by, when your waggish deities would descend upon the terraqueous globe, in their own proper persons, and play their pranks, upon its wondering inhabitants. . . . Certain it is, no mention has been made of them by any of our modern navigators (71–72).

Twenty pages later, however, Knickerbocker is treating the expedition to the mouth of the Hudson as a comic epic:

In the joyous season of spring then, did these hardy adventurers depart on this eventful expedition, which only wanted another Virgil to rehearse it, to equal the oft sung story of the Eneid — Many adventures did they meet with and divers bitter mishaps did they sustain. . . . In all which cruize they encountered as many Lystrigonians and Cyclops and Syrens and unhappy Didos, as did ever the pious Eneas, in his colonizing voyage (93-94).

Without consciously knowing what he was doing, Irving demanded that the historian, in order to serve his culture well, must be its mythographer. To substitute the term *artist* for that of mythographer resolves the problem too easily; it disposes of it in fact. The *Iliad* and the *Odyssey* are true histories; so is the Old Testament, and one need not be a fundamentalist to be able to assign a value to that statement. The novel has been traditionally considered, not in opposition to history (some sense of it at least), but as private or little history. In a sense that Irving understood, *The Scarlet Letter* and *Moby Dick* are far truer histories of America than Bancroft's *History of the United States.* Most true histories tend to be more or less dark, weighted down or infected by that other history which cannot be dismissed because it unfortunately is. The world's literature offers very few examples of histories of wholeness and festive celebration. Irving believed that a new world might at least provide such an occasion. It was a naive but understandable belief.

Burlesque Comedy in a Fallen World

In Irving's treatment of the reign of Peter Stuyvesant, he attempted once again to test the possibilities of nonsatiric comedy. To a certain extent he was successful, but the nature of the subject matter, particularly the encroachment of the Yankee into once-sacred territory, apparently limited his comic imagination. Correspondingly, he turned to lower, more familiar forms of burlesque — that confused range of comic effects referred to by a variety of almost indistinguishable terms; mock-heroic and romance, high and low burlesque, travesty, etc.

The major sources of epic structure in *The History* were the *Iliad* and the *Aeneid;* and of romance, Ariosto, Cervantes, and Malory. Although other works, like the *Argonautica* and the *Pharsalia,* are alluded to, the references are so general that I do not think that Irving had even read them. None of the parallels to epic and romance, however, exist with the precision necessary for mock-heroic; in fact, what there is of traditional mock-heroic and travesty in *The History* is uneven and incoherent. The comedy of this section is another mode of comic heroics — *burlesque* or *Rabelaisian epic.* In a sense, it is a return to early childhood for Irving, when he sallied forth "into the yard of his father's house, the grand theatre of his youthful exploits, with wooden sabre to encounter some youthful playmate."[41] For what we also have in Rabelais is the celebration of heroism as child's play, with wooden swords in an orchard, garden, or barnyard; because of its setting, one could equally call it *food epic.* This form of comic heroic was a minor tradition of British comedy; it can be found in *I Henry IV* and *Hudibras,* for example, and in burlesque ballads, like those of Tom D'Urfey and George Huddesford. It had not been at the center of comedy since the time of Rabelais, unless in the oblique form of

Uncle Toby's and Corporal Trim's pastoral war play.

Hudibras stands in almost the same relationship of Irving's burlesque heroics as Sterne's *Tristram Shandy* does to his whimsical humor and Rabelais to the fools' paradise. While the extent of Samuel Butler's influence is not so large as that of the latter two writers, it is certain that Irving had Butler's brand of burlesque heroics in mind while treating the period of Stuyvesant; the central battle in *The History* is modelled after the battle between Hudibras and the mob in Book I, Canto 2 of Butler's poem. Large sections of *Hudibras* had been used as framing quotations in *The Corrector,* and Butler is mentioned and his work alluded to several times in *Salmagundi.* Irving's adaptations from Butler are quite free, but the following simile, for example — "And now the ruddy-faced Aurora, like a buxom chamber-maid, draws aside the sable curtains of the night, and out bounces from his bed the jolly red haired Phoebus, startled at being caught so late in the embraces of Dame Thetis" (399) — is taken from the first part of Butler's famous simile:

> The sun had long since, in the lap
> Of Thetis, taken out his nap,
> And like a lobster boil'd, the morn
> From black to red began to turn; II.ii.29–32.[42]

Irving had touched upon this mode of comedy as early as the "Letters," in an isolated simile: "like the warrior in the fable, who, deprived of the pleasure of slaughtering armies, contented himself with cutting down cabbages" (*LJO,* 62). In *The History,* the simile has grown in fact and in comic spirit to the point where it gives a distinctive flavor to the heroic days of New Amsterdam. The "warrior" is General Jacobus Van Poffenburgh (a parody of General James Wilkinson):

For at such times, when he found his martial spirit waxing hot within him, he would prudently sally forth into the fields, and lugging out his trusty sabre . . . would lay about him most lustily, decapitating cabbages by platoons — hewing down whole phalanxes of sunflowers, which he termed gigantic Swedes; and if peradventure, he espied a colony of honest big bellied pumpkins quietly basking themselves in the sun, "ah caitiff Yankees," would he roar, "have I caught ye at last!" — so saying, with one sweep of his sword, he would cleave the unhappy vegetables from their chins to their waistbands (292).

This figure is a burlesque of the madness of the hero of epic and romance,[43] but it is free of all mock-heroic ties; it is no longer a framework for human discrepancy but an immediate comic world.

As his name suggests, General Poffenburgh is Irving's version of the bragging captain who had often been associated with food: Falstaff's sack, for example, dramatically punctures the battle of Shrewsbury. Among the representatives of this type alluded to in *The History* are Pantagruel, Falstaff, Hudibras, and Ben Jonson's Bobadil:

[Poffenburgh], though like captain Bobadel [*sic*], . . . had only twenty men to back him, yet in the short space of six months he had conquered and utterly annihilated sixty oxen, ninety hogs, one hundred sheep, ten thousand cabbages, one thousand bushels of potatoes, one hundred and fifty kilderkins of small beer, two thousand seven hundred and thirty five pipes, seventy eight pounds of sugar-plumbs, and forty bars of iron, besides sundry small meats, game, poultry and garden stuff. An achievement unparalleled since the days of Pantagruel and his all devouring army (304-5).

Warlike activity in general in New Amsterdam is treated in terms of food: "Every love sick maiden fondly crammed the pockets of her hero with gingerbread and doughnuts" (335). Food and drink are also the weapons of this military campaign, as they were in *Hudibras:*

> His breeches were of rugged woolen . . .
> Thro' they were lined with many a piece
> Of ammunition-bread and cheese,
> And fat black-puddings, proper food
> For warriors that delight in blood . . .
> His puissant sword unto his side,
> Near his undaunted heart, was tied,
> With basket-hilt, that would hold broth,
> And serve for fight and dinner both.[44]

In the garrison, the force of Jacobus Van Curlet was "reduced nearly one-eighth, by the death of two of his most valiant, and corpulent soldiers, who had accidentally over eaten themselves on some fat salmon" (188-89), and in the field:

But here a strange murmur broke out among his troops . . . spreading from man to man, accompanied with certain mutinous looks and discontented murmurs. For once in his life . . . did the great Peter turn pale. . . . But soon did he discover to his great joy, that . . . the cause of this agitation and uneasiness simply was, that the hour of dinner was at hand. . . . Beside it was an established rule among our valiant ancestors, always to fight upon a full stomach, and to this may be doubtless attributed the circumstance that they came to be so renowned in arms (349).

The three major heroic modes are all reinterpreted in terms of food:

classical history —

A grand triumph therefore was decreed to Stoffel Brinckerhoff, who made his triumphant entrance into town riding on a Naraganset pacer; five pumpkins, which like Roman eagles had served the enemy for standards, were carried before him — ten cart loads of oysters, five hundred bushels of Weathersfield onions, a hundred quintals of codfish, two hogsheads of molasses and various other treasures, were exhibited as the spoils and tribute of the Yankees (200–201);

romance —

[Peter] verily believed that . . . the festoons of dried apples and peaches which ornamented the fronts of their houses, were so many decorations in honour of his approach; as it was the custom in days of chivalry, to compliment renowned heroes, by sumptuous displays of tapestry and gorgeous furniture (402);

and epic —

Like as a mighty alderman, when at a corporation feast the first spoonful of turtle soup salutes his palate, feels his impatient appetite but ten fold quickened, and redoubles his vigorous attacks upon the tureen, while his voracious eyes, projecting from his head, roll greedily round devouring every thing at table — so did the mettlesome Peter Stuyvesant . . . (343).[45]

The climactic battle in *The History* between the Dutch and the Swedes is partly treated as food burlesque. The battle opens with an epic echo translated into terms appropriate to this contest: "'Now had the Dutchman snatch'd a huge repast'" (350). Knickerbocker quotes from John Grub's burlesque ballad of Guy of Warwick, as the Dutch move into battle "'Brimful of wrath and cabbage'" (353).[46] The first Swedish volley, although it misses the Dutch, was not fired in vain:

. . . for the balls, winged with unerring fate, went point blank into a flock of wild geese, which, like geese as they were, happened at that moment to be flying past — and brought down seventy dozen of them — which furnished a luxurious supper to the conquerors, being well seasoned and stuffed with onions (355).

The height of the battle is the single combat between Stuyvesant and Risingh:

At length the valiant Peter . . . aimed a fearful blow . . . but Risingh . . . warded it off so narrowly, that glancing on one side, it shaved away a huge canteen full of fourth proof brandy, that he always carried swung on one side; thence pursuing its tranchant rouse, it severed off a deep coat pocket, stored with bread and cheese — all which dainties rolling among the armies, occasioned a fearful scrambling between the Swedes and Dutchmen, and made the general battle to wax ten times more furious than ever (362).

Stuyvesant finally vanquishes Risingh by throwing Van Corlear's pocket pistol at him "charged to the muzzle with a double dram of true dutch courage" (363); this must surely be an echo of the pistol of sack wielded most manfully by Falstaff at the battle of Shrewsbury.

"The most horrible battle ever recorded in poetry and prose" as mock-epic appeals nominally to the epic combats in the *Iliad* and the *Aeneid* as well as to legendary combats of romance: "The far famed battles of Ajax with Hector, of Eneas with Turnus, Orlando with Rodomont, Guy of Warwick with Colbrand the Dane, or of that renowned Welsh Knight Sir Owen of the mountains with the giant Guylon" (362). It is primarily a burlesque battle and the culmination of many of the elements that have been discussed in this chapter.

Prior to the battle, Knickerbocker makes it clear that the battle is his creation, subject therefore to the impulses of his mind and not to the facts of the historical past:

Before we part however, I have one small favour to ask of them; which is, that when I have set both armies by the ears in the next chapter, and am hurrying about, like a very devil, in the midst — they will just stand a little on one side, out of harms way — and on no account attempt to interrupt me by a single question or remonstrance. As the whole spirit, hurry and sublimity of the battle will depend on my exertions, the moment I should stop to speak, the whole business would stand still (350).

In the battle itself, Knickerbocker's egotism animates the epic and heroic elements and transforms mock-heroics into a burlesque world of childish miracle and movement:

The world forgot to turn round, or rather stood still, that it might witness the affray; like a fat round bellied alderman, watching the combat of two chivalric flies upon his jerkin. The eyes of all mankind, as usual in such cases, were turned upon Fort Christina. The sun . . . scampered about the heavens, popping his head here and there, and endeavouring to get a peep between the unmannerly clouds, that obtruded themselves in his way (350-51).

The sweat prodigiously streaming, ran in rivers on the field, fortunately without drowning a soul, the combatants being to a man, expert swimmers, and furnished with cork jackets for the occasion (358).

The dreadful shout [of Stuyvesant] rung in long echoes through the woods − trees toppled at the noise; bears, wolves and panthers jumped out of their skins, in pure affright; several wild looking hills bounded clear over the Delaware . . . and all the small beer in Fort Christina, turned sour at the sound! (359).

After the battle is over, Knickerbocker is defensive about the fact that there were no fatalities, but this is also a result of the implicit fiction of child's play which stands behind burlesque heroics; the Swedes, for example, hit no one with their fire, due to their "usual custom of shutting their eyes and turning away their heads, at the moment of discharge" (355), and Peter Stuyvesant falls to the ground with a crash that "would infallibly have wracked his anatomical system, had he not been received into a cushion softer than velvet, which . . . some kindly cow, had benevolently prepared for his reception" (363). This episode probably had its origin in Hudibras:

> For [Talgol] catching foe by nearer foot,
> He lifted with such might and strength,
> As would have hurl'd him thrice his length,
> And dash'd his brains, if any, out:
> But Mars, who still protects the stout,
> In pudding-time came to his aid,
> And under him the bear convey'd;
> The bear, upon whose soft fur-gown
> The Knight, with all his weight, fell down.
> The friendly rug preserv'd the ground,
> And headlong Knight, from bruise or wound; I.ii.860-70.[47]

The battle is thoroughly informed by burlesque touchstones. On one side of the field we see the Van Grolls "horribly perplexed in a defile between two little hills, by reason of the length of their noses" (355-56). The Dutch move into battle by giving a furious puff to their pipes, and charging gallantly, "under cover of the smoke" (354). And the only time during the battle when the Dutch fly in confusion before the Swedes is when their cunning commander orders his soldiers to fire full at the Dutch tobacco pipes (359).

For the most part, however, the third part of *The History* is devoted to the modes and meanings of Irving's later career. The nostalgic and bittersweet treatment of the twilight period of a possible America that Irving had chosen as his cultural ancestry would be repeated in the English essays of the *Sketch Book* and *Bracebridge Hall*, where he either attempts unsuccessfully to move into a past moment of English glory or seeks out in the present English equivalents to his own New Amsterdam, settling in *Bracebridge Hall* for the fading borderline of the squirearchy. The battle between the Dutch and Yankees would be enacted again in the two American tales in the *Sketch Book,* with even less hope of a different outcome.[48]

Irving (like Knickerbocker) desperately needs a spiritual ancestor in order to sustain his alienation in the present. Yet, like Rip Van Winkle trembling before the stony figure of Hendrik Hudson, he cannot bring Peter Stuyvesant fully to life. In the future, he would take the far easier path toward spiritual relief in his matter-of-fact histories of Columbus and Washington. In the failure of Stuyvesant as a literary creation and a cultural hero there is repeated yet again Irving's deepest and most pervasive literary theme and fear — that whatever cold and thin meanings this new world had come to stand for, it was after all and above all a place in which the imagination could not function.

Failing in all his newly discovered artistic needs, Irving fell back for the last time into the world of burlesque comedy. He knew it well and had once thought to live in it, at least for a while. It was now too late, and, however successful parts of the third reign may be as burlesque, they are becoming hollow, like Twain's efforts to return to the boy's world of his heart's delight at the end of *Huckleberry Finn.* Both authors had left their childhood behind them forever.

CHAPTER NINE

POST MORTEM EFFECTS

Irving's emotional investment in his Dutch Americans and in his vision of a festive America was far deeper than he imagined in 1809. When New Amsterdam went down to defeat, Irving accompanied it. Because the book was an immediate success, and what is more, a success in England, it is all the more significant that Irving, as a consequence, dried up as a writer. For the six following years, Irving embraced the shadow of literature, editing and writing reviews and pedestrian sketches for *The Analectic Magazine* and doing a few outside jobs of hackwork. By 1815 even that was finished; in that year he sailed to England to help his brother Peter run the Liverpool branch of the family business. As far as he knew, he would thenceforth devote himself to business.[1]

Irving was released from his creative limbo on an evening in June 1818, when he found himself laughing with relatives "at long-forgotten days in Sleepy Hollow." By the next morning, much of "Rip Van Winkle" had been written.[2] Given the psychological release, the tale had rushed out, because it had first been written in 1809, in the chapter of *The History* devoted to Stuyvesant's voyage up the Hudson, which was also an allegory of the failure of the imagination in America.

The tale treats the same scenery, and the same values in the scenery, as the earlier chapter. The supreme quality of both descriptions is the magic ability of the Catskill mountains to mirror all the changes of the natural day and reflect the spiritual meanings that these represent. In both versions the mountains become "barometers" of the mind, and whatever seems to happen on these magical heights must be read in that light.

Irving was released by memories of Dutch New York, and it is not surprising that from this energy came the two earliest tales that grace our literature. It is not surprising because "Rip Van Winkle" and "The Legend of Sleepy Hollow" are both attempts to go back and test the vision of America that he had been forced to abandon — to ask again the question, "Did it have to fail?" and to answer it again in the same way. The intensity of these tales, from an author who would never again write deeply, can only be understood as the crystallization of a literary career totally devoted to America and comedy.

Both tales are presented as posthumous productions of Knickerbocker *recovered* by Geoffrey Crayon, Gent., and they are posthumous in a double sense. They are published after Knickerbocker's death, that is, after he had been replaced by Crayon as the projection of Irving's literary sensibilities; and, compared with the robust and whimsical voice of the narrator of *The History*, this resurrected Knickerbocker speaks like one half-dead. D. H. Lawrence's phrase for the poetry of Walt Whitman, "post mortem effects," expresses the relationship of the tales to *The History*.

The History was the story of a sacred community, represented at its highest moment by the "Golden Age" of Wouter Van Twiller, which is destroyed by an alien race of Yankees. In *The History*, this fall occurs in spite of the efforts of two able champions, Peter Stuyvesant and Diedrich Knickerbocker, who defend their civilization in history and in art; in "Rip Van Winkle," the fall occurs because the only available champion is sleeping.

Rip lives in "a little village, of great antiquity, having been founded by some of the Dutch colonists, in the early times of the province."[3] Hudson, New York, like New Amsterdam, is a comic utopia, although its status as myth is tempered more by probability. One outstanding feature of this region links Hudson with Communipaw, which is the only place in Knickerbocker's contemporary America that is exempt from the curse of time and politics (*HNY*, 84-85). In Hudson, even "when the rest of the landscape is cloudless," the Catskills "will gather a hood of gray vapors about their summits, which, in the last rays of the setting sun, will glow and light up like a crown of glory" (*RS*, 80); while, in the earlier work, "the cause of the remarkable fog that often hangs over Communipaw of a clear afternoon" is the inveterate pipe-smoking of its inhabitants (*HNY*, 88), and this fog once hid the peaceful little community from a marauding British squadron.

If not specifically timeless, Hudson is at least out of the drift of time: "How sagely they [the inhabitants] would deliberate upon public events some months after they had taken place" (*RS*, 84).

The principal citizens of the village, like those of New Amsterdam, are lubbers of Cockaigne. The great man of the town is Nicholas Vedder, and his daily routine is an adaptation of Wouter Van Twiller's administration of government:

[Vedder was] a patriarch of the village, and landlord of the inn, at the door of which he took his seat from morning till night, just moving sufficiently to avoid the sun. . . . He was rarely heard to speak, but smoked his pipe incessantly. His adherents, however . . . perfectly understood him. . . . When any thing that was read or related displeased him, he was observed to smoke his pipe vehemently, and to send forth short, frequent and angry puffs; but when pleased, he would inhale the smoke slowly and tranquilly (*RS*, 84).

This is the world that Rip leaves on "a fine autumnal day," and when he returns he finds everything changed. The change is only partly a metamorphosis of the colonial into the American, attested by the repainting of George III into George Washington. Rip also finds everything changed into its opposite; his twenty-year sleep was also a step through the looking glass. This is the fundamental pattern, and Irving carefully delineates such relationships in the story. As William Hedges has pointed out, Rip hears a voice calling his name prior to the first appearance on the mountaintop, but when he looks around, he can "see nothing but a crow winging its solitary flight across the mountain" (*RS*, 85). After he awakens, he calls for his dog, but "he was only answered by the cawing of a flock of idle crows, sporting high in the air" (*RS*, 89). We are told of Rip that children "would shout with joy whenever he approached" and "not a dog would bark at him throughout the neighbourhood" (*RS*, 81). When Rip reentered the village, a "troop of strange children ran at his heels, hooting after him," and the dogs too "barked at him as he passed" (*RS*, 89). And on his return, Rip seems to look at himself as in a mirror: his son, Rip Van Winkle, is pointed out to him, and "Rip looked, and beheld a precise counterpart of himself, as he went up the mountain" (*RS*, 92).

The change in Rip's village corresponds to the two major movements in *The History* — the degeneration of Dutch lubbers into disputatious democrats and the conquest of New Netherlands by the Yankees. The two movements are not distinct; they represent the inner and outer (spiritual and historical) aspects of the same degenerative process.

Rip not only finds the appearance of the village strange; he cannot even recognize the inhabitants:

There was a busy, bustling, disputatious tone about it, instead of the accustomed phlegm and drowsy tranquillity. He looked in vain for the sage Nicholas Vedder, with his broad face, double chin, and fair long pipe, uttering clouds of tobacco-smoke instead of idle speeches. . . . In place of these, a lean, bilious-looking fellow, with his pockets full of handbills, was haranguing vehemently about rights of citizens — elections — members of congress — liberty — Bunker's Hill — heroes of seventy-six — and other words, which were a perfect Babylonish jargon to the bewildered Van Winkle (*RS,* 91).

What Rip finds on his return is indeed a new world, the logocracy discovered in America by the Tripolitan prisoner, Mustapha, in *Salmagundi;* and this comic vision of democracy is, for Irving, simply one of the Yankee character written on American politics. Driven out of England originally because of their interminable loquacity, this race of barbarians had vaporized about "liberties" and "rights" from Stuart England to the wilds of Massachusetts.

The conquest of Hudson by the Yankees is subtly invoked. The "lean bilious-looking fellow," however, is characterized in terms of Yankee touchstones from *The History.* Jonathan Doolittle, the new proprietor of the village, has the name of one of the Yankee warriors encountered by Stoffel Brinckerhoff at the battle of Oyster Bay (*HNY,* 199). The new hotel is a "large rickety wooden building . . . with great gaping windows, some of them broken and mended with old hats and petticoats" (*RS,* 90). This is the Yankee "air castle" of *The History,* described in the very terms Knickerbocker had used earlier (*HNY,* 162, 402.)

One last relationship should clarify this level of the tale, and that is the equivalence, by analogy, of petticoat and democratic government. For Rip is terribly henpecked, and the form that his domestic persecution takes is the "ever-during and all-besetting terrors of a woman's tongue" (*RS,* 83). At the end of the tale we are told: "happily [petticoat government] . . . was at an end" (*RS,* 95).

The two types of government were associated throughout the eighteenth century in British political satire. Petticoat government was a popular burlesque fiction for the situation of the parliamentary ruler in Arbuthnot's *John Bull* and its many imitators, and the Punch and Judy farces, which usually had a political level.[4] Mustapha had been told in confidence that many of the leading congressional orators were, in fact, termagant wives, who "certainly are eminently possessed of the qualifications requisite to govern in a logocracy" (*Sal.,* 177). William Kieft, the governor who introduces democratic turbulence into New Amsterdam, "submitted at home to a species of government, neither laid down in Aristotle, nor Plato; in short, it partook of the nature of a pure unmixed tyranny, and is familiarly denominated *petticoat* government" (*HNY,* 185). This connection is made explicitly in "Rip Van Winkle" (*RS,* 95).

The proportions of the story on this level are particularly neat. From Rip's point of view, the village he left represented private turmoil and public tranquillity. At the story's end, Rip enjoys private tranquillity in a village given over to public turmoil. It is almost as if the one is the price that Rip has to pay for the other.

Rip's experience on the mountain is explained to him by the "chronicle" of the village: Henry Hudson keeps a vigil on the mountaintop every twenty years, "being permitted in this way to revisit the scenes of his enterprise, and keep a guardian eye upon the river, and the great city called by his name" (*RS,* 94). But the powers that be must be totally ineffectual, since the tide of Yankee democracy has already swept Dutch virtue before it when the legend is recounted; when, if the legend be true, Hudson is once more awake, watching, with "guardian eye," a Yankee election harangue! Peter Stuyvesant had devoted his life to fighting democrats within and Yankees without the state that he was given in trust. Peter "never could be brought to yield the rites of hospitality . . . [to] an Englishman or a Yankee" (*HNY,* 499); Rip sits in front of Mr. Doolittle's hotel and tells "his story to every stranger" that arrives (*RS,* 95).

The shape of the tale is meaningful. It is untenable that Rip should be allowed to slip back into folk contentment at the end, or that the middle could be a faery adventure, when the village which frames the story is a scene of such a drastic transition. Rip must be responsible for the change, and the adventure must be the datum of his responsibility. Rip is no Peter Stuyvesant, although he "was a descendant of the Van Winkles who figured so gallantly in the chivalrous days of Peter Stuyvesant. . . . He inherited, however, but little of the martial character of his ancestors" (*RS,* 81). Knickerbockers fought in those days as well; even their degenerate descendent devoted his life to saving a civilization, giving it qualitative stability through an artistic vision of the past. "Rip Van Winkle" is a story of the artistic imagination. Unfortunately, Rip is not an artist either, at a time when only a great imaginative effort could have saved the last poor stronghold of Dutch civilization in New York. *But he is the only possible champion;* for only he knows the Yankee. He has been living with one for many years.[5]

I have argued earlier that Irving was slowly working his way toward identifying the festive and creatural qualities of his Dutch lubbers with creative potency. This seems to be a naive premise; it does not accord with what we know of the characters and lives of most artists. Yet Irving asserted it — the identification becomes explicit in "Sleepy Hollow" — probably because he wanted it to be so. To have this tale make sense we must try to see Rip as an artist manqué and his escape into nature as an artistic quest.

One does not save a culture artistically in the field of battle; one withdraws into the depths of the creative imagination and seeks to return to a figurative moment of origin when the values of that culture were fully realized. Knickerbocker had to start his effort with the creation of the world. Rip manages somehow to work his way backward to Henry Hudson and his crew, the first moment of Dutch America.

Rip's faery experience occurs at twilight, which is the time of day in *The History* when imaginings are irresistibly called forth. It is also a time of psychic revelation for Hawthorne, for twilight journies by Goodman Brown and Robin lead to terrifying visions of wife and father. Rip is poised on "one of the highest parts of the Kaatskil mountains," between day and night. On one side he sees the sun-filled Hudson, and "on the other side he looked down into a deep mountain glen, wild, lonely, and shagged, the bottom filled with fragments from the impending cliffs, and scarcely lighted by the reflected rays of the setting sun" (*RS*, 85).

The first ancient Dutchman that Rip sees is an apparition called forth from the depths of his mind, that wild, lonely, and shaggy glen. It emerges very gradually from the darkness below the mountain; it is first heard crying "Rip Van Winkle"; it is then sensed — "Wolf bristled up his back" (*RS*, 85). And as it climbs the mountain with a barrel on its back, the visual effect from Rip's vantage point is that of a fetus (or idea) unrolling.

Rip returns to the very beginning of Dutch civilization in America. On another level, equally significant in the light of Irving's career, he has returned to the vision of America in *The History*. What he witnesses is the replay of a scene from that earlier work; only it is repellent and played in slow motion. The ancient costumes, the cheerful visages, and the corpulent forms that had delighted Diedrich Knickerbocker now appear "odd-looking" and "peculiar." The faces are grotesque: "One had a large beard, broad face and small piggish eyes: the face of another seemed to consist entirely of nose" (*RS*, 87). Rip is looking at the face of a typical Dutch lubber and the "jolly" face of Anthony Van Corlear — the favorite of New Amsterdam is now a freak.

As Irving had conceived it in 1809, old New York was to be a burlesque paradise of play and nourishment. It still is, but atrophy has set in. Hudson and his men play at ninepins without amusement; they drink "in profound silence"; and "they maintained the gravest faces, the most mysterious silence, and were, withal, the most melancholy party of pleasure he had ever witnessed.... As Rip and his companion approached them, they suddenly desisted from their play, and stared at him with such fixed statue-like gaze, and such strange, uncouth, lack-lustre countenances, that his heart turned within him, and his knees smote together" (*RS*, 87).

Whether external apparition or internal imagining, these creatures are stillborn, unwarmed by life. Could they be appealing to Rip for help?

When Rip first heard his name called, he supposed it to be "some one of the neighbourhood in need of his assistance, [and] he hastened down to yield it" (*RS*, 86). Hudson and his crew make signs to him; Rip assumes that he is being asked to serve them, so he pours out more liquor. Rip received their gestures with "fear and trembling," an Abraham unwilling to make the sacrifice demanded of him.

Hudson did not cast Rip into a magical sleep; Rip sneaked a "quieting draught" when no one was watching. Drunkenness would remove this abortive vision and the responsibilities that only he could be aware of; and he found in the liquor the surcease he desired. When he finally awoke, nothing could be demanded of him. Rip's sleep on the mountainside and the degeneration of an isolated Dutch village into talk and business are not unrelated incidents. The responsibility of the artist as conceived by Washington Irving and Diedrich Knickerbocker, and imposed upon Rip Van Winkle, was nothing less than to prevent the American Revolution: effectively, to fight history, in order to allow the imagination to flourish in America. It is an insane task. In 1809, Irving created a madman who was willing to undertake it; in 1819 Rip-Irving is afraid even to try. But the dramatization of that responsibility and that failure resulted in Irving's finest American tale.

"The Legend of Sleepy Hollow" is Irving's last attempt to preserve a festive America. Like *The History* and "Rip Van Winkle," it is a tale of a Yankee invasion, but in it the Yankee is temporarily defeated, and his defeat is due primarily to the Yankee-American inability to assign any value to the world of dreams and imaginings. There is a hint of this theme toward the end of "Rip Van Winkle": the villagers who doubt the reality of Rip's tale and insist "that Rip had been out of his head, and that this was one point on which he always remained flighty" (*RS*, 95) are the new Yankees who have conquered the sleepy community of Hudson, New York, and converted it into a secular logocracy. They can only identify imaginative vision as madness (which, in a positive sense, it is).

The identification of the American Cockaigne as the proper field for imaginative activity had been implicit in *The History* and "Rip Van Winkle," but in this tale it is manifest:

A drowsy, dreamy atmosphere seems to hang over the land and to pervade the very atmosphere . . . the place still continues under the sway of some witching power, that holds a spell over the minds of the good people, causing them to walk in a continual reverie. They are given to all kinds of marvellous beliefs; are subject to trances and visions; and frequently see strange sights, and hear music and voices in the air (*RS*, 143).

Like almost all of the major American writers of the nineteenth century, Irving was concerned with the question of whether the creative imagination could take root in a country of such thin traditional soil; a country, moreover, which had been devoted by Adams and Jefferson to the practical arts alone. They had reasoned that the level of economic luxury necessary to foster a class of fine artists was incompatible with the nature of a democracy. But Irving did provide a formula for art in America. And while it may be difficult to take seriously the conception of an American culture growing out of Lubberland, the location of art (especially a comic art) within the context of creatural comfort, ceremony, festivity, and play does have validity.

On the other hand, Irving's aesthetic vocabulary — the passive and self-indulgent concept of the imagination suggested by words like *reverie* and *dream,* and the folk or fairy-tale vocabulary of spells, bewitching, and entrancement (which would be taken over by Hawthorne) — introduces yet again that note of ambivalence which is always found when Irving touches this subject.[6] In other essays in *The Sketch Book,* particularly "Westminster Abbey," Irving's doubts take the form of a fiction in which the imagination is unable to function at all. And in the later "Stout Gentleman" (the inner fusion of sense data and associations), it is not merely ineffectual, it is also morally reprehensible, resented by the stout gentleman, who, at the end of the tale, rebukes the artist by thumbing his ass at him without ever giving him a sight of his face:

This was the only chance I would have of knowing him. I . . . scrambled to the window . . . and just caught a glimpse of the rear of a person getting in at the coach-door. The skirts of a brown coat parted behind gave me a full view of the broad disk of a pair of drab breeches. . . . and that was all I ever saw of the stout gentleman!

At any rate, Sleepy Hollow *is* a dreamer's paradise, and the narrator sees it as "a retreat, whither I might steal from the world and its distractions, and dream quietly away the remnant of a troubled life" (*RS,* 142–43).

The Yankee of *The History* and "Rip Van Winkle" had consisted of a body of generic traits associated with a name; in "Sleepy Hollow," it is a single individual, Ichabod Crane, a "native from Connecticut." Crane has many of the qualities of Irving's earlier Yankees, and it will be useful to draw attention to these similarities, since criticism of the tale has raised questions about Irving's attitude toward Crane.

The first thing we are told of Ichabod is that he "sojourned, or, as he expressed it, 'tarried,' in Sleepy Hollow" (*RS,* 144), and the first thing that we are told of the earlier Yankee type is that he "is in a constant state of migration; *tarrying* occasionally here and there" (*HNY,* 161). While Crane believes that he might one day possess Katrina Van Tassel's fortune, he dreams of investing the money "in immense tracts of wild land and shingle palaces in the wilderness":

Nay, his busy fancy already realized his hopes, and presented to him the blooming Katrina, with a whole family of children, mounted on the top of a wagon loaded with household trumpery, with pots and kettles dangling beneath; and he beheld himself bestriding a pacing mare, with a colt at her heels, setting out for Kentucky, Tennessee, or the Lord knows where (*RS,* 152).

This is precisely the life story of the earlier Yankee: "His whole family, household furniture and farming utensils are hoisted into a covered cart . . . which done he . . . trudges off to the woods. . . . A huge palace of pine boards immediately springs up in the midst of the wilderness . . ."

. . . He soon grows tired of a spot, where there is no longer any room for improvement — sells his farm, air castle, petticoat windows and all, reloads his cart, shoulders his axe, puts himself at the head of his family, and wanders away in search of new lands — again to fell trees — again to clear corn-fields — again to build a shingle palace, and again to sell off, and wander (*HNY,* 163).[7]

In *The History* there is even a specific anticipation of Ichabod Crane in the "long sided Connecticut schoolmaster" who kidnapped and severely flogged Knickerbocker's grandfather when he was a boy (*HNY,* 263).

It has been argued by several critics that Sleepy Hollow dramatizes the conflict between the active and the imaginative life, and that Ichabod, despite the ridiculous figure he is made to cut, is a Quixotic projection of the artist — deliberately ridiculous as an emblem of the slightly comic position of the artist in America.[8] If, after fifteen years of trying, Irving finally managed to paint his enemy in rich colors, this can hardly be taken as evidence of an awakened sympathy for the type. For Ichabod Crane is definitely the enemy. Crane is not only a Yankee of Franklin's stamp, he also possesses many of the qualities of his earlier Puritan ancestors. Both attitudes involve a manipulation of nature, one for the purpose of accumulating material wealth and the other for the purpose of arousing piety through terror.

Irving's comic feud with schoolmasters and natives of Connecticut can be seen as early as *The Corrector,* and it was sustained throughout his subsequent works. The treatment of neither in "Sleepy Hollow" suggests

any grounds for sympathy. Ichabod also corresponds to several other negative types in Irving's work. He is, for example, the sophisticated foreigner
who debauches the tastes of the simple country girls (*RS*, 147), the home-
grown equivalent of the French *émigré* in *Salmagundi*.

Ichabod Crane simply cannot be identified with the artistic imagination; there is too much sound evidence against this association. We are told
"in fact" that Ichabod was "an odd mixture of small shrewdness and
simple credulity" (*RS*, 148); these qualities are not imaginative, but they
do relate directly to the Yankee-Puritan coupling referred to above.

Three times in the tale, Ichabod is seen engaged in "artistic" pursuits: he would amuse the maidens on Sunday by "reciting . . . all the epi-
taphs on the tombstones" (*RS*, 147), and a sheet of paper is found,
"scribbled and blotted in several fruitless attempts to make a copy of
verses in honor of the heiress of Van Tassel" (*RS*, 171). The third instance
plays with the terms of creativity:

As the enraptured Ichabod *fancied* all this, and as he rolled his great green
eyes over the fat meadow-lands, the rich fields of wheat, of rye, of buck-
wheat and Indian corn, and the orchards burthened with ruddy fruit . . .
his *imagination* expanded with the idea, how they might be readily turned
into cash, and the money invested (*RS*, 151-52; italics mine).

Ichabod Crane is a petty capitalist and speculator.

Arguments linking Crane and the imagination generally hinge on his
capacity for swallowing tales of the marvelous. Old Dutch wives tell him
"marvellous tales of ghosts and goblins, and haunted fields, and haunted
brooks, and haunted bridges, and haunted houses, and particularly of the
headless horseman, or galloping Hessian of the Hollow."

He would delight them equally by his anecdotes of witchcraft, and of the
direful omens and portentous sights and sounds in the air, which prevailed
in the earlier times of Connecticut; and would frighten them wofully with
speculations upon comets and shooting stars; and with the alarming fact
that the world did absolutely turn round (*RS*, 149).

Ichabod's voracious appetite for the supernatural is both "gross" and
"monstrous." It is associated with his insatiable physical hunger which, as
we shall see, is essentially sterile, an absorption which does not nourish.

There is a sense in which Crane does "create," however; he works at
night, transforming nature into a place of terror:

What fearful shapes and shadows beset his path. . . . How often was he
appalled by some shrub covered with snow, which, like a sheeted spectre,

beset his very path! . . . and if, by chance, a huge blockhead of a beetle came winging his blundering flight against him, the poor varlet was ready to give up the ghost, with the idea that he was struck with a witch's token (*RS*, 149, 148).

This is comparable to the world of Hawthorne's "Young Goodman Brown"; Crane is not imagining; he is projecting the terror of his isolation (the spiritual isolation of the mobile and manipulative Yankee) upon the neutral darkness of nature. By transforming nature into a place of terror he expresses his fear of the natural and his own body, just as the transformation of the abundance of the Van Tassel farm into the neutral sterility of money expresses a similar fear. And the images that are evoked by his "excited imagination" terrify him in turn: "His only resource on such occasions, either to drown thought, or drive away evil spirits, was to sing psalm tunes" (*RS*, 148). True creativity in "Sleepy Hollow" is represented by the Van Tassel farm and by Brom Bones.

Brom Bones, Ichabod's opponent, is Irving's final version of the traditional *buck* of *The Spectator*. He is a sympathetic character: "with all his overbearing roughness, there was a strong dash of waggish good-humor at bottom" (*RS*, 154). Although Ichabod Crane is not an artist, a case could be made for Bones — an artist, moreover, whose productions suggest Irving's own. After all, Brom Bones creates the legend of Sleepy Hollow out of the rumors of the community; its plot is the defeat of a Yankee, and its form is a hoax. Bones is a parodist — he "had a scoundrel dog whom he taught to whine in the most ludicrous manner, and introduced as a rival of Ichabod's . . . in psalmody" — and a burlesque artist — he "broke into the school-house at night . . . and turned everything topsy-turvy" (*RS*, 156).

Although the conflict at the center of "The Legend of Sleepy Hollow" is comparable to that of *The History*, Irving uses the symbolism of the earlier work in a contrapuntal way to express the conflict. It is Ichabod who is given the classical vision of Cockaigne — ". . . he pictured to himself every roasting pig running about with a pudding in his belly, and an apple in his mouth" (*RS*, 151) — but it is here contrasted unfavorably with the natural abundance of Sleepy Hollow and becomes simply a sign of Ichabod's avarice. Ichabod, like Pantagruel, is a huge gullet; not only does he eat enormous quantities of food, but he eats superstition as well, with a "capacious swallow" (*RS*, 148). He is a "huge feeder" (*RS*, 146), and Katrina Van Tassel is "plump as a partridge; ripe and melting and rosy cheeked as one of her father's peaches" (*RS*, 150). But although he eats voraciously, he remains as lean and skeletal as ever. The eating of Crane is likened to the devastations of a plague: he is compared to the grasshopper (*RS,* 158); and "to see him striding along the profile of a hill on a windy day, with his clothes bagging and fluttering about him, one might have mistaken him for the genius of famine descending upon the earth" (*RS,* 145).

Ichabod Crane is literally defeated and expelled from Paradise as a result of a prank played on him by Brom Bones. The essential cause of his defeat, however, is his fear of the powers of the imagination, his fear of art — common to both the Puritan and the Yankee. This is reinforced in the contrast between his aversion and Brom Bones's easy entrance into the very legend that sends Crane flying:

[Brom Bones] made light of the galloping Hessian. . . . He affirmed that, on returning one night from the neighbouring village of Sing Sing, he had been overtaken by this midnight trooper; that he had offered to race with him for a bowl of punch, and should have won it too, for Daredevil beat the goblin horse all hollow (*RS,* 164–65).

The defeat of Ichabod Crane is the most glorious moment of Irving's career, artistically and, perhaps, psychologically as well; for it fuses into one image the various meanings that made up Irving's American period. Within the context of *The History,* Ichabod is defeated by his own conquest: the pumpkin was the Yankee emblem in that work, and it signaled the Yankee conquest of Fort Goed Hoop, where it "was hoisted on the end of a pole, as a standard — liberty caps not having as yet come into fashion" (*HNY,* 193).

Ichabod Crane is also defeated by his historical conquest. Irving has finally succeeded in undoing for a moment the American revolution by identifying the Dutch protagonist of his tale with the two historical enemies of Yankee America, the Hessians and the British in the person of Major André.[9] In the third place, the Yankee is defeated by that value to which he had devoted his existence, and that is mind to the exclusion of body. The Horseman throws his head at Ichabod as if to say that he does not much need it, that he is quite comfortable in his subsequent untroubled state. Finally, Ichabod is defeated by American art, Dutch art; for the legend is a creation of the Dutch community generally and Brom Bones particularly.

Ichabod Crane, however, is not defeated for long. The qualities that keep him thin in Sleepy Hollow allow him to grow and prosper in the outside world of American history, where his path is that of the *democratic toadeater* as defined in *The Corrector* and *Salmagundi:* after his dismissal by Katrina he had "studied law . . . been admitted to the bar, turned politician, electioneered, written for the newspapers, and finally . . . been made a justice of the Ten Pound Court" (*RS,* 172). The qualities represented by Ichabod Crane must overwhelm Sleepy Hollow as they did Hudson. This has already happened at the time the story is told: the tale is set "in a remote period of American history, that is to say some thirty years since . . . " (*RS,* 144). In the story itself, the abundance, which had been growing throughout Irving's early work, is an autumnal feast; it is a farewell banquet (*RS,* 158–59).

Like "Rip Van Winkle," "Sleepy Hollow" is provided with a framework which seems to produce the tensions that we associate with the literary hoax. The tale is related at a meeting of the New York Corporation. And when doubts are raised as to the historical veracity of the tale, the story-teller ends the postscript by admitting, "Faith, sir . . . as to that matter, I don't believe one-half of it myself."

The story-teller is a "pleasant, shabby, gentlemanly old fellow, in pepper-and-salt clothes, with a sadly humorous face," and Knickerbocker strongly suspects him of being poor. His identity as a defeated Dutchman is conveyed by a device that Irving had used in "Rip Van Winkle": the tale is approved and laughed at only by two or three deputy aldermen who are clearly Dutch, since they "had been asleep the greater part of the time."

The postscript is a reprise of the conflict between Dutch and Yankee, and this time overtly on the level of the imagination, since it is the value of the tale itself that is in contention. The story-teller's opponent is the artist's traditional foe, the Shandean man of gravity: a "tall, dry-looking old gentleman, with beetling eyebrows . . . [and] a grave and rather severe face." I suspect that Irving meant us to entertain the possibility that he is Ichabod Crane. At any rate he demands to know "what was the moral of the story, and what it went to prove." In one sense, he is withholding both laughter and approval until he can be convinced that the tale is either socially useful or true. In a deeper sense he is asking what the world of Dutch abundance (and Irving's literary efforts) *mean* to an America of politics and business.

The major proportions of the postscript are the reverse of the tale. Here, the Yankee and his values are triumphant; the shabby Dutchman in that world can only recreate the past as an idle diversion and one whose meaning is not comprehended. And yet within the postscript the Yankee is defeated once again, for the Dutchman responds to his questioner with a triumphant leer and overwhelms him with a weapon which has a comfortable place in the work of at least one writer of burlesque comedy — a nonsense syllogism.

How shall we finally read the final line — "Faith, sir . . . as to that matter, I don't believe one-half of it myself" (*RS,* 385)? It would be tempting to hear Irving defending his Dutch American vision as American imagining, made up in defiance of American fact *but still meaningful, still valuable.* It is more likely, however, that in this statement Irving is gently bidding farewell to his career as an American writer and a writer of burlesque comedy.

CHAPTER TEN

THE SENSE OF A BEGINNING

There had been a number of attempts to provide America with a fine literature before Irving. Almost all of these works have very little artistic energy in their own right, but, more importantly, they fail to cast any shapes into the future. Either their premises are slavishly retrospective, devoted to the worship of European fathers; or, as in the cases of Royall Tyler's *The Contrast* and Hugh Henry Brackenridge's *Modern Chivalry*, they attempt to create an American literature *reasonably*, by adding the coloring of fiction to the commonplaces of Republican rhetoric.

If, as I have asserted or implied in this study, Irving's American writings are the proper beginning of many significant strains in our national literature,[1] then his literary premises (also retrospective in a sense) must have been paradigmatic in their implications if not in their finished form. Among these premises are the following: the choice of a whimsically mad historian to stand for the American voice in literature; the decision to begin *The History* with the creation of the world, that is, the choice of a testamentary rather than an historical form as the appropriate vehicle for American fiction; and an understanding of the essential enmity between a national literature and the historical nation. This led to the association of festive values and burlesque comedy with an ethnic strain in colonial America that had already been written out of history by 1809.[2]

Diedrich Knickerbocker is the first narrative voice in American literature that rings true, and it should have been one of the least expected — the voice of a mad egotist, unable to order his story in his mind, unable to exert any control on the story he earnestly wishes to tell, unable to decide whether that story is fact or myth, actual or marvelous.

The voice of the exemplary American of contemporary drama and fiction — Tyler's Manly, William Dunlap's Bland, Brackenridge's Farrago, even Cooper's Natty Bumppo — is stiff and often painfully verbose. We may attribute this to the authors' lack of talent if we will, but a more basic reason involves the premises which guided them into their comatose existence. Facing the problem of what the representative American character should be, these authors took an obvious and very reasonable course. They translated the rhetorical definitions of the American (as he appeared in the prose of Paine, Adams, Franklin, Jefferson, Hamilton, etc.) into literary character and attempted to set this character loose in a fictive world. The result was that characters such as these could do nothing but talk, and their talk consists largely of the rhetorical formulations that called them into being. It is ironic that the most obvious means of creating American character should result in such inflexibly sententious puppets, considering how vigorous the personae of Paine's *Common Sense* or Franklin's *Autobiography* are as literary presences.

The voices of these early characters cannot take on human intonations because of the burden of Republican importance their talk must carry; they are continually in council. Manly, for example, is the dead center of his own play. He may remind us in retrospect of George Babbitt, but the vitality of Lewis' character is due to a revolutionary turn in the relation of the American to his public speech. Among other things, *Babbitt* dramatizes the living death of an abandonment to institutional rhetoric. Between Royall Tyler and Sinclair Lewis, Thoreau had worked out these implications within the drama of language itself.

In *Babbitt,* the life of the body has been frozen into a set of mechanical gestures, while the mind and mouth of man repeat prerecorded political, social, and cultural commercials whenever the appropriate verbal cue is given. The success of Natty Bumppo as a character also involves a recognition of the emptiness of American talk: Cooper keeps Natty's mind and body in isolation from one another; he is a literary schizophrenic. He lives with the savages, the dark races of the American continent, yet he talks continuously of the legitimacy of racial separation. His talk often seems endless, but he can act. His behavior, when it is most exciting, is native. His mouth is in the constant service of the light dose of revelation he received in the settlements, but his body fully accepts the reality of that unchristian nature where he has chosen to live out his life.

The most illuminating failure to create American character is that of Brackenridge's Captain Farrago. Referring to his importation of an Irishman, Teague O'Reilly, to provide the low comedy for his novel, Brackenridge claimed that he could not find an appropriate comic figure in

America: "The American has, in fact, no character; neither the clown nor the gentleman; so that I could not take one from our country, which I would rather have done as the scene lay there."[3]

But Farrago himself was supposed to be a comic character. The title of his novel, *Modern Chivalry,* and the structure of the work, make it clear that he was to be still another reincarnation of Don Quixote. The name Farrago has definite comic associations. Joseph Dennie, Brackenridge's contemporary, had written a serial with that title in 1792. Like *Salmagundi,* it refers to that mixed bag of styles, tones, and subjects, which was one of the comic forms that claimed its descent from the Latin *satura* (hodge-podge).

When Brackenridge claims that there are no comic types in America, he is in fact claiming that *there cannot be;* for America was rhetorically dedicated to the elimination of high and low, clown and gentleman. Yet, in almost every incident in *Modern Chivalry,* Farrago is involved with low, ignorant, debased, Americans. The only possible relationship that Brackenridge can set up between them is to have Farrago define at great length the Republican rhetorical model he embodies. The American crowd, the American democrats, ignore him and choose Teague as their model.

Brackenridge cannot bring himself to cast his American in a truly comic role, because the forms of thought and behavior that belong to Quixote are incompatible with the delineations of American rhetoric. On a superficial level, he cannot have him beaten or made the butt of endless practical jokes. Essentially, *he cannot have him mad.* The English had no inhibitions against casting young country Squires, dotty vicars, and old maids in the role of Quixote, but a formula for radical irrationality as an essential part of the American character was unthinkable for Brackenridge. Not so for Hawthorne, Melville, Whitman, or Thoreau.

Diedrich Knickerbocker possesses in full that vital madness, the openness to impulse and incoherence that the political and ethical rhetoric of America would not allow. Knickerbocker is a living example to American society of the value of living in two worlds at once — the linear world of history and the ritual world of comedy — and he exposes, by that very madness, the sterility of the distinction between the two.

Beginnings are difficult enough in themselves, but to begin a beginning is a task to be undertaken at the risk of one's sanity. No risk, however, is too great for Diedrich Knickerbocker in the fulfillment of his life's work, considering also that he has little sanity to risk. His life has been gladly devoted to the production of one great work: an account of the history and nature of Dutch civilization in America, one of *several possible American civilizations.* As literature, however, as a legend of happy origins where prelapsarian values shine for a moment before they are swept away by the intentions of history, it is a realization of that unkept promise, a second creation of these values in the present. Knickerbocker knows that an act of such cultural significance must rest upon the most solid foundation imaginable; so he anchors his history in the aboriginal void. Driven ever backward by a mad inner necessity, Knickerbocker begins his history with the creation of the world — the origin of all origins. It is the only way that Irving's and Knickerbocker's history of America can begin. The opening book is literally the enactment of a beginning, the new beginning of America. Irving's America is the result of a sacred act of creation which is also the act of artistic creation.

This is, in a sense, the beginning of every work of art, although it is explicit in proportion to the self-consciousness of the work. Every art work creates a world out of nothing, and that sacred world is continually threatened by the historical presence of the world which occupies the heavier time and space in which the author (and narrator) sits and writes. Strategies for abolishing that heavier world — gestures of exorcism and purification — are also present in most art works, although rarely as overtly as in Irving's *History,* and these can also be regarded as a series of strategies designed to destroy the two enemies of art — time and the rational mind. In the opening of *The History* Knickerbocker is, to quote a twentieth-century Shandean, Valeriy Tarsis, engaged in playing "shuttlecock with time and space." And his racquet, or Harlequin's wand, as Knickerbocker prefers to call it, is the radical disorder of his own mind, his almost total solipsism.

This is the magic to which Irving devotes the opening book, a magic that he would attempt once more in "Rip Van Winkle." But just as Shakespeare's Richard II finds the freedom in his prison cell to spin a world out of his own mind and then has that world exploded by Bolingbroke and time, which are, tragically, part of the contents of his mind; so the history of Yankee America is also inescapably a part of Knickerbocker's madness. And he is doomed to write a work in which the Yankees engage and destroy that far superior world of comedy, committing America again, now in art, into the meanings of Yankee history.

The early chapters of Knickerbocker's *History* anticipate a deep sense of the beginning which seems to be peculiar to American literature. The art work of an original or aboriginal continent should be an original creation, in the literal sense of that term. The literature of a continent outside of time should be similarly timeless, and, in a culture that lacks traditional ceremonial and festive structures through which sacred time and space can be evoked, Irving's mythic gesture seems the most obvious way of accomplishing this end: returning to the moment of original creation, beginning at the ultimate beginning; working to that moment from the present in order to insure the purity of such an opening. Two opening fictions in particular bear a close resemblance to Diedrich Knickerbocker's backwards flight — the search for *The Scarlet Letter* in the "Custom House" and the transportation of Hank Morgan back to Arthurian England in Twain's *A Connecticut Yankee in King Arthur's Court.*

Hawthorne's "Custom House" is not a preface to *The Scarlet Letter,* and yet it stands in a necessary prefatory tension with the romance that follows it. Before Hawthorne can write his greatest American story, he must fight his way through other senses of the American past, other American values, each claiming in hollow, ghostly tones to be the central meaning of America. The essay enacts a search for the only proper and possible origin of American literature.

Immediately after Hawthorne has conducted us into the Custom House for the first time, he moves into what seems to be an autobiographical digression. It is one of several set pieces in the "Custom House," and it is woven about the theme of Hawthorne's ambivalence toward the validity of imagining in America.

He moves back along the path he has just taken into the "old town of Salem" and wonders why it should have such a deep hold on his affections, considering its flat, unvaried surface, like a "disarranged checkerboard." The thin soil upon which he stands, however, is identified with the funeral ashes of his ancestors, and it is this in which he is rooted. Up from this widespread tomb come the voices of his two earliest American ancestors, William and John Hawthorne. They upbraid him for being a writer of storybooks. Whatever their faults, they at least acted in the world. William, particularly, was a large figure "as a man of war and peace . . . a soldier, legislator, judge . . . a ruler in the church."

The opposition here is not between the man of action and the man of imagination. William and John have not emerged from their tombs to walk about the earth a space merely to put their worthless descendent down as a frivolous and useless being. They have come to demand that he, like Hamlet, devote his talents to vindicating their lives: in this case, writing, rather than acting out, their scenario for America. They implicitly demand that the work he is contemplating be a public history of the early days of the colony, a history, that is, of their devotion, sacrifices, pioneer vigor, and above all of the legitimacy of their severity to Indian, Quaker, and witch. This meaning is made clear by the structure of the essay as a whole, and it is implied by their words of reproach: "What mode of glorifying God, or being serviceable to mankind in his day and generation, — may that [writing storybooks] be?"

The "Custom House," like most Romantic essays, dramatizes a withdrawal from a present that is felt to be valueless and a psyche that is fragmented and "tarnished." It records a voyage after lost values that leads the submissive psyche into death, the past, and the depths of the creative imagination. As Hawthorne moves into the past or, correspondingly, through the various architectural levels of the custom house, he is waylaid and tempted by a series of false fathers — King Derby, the old General, William and John Hawthorne — all of whom are likened to voices speaking from moldering open graves or ruins: the General, for example, is like the "gray and broken ruins" of an old fortress like Ticonderoga. And each of them implicitly demands that he shall stop there and tell their story — the story of New England maritime commerce, of Revolutionary heroism, of Puritan integrity — as *the true American story*, the American story of most value to a foundering present. Hawthorne is attracted but resists them all until "one idle and rainy day," in the upper recesses of the custom house, he is visited by the headless ghost of his true father, Surveyor Pue, who gives him his inheritance, "a certain affair of red cloth." "With his own ghostly voice, he has exhorted me, on the sacred consideration of my filial duty and reverence towards him, — who might reasonably regard himself as my official ancestor, — to bring his mouldy and moth-eaten lucubrations before the public." And Hawthorne immediately acquiesces.

Hawthorne's ghostly fathers, false or true, are also guides into the American past, and the time periods over which they guide him are very precisely calculated. Ultimately Pue takes him back, through his antiquarian researches, to the early days of Massachusetts. But William could have led him there much more easily! The tension between William and Pue is the major structural element in the essay. William would have taken him back so that he could have written a public history of Puritan necessities. Hawthorne perversely makes his own way back *to that period* to write instead a private history, which is far truer than the historical mandates of intense faith and pioneer life. He returns to write the story of the first heartbeat in the wilderness of America.

The opening of *A Connecticut Yankee* is the opposite of Irving's *History*, for Twain is attempting to validate the historical present, America as an industrial democracy, or at least to test its validity — not to annihilate it in the service of superior cultural values. Malory's England is the corresponding culture of ceremonial values and, insofar as it is a literary past (myth rather than history), the civilization that Hank Morgan attempts to set on the right track is Twain's parallel to Irving's colony of Dutch lubbers. Neither the historical fiction nor the literary myth, however, is seen as in any sense valuable by the two Victorian moralists and utilitarians (Morgan and Twain) who wander selectively through it.

The use of parody as a means of rendering the past is as destructive as Irving's festive comedy is potentially rejuvenating. Cooper, Hawthorne, and James would regret the absence of dukes and dauphins in America. Where the simplistic American eye sees a history of crime and exploitation, a more respectful sense of the past sees the texture of alternatives, out of which time has in fact ruthlessly stripped one thread and that, too often to the eye of the artist, the worst. Even Twain is betrayed by a desire for a rich past. When he gives us the Duke and the Dauphin in *Huckleberry Finn,* he celebrates them against his will. For all their moral worthlessness, they intuitively create festive rituals which bring an apathetic river-shore democracy to life for a brief moment. If that life is one of thoughtless violence, it is partly because historical America no longer has a sense of how one participates in a religious ritual, a Shakespearean drama, even a low vaudeville.

Born and bred a Yankee democrat, reared to the crafts and trades of a mechanistic civilization, Hank Morgan is sent back to the moment of origin in order to test whether the two values of political democracy and the efficient harnessing of power — *if present from the beginning* — can save the only civilization which he believes has any potential for the future. It needs to be saved because of certain discoveries Twain unwillingly made about America in *Huckleberry Finn.* There is an element of incoherence in Twain's fiction but one that Benjamin Franklin would have enthusiastically approved of; for what Twain is asking us to believe in is a vision of man in which the appropriate introduction of street-lighting, garbage disposal, electricity, and balloting into his social environment will redeem essential human nature, so that man in the future will be as spiritually clean as the institutions he has evolved.

It is appropriate that Hank Morgan, doomed to die as a sorcerer, should conquer and dominate feudal England through his mastery of time, his ability to predict an eclipse of the sun. He reminds us of another Yankee from further north, Sam Slick, whose profession is that of persuading Americans of the value of buying and knowing time. Morgan, ironically, controls this early society through his use of magical forms, but, like Ahab, he uses them in an efficient and Machiavellian spirit.

The return to some moment of ultimate origins as the only possible way of beginning the American fiction could be traced in *Moby Dick, Walden,* and "Song of Myself," but in these the structure is present as a continual tug of war between art and history, past and present, the sacred and the profane.

By beginning his work with the original creation, Irving is also able, or impelled, to raise a question that would continue to produce tensions in many of the major works of the following decades. Briefly stated, the question is whether the proper form of the American literary work is the history or the bible. Although one hesitates to consider Irving within the context of Puritan art and society, it is not surprising that there is a deep tendency in American artists to reproduce sacred forms, considering that the Puritans saw their lives and their settlement in revealed or promissory and not historical terms.

Knickerbocker wants to write a history, but what he produces, as a consequence of his opening strategy, is a testament. And in the literature to come, Emerson, Hawthorne, Melville, Thoreau, Whitman, and, in our century, Henry Miller would all involve their fictions in more or less overt testamentary form. The opposition of historical and biblical form can be accommodated, without too much distortion, to the opposition of the novel and the romance which Hawthorne discussed in his preface to *The House of the Seven Gables*. Whatever else the term suggests, American romances are deliberately ahistorical in that they refuse to reproduce the density and texture of the social present.

The testamentary form of *The History* obviously contributes to the annihilation of the world of history which is the aim of the opening book. But this work is also accomplished by a self-conscious drama which exists in Knickerbocker's mind as a continual conflict between the demands of fact and the impulse to create significance through what Knickerbocker calls "poetry." The real terms of this struggle are whether myth or history is more appropriate to a country like America. And in fact Diedrich Knickerbocker ignores history completely and reconstructs the history of America according to imaginative structures. It is ironic that his creator should spend the latter part of his career as an authentic historian – turning out inferior histories and biographies.

The more conventional view of the place of Irving's *History* in American literature is that of Marcus Cunliffe, whom I have quoted in the beginning of this study, asking if Irving was "so much to blame in judging his *History* a dead end, when it was only a false start?" We have not been able to feel any strong kinship between *The History* and works like *Walden,* "Song of Myself," and *Moby Dick,* but in several significant respects they belong to the same order of imaginative nationalism as it attempts to destroy the history that *is* in order to create a culture.

The identification of colonial Dutch America as the potential ground for artistic creativity in America may seem shallow and eccentric, but it is present, although it is weakened, as always, by Irving's limp aesthetic vocabulary. Hawthorne's aesthetic vocabulary is deceptively similar because he is also ambivalent toward imaginative activity. In Irving, however, there is no contrary principle of power that would continue to hold his aesthetic vision in any kind of productive tension. In the two American tales in *The Sketch Book,* both attributed to a now dead Knickerbocker, Irving returns to the locale and the concerns of *The History,* but it is the implicit prominence of his aesthetic equation that gives these tales, especially "Rip Van Winkle," their real power. In the "Legend of Sleepy Hollow" the equation of Dutch lubberland and imaginative potency finally becomes explicit.

Irving's literary response to the questions of whether or not America could produce an imaginative literature of its own and what the form and content of that literature should be may also seem shallow in the light of the more complex statements and investigations raised after him by Hawthorne and James; but he had, after all, the benefit of very few examples and almost no dialogue to provide him with more adequate terms. He does not see the problem in terms of East and West, England and America, old and new; he begs the paleface-redskin debate completely. Cooper's easy answer that culture is a product of the capital held no appeal for this cosmopolitan New Yorker and future citizen of the world. He believed, at least in his early fiction, that America was incapable of generating a literary culture because it had fallen into the hands of the Yankees and the spiritual traits which they represented. There was substance to Irving's attitude. Here, according to Constance Rourke, are the designs of the Yankee regarding art in America:

[Franklin] spoke on this subject with customary precision. "All things have their season, and with young countries as with young men, you must curb their fancy to strengthen their judgment. . . . To America, one schoolmaster is worth a dozen poets, and the invention of a machine or the improvement of an implement is of more importance than a masterpiece of Raphael. . . . " At about the same time Washington declared "that only arts of a practical nature would for a time be esteemed," adding that it was easy to perceive the causes which have combined to render the genius of this country scientific rather than imaginative. . . .
. . . Adams condemned the arts altogether, anticipating by almost a century, as had Franklin, an opinion of Mark Twain's Connecticut Yankee about the art of Raphael: "I would not give sixpence for a picture of Raphael or a statue of Phidias." He went on with heat, "The age of painting has not yet arrived in this country, and I hope it will not arrive very soon."[4]

With few exceptions, all of the artists in Hawthorne's tales and romances are practitioners of the mechanical arts, although they are able to create art products which transcend the limitations of craft and achieve the effect of fine art: Owen Warland, for example, is a watchmaker, Hester Prynne a seamstress. Dame Rigby creates Feathertop out of a scarecrow. Holgrave the photographer belongs in this category. Shem Drowne was an actual crafter of weather vanes and figureheads; in the tale "Drowne's Wooden Image," Hawthorne has John Singleton Copley call Drowne a man of genius.

Irving's imaginative response to the question of American art is simply to annihilate an America which he believed was incapable of giving itself to the impulses behind art and re-creating in its stead one that possibly could. The virtues of his Dutch lubbers are those of creatural comfort — eating, sleeping, smoking, silence, and, to a limited extent, bawdy and scatological play. They are also the ability to live in one's body, to live in the festive present, values that would later be celebrated by Thoreau and Whitman.

How Emerson, Thoreau, and Whitman, in their various ways, managed to adjust economy and festivity are long and complex stories as yet unexplained. *Walden* and *Nature* both begin in the world of economy and move, through the delicate operations of the irrational mind, to realms of finer values — although in Emerson they do not seem to be related to creatural comfort. In Whitman, it is not so much an adjustment as a fusion carried off by the sheer power of a Rabelaisian consciousness that refuses to accept the distinction. Hawthorne and Melville do not seem to be concerned with this vision of America, and yet it informs one of the several structures used by Hawthorne to define the Puritan legacy to America, and it shapes the development of Melville's early writing.

Hawthorne's "Maypole of Merry Mount" resembles Irving's *History* more closely than does any other single American work, although my view of the tale runs counter to almost all the accepted readings of it. Merry Mount does not fall because its values are false, but because of the author's inability to sustain its values. For Hawthorne, this takes the form of psychological fear rather than artistic inefficacy. Nevertheless, I believe that in this tale, Hawthorne is sincerely testing the possibility of establishing a festive, *and an artistic,* civilization in America:

Bright were the days at Merry Mount, when the Maypole was the banner of that gay colony! They who reared it, *should their banner be triumphant,* were to pour sunshine over New England's rugged hills, and scatter flower seeds throughout the soil. *Jollity and gloom were contending for an empire* (italics mine).

Merry Mount is a totally festive culture. Its calendar is *The Book of Days,* and it has no entries relating to the historical occurrences and exigencies of the seventeenth century in America. Merry Mount is also a source of artistic inspiration: its "true History," says Hawthorne, is "a poet's tale."

Merry Mount is overtly identified with the Golden Age, a place where "May, or her mirthful spirit, dwelt all the year round." But its implicit relationship to the Puritan settlement is that of a younger, though older, England. It is Old England, Merry Old England, treated as a myth of prelapsarian gaiety. Even more than the Dutch and Yankee civilizations in *The History,* Merry Mount is in necessary conflict with the grim and weighty existence of the Puritans: these two colonies are the youth and maturity of one civilization.

In England, Merry Mount has already been destroyed; there the maypoles have already been cut down. It is as if an earlier England had struggled to establish itself again in the timeless space of the New World — "all the hereditary pastimes of Old England were transplanted hither" — only to be challenged again by the secular and alienated consciousness of the Reformation.

Jollity, it turns out, cannot struggle successfully against gloom, and yet even Endicott feels some need to effect a partial marriage between the two. So he adopts the Lord and Lady of the May, and in "garments of more decent fashion," the youth's hair cropped "in the true pumpkinshell fashion," they are led east of Merry Mount into American history.

After Hawthorne has opened his tale, he indicates a number of times that the gaiety of Merry Mount is merely a false glitter: the leaders of the colony are "sworn triflers of a lifetime," who know that mirth is but the counterfeit of happiness. Yet such assertions are in flat contradiction to the opening two paragraphs of the tale. Moreover, a conflict between men who really understand the grave truths of human life and degenerates who counterfeit impossible values badly is hardly worth the telling.

The contradiction between the opening paragraphs and the later denials points to the deeper interest of the tale. The jollity of Merry Mount is not false, but the narrator realizes that it is potentially wild, and he, therefore, begins to distort his festive vision almost as soon as he has premised it.

Merry Mount goes down to defeat, not because of the Puritans, but because of the ambivalence of the dreamer. Hawthorne dreamed of a Golden Age in America as Melville dreamed of Typee. As Hawthorne dreams he suddenly becomes aware that on the underside of Paradise there is the possibility of bestiality and violence. Is this the truth of an American Paradise or the sexual fear of the dreamer? Hawthorne is by far the greater artist, but Irving, perhaps because of his youth and artistic irresponsibility, dared to dream out his dream, to sketch the values that are possible in art and impossible in life.

Immediately after the apostrophe to the flowers of the Golden Age, which the maypole of Merry Mount brings to life again, Hawthorne suddenly notices a "wild throng" clustered about it. He denies that they could possibly be the fauns and nymphs of the "classic Groves." They are Gothic monsters, although, he admits, "perhaps of Grecian origin": one has the "head and branching antlers of a stag"; another "the grim visage of a wolf"; while a third "showed the beard and horns of a venerable he-goat."

After Hawthorne works his way through the animal possibilities of the maypole, he shifts to another source of adult disgust, the blown-up features of the child, in the giants of Mardi Gras, for example, or the cinema Frankenstein monster: "Other faces wore the similitude of man or woman, but distorted or extravagant, with red noses pendulous before their mouths, which seemed of awful depth, and stretched from ear to ear in an eternal fit of laughter." This is remarkably parallel to Rip Van Winkle's reaction to the lubber faces, lovingly dreamed into existence by Knickerbocker, which he sees in the Catskills.

Hawthorne, like Irving, has attempted to dream of an America that opposed in every respect the civilization he had inherited. And like Irving he framed it as one version of the origin of settlement in America.

Typee was Melville's first successful work of literature, and it overtly represents an attempt on the author's part to escape to a festive and creatural culture. Like Hawthorne, however, he treads warily from the start. He escapes into a world in which he clearly cannot exist for long; its qualities are too static and restrictive. It is, moreover, outside of America in every sense; it has no values that can be easily substituted for those that are shaping the American present, because its primitivism is so extreme. Melville later accepted the challenge of meeting the American historical present and future head-on. When he next sees the beautiful creatures of his earlier dream, in *Omoo,* their bodies are rotting with venereal disease.

Melville brings his body to Typee, but his mind also accompanies him. It is active from the start, projecting mild forms of guilt and anxiety at first — a sense of unease at the pleasure and indolence that characterize the culture — and it manifests itself in a structure which defines him as a prisoner of enjoyment: the knowledge that he cannot leave tarnishes the values of Typee for him. But he is the author of the book and responsible for its structures. The terrestrial paradise becomes unbearable when Melville seems to discover what he knew all along, that the inhabitants of this edenic realm are *headhunters.* Unlike Brom Bones, he cannot live without his head, and he is probably right. Other solutions are possible, however. In *Moby Dick*, he finally makes peace with his earliest dream and nightmare. Here, a narrator who greatly resembles Diedrich Knickerbocker meets a headhunter and marries him.

As early as *Salmagundi,* Irving was sketching his cultural vision of the true America, and the nature of his terra incognita was that of burlesque comedy. He tried hard to see an America devoted to festivity and celebration, childishly free to play and, hopefully, to dream. His America was also as receptive as a hard moral past could allow it to be to the mysteries of obscenity and scatology. But even in the nineteenth century, no one could begin to treat these values with the boldness of Shakespeare or Rabelais, and Melville and Thoreau go to great lengths to bury the connection between their fictions and the life of the body.

Irving belongs in the company of the major writers of nineteenth-century America only because he knew in his early period what the American writer would have to do to write American literature.

NOTES

Preface

1. Marcus Cunliffe, *The Literature of the United States* (London, 1954), p. 56.

2. The statement is essentially if not literally true; there are a very few exceptions to it. Irving does move through the period of the Revolution in some of his later American tales, but the oblique track along which he moves into the national period actually lends support to this generalization. In "Wolfert's Roost" (1839), for example, he traced the history of a Dutch "mansion." It is located in Westchester County, and, during the period of the Revolutionary War, it had been a neutral territory between the opposing camps (Cooper had treated this area in a similar manner earlier in *The Spy*). For Irving, however, it seems to be inhabited only by the Dutch: "a race of hard-headed, hard-handed, stout-hearted yeomen, descendents of the primitive Nederlanders." Of the three forces involved in Irving's vision of Revolutionary America, the Dutch alone are exemplary. Eventually they are drawn into the war against their will, and they fight off both the British and the Colonials who are foraging for food in their territory. A few pages later, the Dutch seem to be fighting only the British. There is, however, no appeal made to future nationalism. The rebels fade out of the sketch, and the Dutch seem quite capable of winning the war by themselves: At Wolfert's Roose "was concocted the midnight invasion of New York Island, and the conflagration of Delancy's Tory mansion. . . . Nay, more, if the tradition of the Roost may be credited, here was meditated, by Jacob Van Tassel and his compeers, a nocturnal foray into New York itself, to surprise and carry off the British commanders, Howe and Clinton, and put a triumphant close to the war."

The third chronicle begins with the statement that the Revolutionary War was over, but there is no reference whatsoever to the fact that a new nation has emerged; the region remains Dutch to the end of the tale.

NOTES

Chapter I

1. *American Folklore* (Chicago, 1959), p. 8.
2. Stuart Tave, *The Amiable Humorist* (Chicago, 1960).
3. The need for a taxonomy of the comic is not a mere academic exercise. We must have conceptions and a language that fit and expressively delineate the differences we all know exist in this confusing and disarming category of literature. Ruth Nevo, in an article, "Toward a Theory of Comedy," *Journal of Aesthetics and Art Criticism*, XXI (1962–63)[327], puts the problem well: "What formal principles can provide a valid approach to works as rich, as complex, as marvellously different from one another, as, for random example, *Lysistrata, As You Like It, . . . Volpone, . . . Tartuffe, The Way of the World, . . . The Barber of Seville, Cyrano de Bergerac, Pygmalion, The Playboy of the Western World, . . . The Good Woman of Szechuan, The Italian Straw Hat,* and *City Lights?* And this excludes works which are not indeed dramas, but to which a theory of comedy can hardly fail to apply, such as *Don Quixote, Gargantua,* and *Tristram Shandy.* The list could be extended almost indefinitely . . . " But her own distinctions are terribly disappointing: "If the dynamic of human nature — the irrational, the libidinous, the egoistic, the 'ugly,' which is comedy's subject matter — is regarded with tolerance, even with the respect accorded to a vital energy . . . the result is Aristophanic or Rabelaisian comedy, the comedy of licence from inhibition. . . . If, however, this original human stuff is regarded with anger or contempt, if it is called folly or vice, and so chastised . . . then the comedy has become satire" (332). It is not that she is wrong but that she has given us far too little to think and work with, and yet this is one of the two most usual approaches to the problem of the comic: to set up a continuum which moves from a pole of joy to one of anger, which suggests that whether or not the author cares for his subject matter is the primary, possibly the only, determinant of comedy. Such a distinction would be quickly exposed if applied, for example, to the romance, or tragedy, or the lyric.

The inherited vocabulary of comedy may be of some value, but not as it has been used. On the one hand, there are terms like *parody* or *travesty* which claim to tell us what a form is and what it is doing, but in fact only tell us that in these cases satire may not possess its necessary fund of moral seriousness. The more general terms seem to be kept almost deliberately vague. It is a rare study of the comic that does not communicate to us, through the way comic terms are used, that wit and humor, wit and satire, irony and satire, etc., are synonymous or at least overlapping terms.

It has become fashionable, in extended studies of the comic, to provide the reader with a schema in chart form of the subdivisions of the comic. In Walter Sorell's *Facets of Comedy* (New York, 1972), p. 18, the poles of the comic are "Joy" to "Criticism," or "Fun for fun's sake" to "The ridiculous and the sublime," and the parts of this continuum are: "Horseplay, Farce (Burlesque), Clowning, Humor (Pun, Nonsense), Wit, Parody, Irony, Caricature, Satire." The principle of differentiation is nowhere explained, and the terms are never defined. The list itself is, I believe, intellectually impenetrable, and some of the appositions and positions of terms seem quite perverse.

Marie Collins Swabey's *Comic Laughter* (New Haven, 1961) is a very interesting book, but her schema suffers from the same faults as Sorell's. There is only one categorical term, the comic or the ludicrous, and six subdivisions: the comic, wit, humor, satire, irony, and etc. The footnote to the last category is extremely pertinent: "In addition to the chief varieties of the ludicrous, other minor subdivisions might be added, such as the whimsical, the grotesque, and the ridiculous. These, however, hardly warrant separate treatment" (p. 4).

4. See also Wayne C. Booth, *The Rhetoric of Fiction* (Chicago, 1960), p. 230.

5. *Gargantua,* trans. by J. M. Cohen (Suffolk, 1957), p. 75 (hereafter Rab.).

6. In Robert C. Elliott's *The Power of Satire* (Princeton, N.J., 1960), p. 187, *The Praise of Folly, Gargantua, The Anatomy of Melancholy,* and the *Alice* books are called the "great mavericks" of comedy.

7. Erasmus, *The Praise of Folly* (Ann Arbor, Mich., 1958), p. 2.

8. Ibid., p. 3. Cf., ". . . the Victorians saw in the exhibitionism of *Tristram Shandy* (and of Sterne) a further disquieting instance of the play impulse. Sterne seemed almost to embody the spirit of display, display for its own sake, as a game"; Richard A. Lanham, *Tristram Shandy: The Games of Pleasure* (Berkeley, Calif., 1973), p. 51.

9. *Mimesis,* tr. Willard Trask (Princeton, N.J., 1953), pp. 275–77.

10. Ed. G. B. Harrison (London, 1927), p. 100.

11. (Princeton, N.J., 1962), pp. 155, 176.

12. Wayne Booth, in an article, "The Self-Conscious Narrator in Comic Fiction before *Tristram Shandy,*" *PMLA*, LXVII (March, 1952), 164 and 175, uses the terms "nonsense fiction" and "facetiae." Both of these terms are belittling and reflect attitudes on the part of readers in the past to the work of Rabelais and Sterne. A more common designation for this type of comedy is the term *grotesque:* Marcel Tetel, in his study, *Rabelais* (New York, 1967), uses that term for the comedy of Rabelais; David Worcestor, in *The Art of Satire* (Cambridge, Mass., 1940), p. 60, labels Rabelaisian comedy "Grotesque Satire"; and Rabelais' work exhibits the qualities examined by Wolfgang Kayser in *The Grotesque in Art and Literature* (New York, 1963). It seems to me, however, that this term suggests that the celebratory qualities of burlesque comedy have either turned ugly, as they have in much twentieth-century literature that extends this comic tradition, or they are felt to be so by the critic; Kayser would seem to agree: "Serenus Zeitblom, the narrator of Thomas Mann's *Doktor Faustus,* may turn away in disgust from the "grotesque" landscapes of an ambiguous nature and an inharmonious art in order to dwell solely in the noble realm of the humanities where one is 'safe from such nightmares.' The historian, however, would be at fault if he averted his eyes from the wealth of works from the past which pertain to that strange realm," p. 11.

The definitions and historical illustrations given for the term *burlesque* in the *New English Dictionary* exemplify that slippery career of meaning between celebration and abuse that characterizes most of our terms for the comic. The first illustration given, however, in a glossary of 1656, defines the term's meaning as "drolish, merry, pleasant." What most recommends the term is the pressure it exerts on writers on comedy, almost forcing them to associate it with the vital and the creatural: " . . . presentation of the burlesque side of life shows us man's crudities, ignorance, and embarrassments" (Swabey, *Comic Laughter*, p. 168); the clown "is at home with any kind of horseplay, farcical trick, and burlesque bawdiness"; *commedia dell'arte* "usually revolved around the burlesque of cuckoldry"; and in "a burlesque scene . . . [Aristophanes'] Sausage Seller belabors the Tanner with tripe and prepares himself for his speech to the Assembly by eating garlic" (Sorell, *Facets*, pp. 19, 95, and 45). In order to keep his book, *Burlesque* (London, 1972), down to 72 pages, J. D. Jump begins by eliminating this troublesome linguistic tendency: "For many Americans today, a burlesque is a kind of variety show with a heavy emphasis on sex, featuring broad comedians and striptease dancers. This is not the sense that concerns us here."

13. Henry Fielding, *Joseph Andrews*, ed. Douglas Brooks (London, 1970), pp. 4–5.

14. Merrill F. Heiser, "The Decline of Neoclassicism 1801–1848," in *Transitions in American Literary History*, ed. H. H. Clark (Durham, N.C., 1953), pp. 136–37.

15. See Barrett Wendell, *A Literary History of the United States* (New York, 1905), pp. 172–73; F. L. Pattee, *The First Century of American Literature* (New York, 1935), pp. 243–44; Stanley T. Williams, *The Life of Washington Irving* (New York, 1935), I, 116 [hereafter, *STW*]; Floyd Stovall, *American Idealism* (Norman, Oklahoma, 1943), p. 29; Cunliffe, *Literature*, p. 56; and William Hedges' *Washington Irving: An American Study* (Baltimore, 1965), pp. 78–79, and 98.

16. William Irving, James Kirke Paulding, and Washington Irving, *Salmagundi; or, the Whimwhams and Opinions of Launcelot Langstaff, Esq., and Others*, ed. E. A. Duyckinck (New York, 1860), pp. 329–30. Citations to this work will be by page number alone in the chapters that treat it directly; in the other chapters it will be identified as *Sal.*

Salmagundi was first published in 1807–8, and during the century it was reprinted frequently, both separately and as part of Irving's complete writings. All of these editions are of doubtful authority, considering Irving's ambivalence toward the work. Perhaps it would be most prudent to refer the reader to the original volumes, as Lewis Leary does in his pamphlet, *Washington Irving* (Minneapolis, 1963), but this work is not readily available. Stanley Williams, I, ix, claims to have used the volume in the Riverside edition, 1864–69, although no such edition can be found in his *Bibliography of the Writings of Washington Irving* of a year later, published with Mary Allen Edge (New York, 1936). William Hedges used the volume from the revised edition of 1860–61. I have rejected any revised edition on principle and chosen to use the first edition identified as "printed from the original edition . . . " The edition which I have used runs to 502 text pages and seems to be identical with that listed in Williams' bibliography on page 100. Duyckinck's edition, however, is not printed from the original; it is a revised edition with one or two exceptions which one is at a loss to explain. The fact is that with *Salmagundi* one must make the best of a bad bargain. The only comfort I can offer a reader who desires to trace references to this work is that the pieces are very short for the most part and generally diverse in subject.

A sound edition of this work is badly needed. Such an edition does exist, prepared by Bruce Granger and Martha Hartzog Stacker for the University of Wisconsin's edition of Irving's works. It lies mouldering in typescript, however, because the financial support for this project seems to have dried up. Of all Irving's works, *Salmagundi* stands most in need of editorial correction, and one hopes that a publisher for it will soon be found.

17. Quoted in *STW*, II, 275.
18. Cunliffe, *Literature*, p. 56; Edward Wagenknecht, *Washington Irving* (New York, 1962), p. 9; and William Hedges, "Washington Irving," *Major Writers of America*, ed. Perry Miller (New York, 1962), I, 184.
19. Perry Miller, quoted in Hedges, *Washington Irving*, p. 104.

Chapter II

1. For a full discussion of these pieces, see my introduction to *Washington Irving's Contributions to the Corrector* (Minneapolis, 1969) [hereafter cited as *Corr.*].
2. Washington Irving, *Journals and Notebooks*, Vol. I, 1803–1806, ed. Nathalia Wright (Madison, Wisc., 1969). Citations to this volume will be by page number alone in this chapter but with "Wright" elsewhere. Citations to letters in Pierre M. Irving, *The Life and Letters of Washington Irving* (New York, 1864) [Hereafter cited as *PMI*] Vol. I will be cited in this chapter as "Ltr." along with the page number. I have normalized the Wright text — omitted excisions, restored punctuation, etc. — to make it more readable.
3. George S. Hellman, *Washington Irving, Esquire* (New York, 1925), pp. 30–31.
4. This was based on Laurence Sterne, *A Sentimental Journey;* see *Works* . . . (Oxford, 1927), pp. 32–33 and 37.
5. A letter in *STW*, I, 49, of July 20, 1804. This is taken primarily from *A Sentimental Journey*, pp. 147–48; even the quotation in Irving's letter is Sterne misquoting Addison's *Cato*. Compare also the following from Sterne's work: "The young fellow, said the landlord . . . has but one misfortune in the world . . . 'He is always in love.' — I am heartily glad of it, said I — 'twill save me the trouble every night of putting my breeches under my head. In saying this, I was making not so much La Fleur's eloge, as my own, having been in love with one princess or another almost all my life, and I hope I shall go on so till I die, being firmly persuaded, that if ever I do a mean action, it must be in some interval betwixt one passion and another" (p. 39). See also pp. 52 and 106 of Sterne's work.
6. *STW*, I, 55. The corresponding passage in the rough notes in Wright (pp. 477–78) is terribly disjointed, and Williams' passage is a fair reconstruction.
7. The three quotations are from pp. 142 and 147–48. The episode itself is on pp. 152–58.
8. Pp. 108–9. There are several other possible borrowings from Sterne. Irving's description of the scene in the catacombs of the Church of St.

NOTES

Michel (pp. 44–45) owes something to the chapter, "Le Patissier," in *A Sentimental Journey*, p. 99; and the anecdote related on March 21, 1805, to Sterne's chapter, "Nampont – The Dead Ass," pp. 47–49. Cf. also the anecdote in *PMI*, I, 153 and *A Sentimental Journey*, pp. 106–7. In addition, Sterne is directly alluded to in the journals on pp. 233, 271, and 482.

9. *The Early Masters of English Fiction* (Lawrence, Kansas, 1956), p. 190.
10. A letter of Jan. 1, 1805; *STW*, I, 59.
11. *STW*, I, 395.
12. Washington Irving, *Diedrich Knickerbocker's A History of New York*, ed. Stanley T. Williams and Tremaine McDowell (New York, 1927), pp. xi ff. This is the 1809 edition and will be cited as *HNY* except in those chapters which treat the work, where only a page number will be used. For Irving's lifelong infatuation with the theater, see the unpublished MA thesis by M. M. Raymond, "Washington Irving and the Theatre" (Wellesley College, 1940).
13. Ltr., Dec. 20, 1804, p. 90; Wright, p. 122; Wright, p. 195; Ltr., Apr.4, 1805, p. 123; and Wright, p. 137.
14. Hellman, *Washington Irving*, p. 36.
15. Ibid., p. 22
16. A letter of July 20, 1804; *STW*, I, 48. This sprightly form of burlesque myth and epic becomes one of the more important comic strategies in *The History*. It is Irving's playful response to a literary habit of travel writers, that of coupling the epic description with their own observation of places treated by Homer or Virgil.
17. A letter of Jan. 20, 1805; *STW*, I, 60.

Chapter III

1. In using material from *Salmagundi*, I have tried to restrict myself to sections that Irving contributed or collaborated on. I have made a determination of the contributions on the part of the three collaborators which satisfies me. The evidence for this, however, would probably run as long as this book itself.
2. Tave, *Amiable Humorist*, pp. vii and viii.
3. Ibid., 148.
4. The notion that character in comedy was based on uniqueness was a complete reversal of the dominant principle of comic typology as announced by Aristotle in the *Poetics*. It can be found in English literature much earlier than Sterne, but it is found rarely and then usually in low-comic works. In his *Amusements Serious and Comical* (1700), Tom Brown, for example, announces that "I have a great mind to be in print, but above all, I would fain to be an original, and that is a true comic thought" (London, 1927), "Amusement I." A defense of novelty can be found in Addison's and Steele's *The Spectator*, ed. Donald F. Bond (New York, 1965), No. 626 [hereafter, *Spec.*].
   Tave quotes a contemporary evaluation of Smollett's Tom Bowling: "This is indeed Nature itself; original, *unique*, and *sui generis*," *Amiable Humorist*, p. 167. See also Jack F. Stewart, "Sterne's Absurd Comedy," *University of Windsor Review*, V, No. 2 (1970), 83.

5. *Tristram Shandy*, ed. James A. Work (New York, 1940), p. 65 [hereafter *TS*]. Cf.: "[the gait and figure of Toby's Hobby-Horse] was so strange, and so utterly unlike was he, from his head to his tail, to any one of the whole species, that it was now and then made a matter of dispute — whether he was really a HOBBY-HORSE or no" (*TS*, 78). See also *TS*, pp. 63–64 and 285; and *Sal.*, p. 65.

6. Tobias Smollett, *The Expedition of Humphry Clinker*, ed. Lewis M. Knapp (London, 1966), p. 8.

7. *Humor*, even in the time of Jonson, had had a secondary meaning of "unreasonable caprice." Despite the overlap of meaning between *humor* and *whimsy*, there was an intelligible area of semantic difference, and there was a significant difference in their application as principles of comedy.

8. "The increasing admiration for the humorist ran parallel with the development of the concept of the genius as someone strikingly different from all other men. Both humorist and genius were highly individual, possessors of rare temperament who valued their singularities; both were 'originals'; and at times they were identified"; Tave, *Amiable Humorist*, pp. 170–71.

For another approach to the relationship between Shandean and Romantic aesthetics, see Earl R. Wasserman, *The Subtler Language* (Baltimore, 1959), chapter 5.

9. *Selections from Ralph Waldo Emerson*, ed. Stephen E. Whicher (Boston, 1957), p. 150; and *The Journals of . . . Emerson*, ed. Robert N. Linscott (New York, 1960), p. 18

10. The following are a few random examples of the earlier moral force of *whimsy:* "falling into the oddest Whimsies that ever a sick brain conceived," Jonathan Swift, "Tale of a Tub," *The Prose . . .* (Oxford, 1957–59), I, 88; "This case seems to me to be plainly hysterical; the old woman is whimsical," John Arbuthnot, *The History of John Bull* [1712–13], in *The Life and Works . . .* , ed. George A. Aitken (Oxford, 1892), p. 250; and "Strange and trivial Reasons/The Whimsical Brain allures," Thomas D'Urfey, *Wit and Mirth: or Pills to Purge Melancholy*, [1719–20] (New York, 1959), I, 81. This corresponds to the pejorative associations the term *imagination* possessed for the eighteenth century.

11. Steele's defense of "whimsicals," in *The Theatre* (1720), is also a defense of reasonable men according to the inversion contained in a phrase like " 'tis folly to be wise": "A Whimsical . . . is a Person who governs himself according to his own Understanding, in Disobedience to that of others, who are more in Fashion than himself . . . all the *Great*, who ever liv'd, were Whimsicals"; Tave, *Amiable Humorist*, p. 101. This kind of figurative premise, rather than a real tolerance of humorists, underlies the conception of Sir Roger de Coverley.

12. The duplicated formation appears in John Fletcher's *Rule a Wife and Have a Wife*. Irving alludes to the play in *Sal.*, 117 and *HNY*, 288.

13. One of the amiable character sketches in *Humphry Clinker* describes the subject as giving "vent to every whimsical idea as it arose," p. 60.

14. This allusion to Voltaire was taken from Sterne's "*Bright Goddess*, if thou art not too busy with CANDID and Miss CUNEGUND's affairs . . ." (*TS*, p. 17). The original magazine issue had the spelling Candid which was

later corrected on the assumption that it was a typographical error. Two paragraphs earlier, Jeremy noted: "sentimental correspondence between a crab and a lobster — digression to Abelard and Eloisa," which sounds very much like Tristram's story "of a nun who fancied herself a shell-fish, and of a monk damn'd for eating a muscle" (*TS*, pp. 479–80).

15. Tave, *Amiable Humorist*, p. 22.

16. Democritus as the laughing philosopher was both a common frame for comic writers and a mask for authorial and editorial characters: See Rab., pp. 79, 166, and 452; *TS*, 483; *Momus, or The Laughing Philosopher* (Dublin, 1777), No. 5; and *Sal.*, pp. 33, 85, and 486.

17. See *TS*, pp. 501–2.

18. The cause of immoderate laughter is discovered by the pedant, Cornelius Scriblerus, in Pliny, who ascribes it to the bigness of the spleen; Alexander Pope, *The Memoirs of the Extraordinary Life, Works, and Discoveries of Martinus Scriblerus* . . . , ed. Charles Kerby-Miller (New Haven, 1950), p. 113.

19. See *TS*, pp. 8 and 215; and *Sal.*, p. 333. The narrator of "A Tale of a Tub" says of his treatise: "The *Superficial* Reader will be strangely provoked to *Laughter;* which clears the Breast and the Lungs, is Soverain against the *Spleen*, and the most innocent of all *Diureticks,"* Swift, p. 117. In his preface to *Joseph Andrews*, Fielding defends burlesque "rather, as it contributes more to exquisite Mirth and Laughter than any other; and these are probably more wholesome Physic for the Mind, and conduce better to purge away Spleen, Melancholy, and ill Affections, than is generally imagined," p. 5.

20. *Humphry Clinker*, p. 28.

21. "Should any gentleman or lady be displeased with the inveterate truth of their likeness, they may ease their spleen by laughing at those of their neighbours" (*Sal.*, p. 28).

22. Pp. 14–15.

23. Pp. 17, 28, and 49. Unkind actions even make his teeth chatter; pp. 22 and 67.

24. Another work which illustrates this transformation and with which Irving was quite familiar was George Colman the Younger's *John Bull.*

For a discussion of the amiable misanthrope in Smollett, see Thomas R. Preston's "Smollet and the Benevolent Misanthrope Type," *PMLA*, LXXIX (Mar. 1964), 51–57.

25. Sept., pp. 474–75.

26 *The Prose Works of Philip Freneau*, ed. Philip M. Marsh (New Brunswick, N.J., 1955), p. 122. See also *The Port-Folio*, ed. Joseph Dennie (Philadelphia), Jan. 31, 1801, and July 12, Aug. 2, and Dec. 13, 1806, for the misogyny and self-love associated in America with the old bachelor.

27. See Bruce Granger's "The Whim-Whamsical Bachelors in *Salmagundi,"* *Costerus* (Amsterdam, 1972), [63]–69.

28. It also follows that the work will be of incomparable value: "We advise the public, therefore, to purchase our numbers merely for their own sakes; if they do not, let them settle the affair with their consciences and posterity" (29); and "I bid my readers an affectionate farewell; exhorting them to live honestly and soberly . . . reading diligently the Bible and almanac, the newspaper and SALMAGUNDI; which is all the reading an

honest citizen has occasion for" (502). Thus *Salmagundi* opens and closes. Compare Rabelais: "Find me a book in any language, on any subject or science whatever, which has such virtues, properties, and prerogatives, and I will pay you a quart of tripe. No, gentleman, no. It is peerless, incomparable, and beyond comparison," p. 502.

29. "A Tale of a Tub," p. 40. See also pp. 28, 40–41 and 70 of that work; *TS*, p. 57; and *Sal.*, p. 329.

30. See also *TS*, p. 313, and *Sal.*, p. 27.

Chapter IV

1. *PMI*, I, 175. The first two essays in *Salmagundi* — the essays corresponding to the conventional prospectus of a magazine and the opening essay of a serial — were largely patterned on the lead essay of the first number of *The Town* (New York), Jan., 1807. And the essay "Theatrics" (*Sal.*, pp. 40–43) was based point for point on comments made in a review in *The Town*, pp. 2–3, of a production of *Macbeth*.

2. No. 142.

3. Several passages from *Salmagundi* used in this study were excised from that work prior to the Duyckinck edition. They appear in the microfilm version of *Salmagundi, American Periodical Series*, 1800–1825, roll 44, no. 587. I believe it will be more convenient, however, to refer to the point in the Duyckinck text where the passage had initially been located. This excision was part of a long passage which had followed the phrase, "equal importance" on p. 255, line 19.

4. *The Poetical Works of Edward Young* (London, 1888), II, 125.

5. (London, 1788), p. 92.

6. In *The Connecticut Wits*, ed. V. L. Parrington (New York, 1926), p. 486. "The Echo" was originally published in *The American Mercury* from 1791 to 1805.

7. An excised passage from the poem, "Tea," which had followed l. 20, p. 472.

8. " . . . he neither wept it away as the *Hebrews* and the *Romans* — or slept it off as the *Laplanders* — or hang'd it, as the *English*, or drown'd it, as the *Germans"* (*TS*, p. 351). See also *Spec.*, Nos. 20 and 135.

9. See *Spec.*, Nos. 15, 45, 277, and 478; Richard Steele's *The Guardian*, No. 10; *Memoirs of the Society of Grub Street* (London, 1737), No. 58; *The Connoisseur* (London, 1754-56), No. 54; and Edward Moore's *The World* (London, 1753-56), No. 75.

10. See also *Spec.*, Nos. 36, 67 and 308; Steele's *The Tatler*, No. 88; and *Guardian*, No. 154. Extravagant dancing was also a common theme in the comic ballad of low life; for example, Thomas Dibdin's "Jack at the Opera," extracted in *The Port-Folio*, Jan. 1, 1803.

11. See Oliver Goldsmith's "Citizen of the World," Ltr. X, *Collected Works*, ed. Arthur Friedman (London, 1966), II, 49, for a parallel passage.

NOTES

Chapter V

1. John Neal, *Blackwood's Edinburgh Magazine,* Jan., 1825, p. 61.

2. The foreign traveller letters were a popular satirical format in the eighteenth century. Goldsmith himself imitated *Spec.* No. 50, which is the transcription of a bundle of letters left behind by the Indians after a visit to London. Swift claimed credit for the idea. They were also popular in American periodicals. The best of many were Freneau's "The Voyage of Timberoo-Tabo-Eede, an Otaheite Indian," *Prose Works,* pp. 137–46; and Francis Hopkinson's "Translation of a Letter, Written by a Foreigner on His Travels," *The Miscellaneous Essays* . . . (Philadelphia, 1792), I, 98–100.

3. An outstanding example of this type is Sir Politic Would-Be in Ben Jonson's *Volpone.* See also the letter from Thomas Quid-nunc, *Spec.,* No. 625, and Goldsmith's *Busy-Body,* No. 6. The editor of foreign and domestic transactions in *The Memoirs of the Society of Grub Street* is a Mr. Quidnunc. In *The Port-Folio,* the first number of a serial, "The Barber Shop," identifies that place as the most frequented resort of quidnuncs, Jan. 24, 1801; and there is a letter from a correspondent named Quidnunc in the issue of Aug. 9, 1806.

4. Jonathan Swift, *Gulliver's Travels, The Prose Works,* ed. Herbert Davis (Oxford, 1939–41), XI, 164.

5. See also Goldsmith, "Citizen of the World," Ltr. V, p. 32.

6. In response to Paddle's explanation, "the old man shook his head, shrugged his shoulders, gave a mysterious Lord Burleigh nod, said he hoped it might be so; but he was by no means satisfied with this attack upon the President's breeches." The allusion in the passage is to the play within a play in Sheridan's *The Critic,* III.i. It does not, however, explain the allusion, but in the first scene there is an argument between Mrs. Dangle, a female quidnunc, and her husband. She tells him that "there are letters every day with Roman signatures, demonstrating the certainty of an invasion, and proving that the nation is utterly undone."

7. See Sheridan Baker's "Political Allusion in Fielding's *Author's Farce, Mock Doctor,* and *Tumble-Down Dick," PMLA,* LXXVII, 1142 (June, 1962); also *Tatler,* No. 81; *Spec.,* No. 497; Goldsmith "Citizen," Ltr. LXXIV; Peter Pindar's [John Wolcut], "Hair Powder," *Works* (London, 1794–1801), IV, 37; and Freneau's "Robert Slender's Idea of a Visit to a Modern Great Man," *Prose Works,* pp. 165–67.

8. Goldsmith, "Citizen," Ltr. LXXIV; also see *Sal.,* pp. 70, 261, 287, and 421.

9. *Jonathan Wild, The Works of Henry Fielding* (New York, 1902), XII, 3 and 9 ff.; and *Sal.,* p. 378.

10. Irving's extended figure of a "ward meeting of politic dogs" (*Sal.,* pp. 261–62) was probably derived from Swift's "republic of dogs," "The Battle of the Books," *Prose Works,* I, 141–42.

11. John Mathias (1754–1835) produced one large book of verse invective and satire, *The Pursuits of Literature, or What You Will* (London, 1796), which he revised and reedited for ten years. For an account of Mathias, see Kenneth Hopkins, *Portraits in Satire* (London, 1958), pp. 194–216.

12. Irving's feud with Fessenden would make an interesting digression in this study, but it represents nothing substantial in the development of

Irving's comic method. Irving also mildly attacked Gifford in a note in Jeremy Cockloft's travel diary: "Archy Gifford and his man Caliban — jolly fat fellows" (*Sal.*, p. 101). Caliban was Irving's nickname for Fessenden, and Archy was the famous jester of James I under whose name many jestbooks were published.

13. Hopkins, *Portraits*, p. 137.

14. *The Looker-On*, No. 41; Hopkins, *Portraits*, p. 82; and *The North Briton* (1763), No. 12.

15. *Democracy Unveiled* [hereafter *DU*], by "Christopher Caustic," (New York, 1806), I, 102.

16. *The Port-Folio*, July 25, 1801. See also *DU*, I, 102, *Port-Folio*, Oct. 29, 1803, and "Modern Economy," in *The Evening Post*, ed. William Coleman (New York), Apr. 11, 1804. This is a prolific strain in the political satire of *The History*, e.g., pp. 147, 186, 201, 207–8, 211, and 413.

17. Richard Alsop, "The Echo," No. 20, Mar. 4, 1805, in *Connecticut Wits*, p. 497; Junius Philaenus [pseud.], *A Letter to Thomas Jefferson* (New York, 1802), pp. 44–47; *Port-Folio*, Jan. 28, 1804, and Aug. 9, 1806; and *DU*, II, 42 ff.

18. [F. S. Philbrick], "Thomas Jefferson," *Encyclopaedia Britannica*, 11th ed. (New York, 1911), XV, 305n; and *STW*, II, 286.

For satire on the dry-dock and gunboat schemes of Jefferson, see *Port-Folio*, Jan. 22 and Feb. 12, 1803; *Post*, Jan. 15, 1803, and Jan. 7 and Mar. 21, 1804; "Echo," No. 20, p. 509; *DU*, II, 67–68, 78, and 79.

19. *DU*, I, 110. See also Thomas Moore, *Epistles, Odes and Other Poems* (London, 1806), p. 211n. While this book was politically agreeable to Irving, it was attacked elsewhere in *Salmagundi* for its lasciviousness and as an example of the anti-American lies of splenetic foreign travellers; pp. 101, 105–7, 141–44, and 183. "[Jeremy] bids fair to be ranked on a par with MOORE, who saw enough of America from a stage-waggon to damn the whole of it" (*Salmagundi* excision from the original ending of "The Stranger in Pennsylvania," p. 246).

20. *DU*, II, 75; *Sal.*, pp. 127, 132, and 224; and *HNY*, pp. 179–185.

21. *Notes* . . . (Chapel Hill, 1955), pp. 31–33 and 159; *Port-Folio*, Jan. 15 and 22, 1803; and *Sal.*, p. 340. Jefferson was also bitterly attacked for his active friendship for Tom Paine: *Post*, Jan. 15, 1803; and "Echo," No. 20, p. 509.

22. *Port-Folio*, Jan. 22, 1803.

23. *Domestic Manners of the Americans* (New York, 1949), p. 72. See also Junius Philaenus, *Letter*, p. 46; *The Wasp*, ed. "Robert Rusticoat, Esq." (Hudson, New York), Sept. 23, 1802; *Port-Folio*, Jan. 15, 1803, Feb. 26, 1803, and "Black and White," Apr. 9, 1803; *Post*, Jan. 6, 1804; Moore, *Epistles*, p. 209; and *DU*, II, 7, 16, and 22–23.

24. *Port-Folio*, Jan. 22, 1803; and *DU*, II, 193.

25. For abuse of Paine, see *Port-Folio*, Jan. 22, Mar. 5, and Apr. 9, 1803, and Jan. 12, 1805; "Echo," No. 20, p. 509; and *DU*, II, 40.

26. *Sal.*, pp. 77, 223, 227–28, 259, 265, 268, 337, and 382; *HNY*, pp. 155, 158–59, 211, 217, and 379. See also Goldsmith, "Citizen," Ltr. IV, pp. 27–28; *Humphry Clinker*, pp. 105–6; and Benjamin Franklin's "Exporting of Felons to the Colonies," in *Representative Selections*, ed. Frank Luther Mott and Chester E. Jorgenson (New York, 1936), p. 215.

27. *Sal.,* pp. 267, 338–39, 341, 343, 344, and 404; and *HNY,* p. 226.
28. *Sal.,* pp. 222–23, 224–25, and 226; and *HNY,* p. 171. See also Hopkinson's "Intelligence Extraordinary," and "A Summary of Some Late Proceedings in a Certain Great Assembly," I, 178 and 184–85.
29. See John Trumbull's "M'Fingal," canto III, *Connecticut Wits.*
30. P. 143.
31. "M'Fingal," canto II, p. 79.
32. See *DU,* II, 27. Fighting by proclamation is used extensively in *The History* to characterize the reign of William Kieft (Thomas Jefferson): see pp. 172, 182–83, 186–87, 204, 227, 235, 255–56, 291, and 348.
33. Canto I, pp. 53–55.
34. Jefferson maintained "that this animal was never yet permitted to talk except in a genuine logocracy; where, it is true, his voice may often be heard, and is listened to with reverence, as 'the voice of the sovereign people'" (*Sal.,* p. 173). See *HNY,* p. 219; also *Hudibras,* II.ii.540.
35. See "A Tale of a Tub," p. 46, and *Spec.,* No. 567.
36. Rab. pp. 94–95.
37. Ltr. CXII.

Chapter VI

1. A. R. Humphreys, *Steele, Addison and Their Periodical Essays* (London, 1959), p. 17.
2. ". . . as some men gaze with admiration at the colours of a tulip, or the wing of a butterfly, so I was by nature an admirer of happy human faces," Goldsmith, *Works,* IV, 19. *The Vicar* is not only part of the background of *Salmagundi;* it was also part of the common literary inheritance of Irving's New York set: see *PMI,* I, 215.
3. See *Spec.,* No. 217; *Momus,* No. 2; *The Massachusetts Magazine* as cited in Ernest C. Coleman's "The Influence of the Addisonian Essay in America Before 1810," unpubl. diss., University of Illinois, 1936, p. 271; and *The Weekly Museum* (New York), Apr. 7, 1793.
4. *Humphry Clinker,* p. 60; see also pp. 6 and 22.
5. No. 2.
6. *Humphry Clinker,* pp. 60–61 and 96.
7. In "The Letters of Jonathan Oldstyle," the "good old times" were a vague "few years since." In the opening number of *Salmagundi,* however, they had been moved back to pre-Revolutionary America: the "chief commendation" that Evergreen can lavish upon a new mode is "'that it is the same good old fashion we had before the war'" (36).
8. (London, 1796), pp. 7, 21.
9. (Paris, 1824), p. 180.
10. (Paris, 1824), pp. 3–4; see also pp. 60 and 81.
11. Ibid., p. 188.

NOTES

Chapter VII

1. See *The Seven Wise Men of Gotham,* cited in *Boswell's London Journal,* 1762–1763, ed. Frederick A. Pottle (New York, 1950), p. 264; Thomas Love Peacock's *The Wise Men of Gotham.* Such collections are alluded to in "Tale of a Tub," pp. 41–42, and *TS,* p. 575.
2. *Momus,* No. 7.
3. Irving also alludes to the nursery rhyme:

> Three wise men of Gotham
> Went to sea in a bowl;
> And if the bowl had been stronger
> My song would have been longer.

4. *TS,* pp. 251–55. The source in Rabelais has not been located. Both Paris and Strasbourg are treated by these authors as *cities of fools:* Rabelais characterizes the Parisians as "such simpletons, such gapers, and such feckless idiots" (Rab., p. 74); see also p. 186. Sterne dramatizes the idiotic scurrying of the Strasbourgers; see particularly p. 252. Irving characterizes New York in this way through the metaphor of New Yorkers as geese or goslings: *Sal.,* pp. 72, 86, and 111.
5. *Scriblerus,* pp. 100 and 200–201.
6. *IV,* 145.
7. See also *Humphry Clinker,* p. 133.
8. Francis M. Cornford, *The Origin of Attic Comedy* (New York, 1961), pp. 136–38.
9. Lucian uses a surly Diogenes in a number of pieces to represent Cynic philosophy, *Selected Works* (New York, 1965), p. xvi; and this Diogenes became a comic touchstone for burlesque writers. See Rab., p. 281, and *Momus,* No. 9. Irving alludes to Lucian's "Feast of the Lapithae," *Sal.,* p. 392.
10. P. 121.
11. See also *Sal.,* pp. 97, 226, 253 (here a piece of choplogic is attributed to Trim, but there is no source for it in *Tristram Shandy*), and 263. For comparable burlesque of syllogistic logic, see Rab., pp. 70 and 75; *Hudibras,* I.i.65–80; "A Tale of a Tub," p. 73; Moore, *Epistles,* p. 336; Freneau's "Report of a Law Case," pp. 146–54; and *DU,* I, 117.
12. Pp. 122–23.
13. See also Rab., pp. 78, 177, and 209; and *TS,* pp. 51, 108, 146, and 331.
14. P. 148. Comic play with comets is quite common in British literature of the eighteenth century. For other parallels see *Gulliver,* pp. 164–65 and *Sal.,* p. 149; and *Gulliver,* p. 210 and *Sal.,* p. 315.
15. Translated by William Arrowsmith (Ann Arbor, Mich., 1962), p. 19.
16. *Hudibras,* I.i.121–26; see also I.i.67–68; II.iii.311–12; "A Tale of a Tub," p. 92; and *Sal.,* p. 48. This affectation of precision is specifically Rabelaisian, according to Huntington Brown in *Rabelais in English Literature* (Cambridge, Mass., 1933), p. 205; and see K. H. Francis, "Rabelais and Mathematics," *Bibliothèque d'humanisme et de la Renaissance,* XXI (1959), 95–96.

17. Actually the term had a wider range of meaning and could be used to refer to a false or absurd expert in any field. In "The Citizen of the World," Ltr. XXXIII, Altangi is forced to eat a formal dinner from a cushion off the floor and have a napkin pinned to his chin:"This I protested against, as being no way Chinese; however the whole company, who it seems were a club of connoisseurs, gave it unanimously against me," p. 143.

18. I, viii.

19. See also *TS*, pp. 103, 180, 198, and 238.

20. P. 97. See also *Three Hours after Marriage* by John Gay, Alexander Pope, and John Arbuthnot, ed. Richard Morton and William M. Peterson (Painesville, Ohio, 1961), *passim;* Arthur Murphy's *Gray's Inn Journal* (1753–54), No. 5; Pope's "The Dunciad," *The Poems* . . . , ed. John Butt (New Haven, 1963), pp. 764–65 and 784–88; Thomas Shadwell's *Virtuoso* (1676); and *Momus, Nos.* 20 and 21.

21. *The Port-Folio,* Aug. 16, 1806; *Modern Chivalry,* ed. Claude M. Newlin (New York, 1937), p. 257; and Freneau's "Rules and Directions How to Avoid Creditors, Sheriffs, Constables, etc.," *Prose Works,* p. 113. See *Sal.,* pp. 213–14.

22. See *Sal.,* pp. 309–10 and 416–17; in early editions of *Salmagundi* passages were set in black-letter. See also George Huddesford, "Bubble and Squeak," *The Poems* (London, 1801), II, 69; and *Flim-Flams,* I, 56, where the author's uncle also has "a delicious gusto for masticating a black-letter book."

23. See also *TS*, pp. 262 and 369.

24. Cf. "Oromedon, who begat Gemmagog — who was the inventor of pointed shoes" (Rab., p. 173).

25. *Joseph Andrews,* p. 19.

26. These references are curious, and, while it is obvious from them that Hebrew has comic weight, it is not at all obvious what its comic associations are. In the second volume of *Gargantua,* Pantagruel and his friends first meet Panurge in Paris, pitifully wounded and in a sorry state. They are interested in Panurge and eager to help him. He addresses several speeches to them, telling them that his story is a sad one, that he will not be able to tell it unless he has something to eat, that he has already asked them for food and they have not responded, that his condition should clearly express what it is he needs, that he is tired of talking and would remind them of the injunctions of the Gospel, etc. Each speech is in a different tongue, some real, some gibberish, and Pantagruel and Epistemon cannot understand his answers in German, Italian, Basque, Dutch, Spanish, and Danish. His ninth response is in Hebrew, at which point Epistemon finally understands him. The point is not that they can only understand the ancient tongues, because three speeches later they cannot understand Latin (bk. II, ch. 9).

Tristram describes an oratorical stance of Trim's and doubts "whether the oldest Fellow of a College, — or the *Hebrew* professor himself could have mended it" (*TS,* 123). See also *Hudibras,* I.i.59–60. The reference in *Salmagundi* is a negative one; though Wizard "is but little versed in Hebrew" (36), he has all the other qualifications for criticism.

27. See *Sal.,* p. 308; *Scriblerus,* p. 108; *Joseph Andrews,* p. 17; *Flim-*

Flams, I, 57; and Freneau's "Philosopher of the Forest," No. 1 — "There are indeed a few niceties in the dialect of the *Kalmuck Tartars* with which I am not so well acquainted; as also, several Chinese characters of inferior note," p. 201.

28. See, for example, "Don Quixote's Curious Discourse on Arms and Letters"; *TS*, pp. 102–3 and 206; and Freneau's "A Discourse on Beards," pp. 98–102.

29. Pp. 102–3.

30. P. 114.

31. Pp. 17–19.

32. See also *TS*, pp. 149 and 616, and *A Sentimental Journey*, p. 129.

33. Joseph Dennie, "Farrago," No. 3, in *The Port-Folio*, Vol. I, No. 4.

34. Cf. "A Tale of a Tub," p. 59.

35. See *HNY*, pp. 81–82, 86, and 226.

36. *Gulliver*, pp. 31 and 234; see also *Humphry Clinker*, p. 17.

37. The celebrated poet is Butler:

> He knew the seat of Paradise,
> Could tell in what degree it lies;
> And, as he was disposed, could prove it,
> Below the moon, or else above it:
> What Adam dreamt of when his bride
> Came from her closet in his side:
> Whether the devil tempted her
> By a High-Dutch interpretor . . . (I.i.173–80).

38. A hint for this essay may have been derived from the following: ". . . if ever Plan independent of all circumstances, deserved registering in letters of gold (I mean in the archives of *Gotham*) — it was certainly the PLAN of Mrs. *Wadman*'s attack of my uncle *Toby* in his sentry-box, BY PLAN" (*TS*, 575).

39. Irving may have had *Spectator* No. 67 in mind here, where a M. Riga-doon appears as a dancing master, and statements like the following on dancing occur: "*Homer* calls *Merion* a *Fine Dancer;* and says, That the graceful Mein and great Agility which he had acquired by that exercise, distinguished him above the rest in the Armies, both of *Greeks* and *Trojans.*" See also *Spec.*, No. 308.

40. Irving paraphrased this passage in a letter of 1810; *PMI*, I, 252.

41. P. 41.

Chapter VIII

1. John Neal, p. 58; Russell Blankenship, *American Literature* (New York, 1931), pp. 247–48; Henry Seidel Canby, *Classic Americans* (New York, 1931), p. 86; Parrington, *Main Currents in American Thought* (New York, 1930), II, 212; A. Fontenay, "La Littérature Américaine: Washington Irving. . . ," *Revue des Deux Mondes*, VI (1832), 515; Cunliffe, *Literature*, pp. 55–56; Wagenknecht, p. 170; and Hedges, *Washington Irving*, pp. 12 and 98.

2. *STW*, I, 114.

3. Charles Churchill, "The Ghost," *Poetical Works* (Oxford, 1956), IV, 369; *Flim-Flams*, p. viii — "wind-catchers" and "cloud-modifiers"; "Echo," No. 20, pp. 507–8 and *Sal.*, p. 224.

4. " . . . stop! my dear uncle *Toby*, — stop! — go not one foot further into this thorny and bewilder'd track, — intricate are the steps! intricate are the mases of this labyrinth! intricate are the troubles which the pursuit of this bewitching phantom, KNOWLEDGE, will bring upon thee. — O my uncle! fly — fly — fly from it as from a serpent" (*TS*, 90).

5. "A Tale of a Tub," p. 33, and *Flim-Flams*, p. 8.

6. Cf., "And various writers . . . anxious for the accommodation of these travellers, have fastened the two continents together by a strong chain of deductions — by which means they could pass over dry shod" (*HNY*, p. 47).

7. Theodore Hornberger, in *The Literature of the United States*, by Walter Blair, Theodore Hornberger, and Randall Stewart (Chicago, 1953), I, 6.

8. Knickerbocker is scornful of the "idea that America is the fairy region of Zipangri, described by that dreaming traveller Marco Polo the Venetian; or that it comprizes the visionary island of Atlantis, described by Plato. Neither will I stop to investigate the heathenish assertion of Paracelsus, that each hemisphere of the globe was originally furnished with an Adam and Eve" (46).

9. See *HNY*, pp. 74–75 and 129.

10. *The Letters of James Kirke Paulding*, ed. Ralph M. Aderman (Madison, Wisconsin, 1962), p. 124.

11. The observation attributed to the "philosopher" is a pointed paraphrase of Paulding's passage on blacks (*Sal.*, p. 479).

12. This is taken from Tacitus, "Germany and Its Tribes," *The Complete Works* (New York, 1942), p. 709.

Rabelais also makes Noah the spiritual ancestor of the Pantagruelines, for Noah "planted us the vine, from which comes that ambrosial, delicious, precious, celestial, joyous and deific liquor which is called *drink*" (Rab., p. 171).

13. It is quite true that American literature has been informed by patterns of sacred, specifically biblical, recognition from William Bradford's *Plymouth Plantation*. I have decided to ignore the literature of the American seventeenth century both for reasons of economy and because it had very little influence on Irving's art, although he had read various works belonging to it.

14. See *HNY*, pp. 80–81 and 107.

15. Cf., "In this dulcet period of my history, when the beauteous island of Mannahata presented a scene, the very counterpart of those glowing pictures drawn by old Hesiod of the golden reign of Saturn, there was a happy ignorance, an honest simplicity prevalent among its inhabitants." (*HNY*, p. 141).

16. P. 269.

17. William Byrd, *Histories of the Dividing Line* (New York, 1967), p. 92 [Mar. 25, 1728].

18. Franklin, *Representative Selections*, p. 452.

19. Although I am not arguing influence in this section, Irving was thoroughly familiar with *Gargantua* and put it to use. In addition to the allusions and borrowings to be mentioned, Irving alludes in *Salmagundi* to "Justice Bridlegoose deciding by a throw of a die, and of the oracle of the holy bottle" (106), and in *The History* to the ink-horn of "the sage Gargantua; which according to the faithful chronicle of his miraculous achievements, weighed seven thousand quitals" (237) and to the means by which Pantagruel protected his army — "by covering it with his tonge" (414). There is also an allusion to Rabelais in a letter of 1811, *PMI*, I, 274.

20. Genital celebration, as opposed to fictions of sexual play, is common in primitive art, whether the poems of Archilochus or English nursery rhymes like "Goosy, Goosy, Gander" or "I Had a Little Nut Tree."

21. P. 55.

22. Devices comparable to this are to be found in great plenty in Rabelais, particularly in the false etymologies of Gargantua (53), Pantagruel (176) and Anarch, king of the Dipsodes (252). I have already mentioned that Noah, as inventor of wine, is a spiritual ancestor in *Gargantua*. Irving's Noah is also associated with nourishment: "Methodius gives him a son called Jonithus or Jonicus (who was the first inventor of Johnny cakes)" (*HNY*, p. 35).

23. See also Rab., pp. 53 and 177; and *HNY*, p. 142.

24. Knickerbocker also surveys the twenty-three systems of fortifications that Stuyvesant did not use, which is probably derived from the works of fortifications in Uncle Toby's library (*TS*, 88–89).

25. *HNY*, 130, 159, and 402.

26. Tagliacozzi is treated comically in *Hudibras*, I.i.281; and *Tatler*, No. 260.

27. John Ferriar, *Illustrations of Sterne* (London, 1788), chap. iv.

28. See also D'Urfey, III, 12 and 322, and IV, 259: "A Ballad of the Nose"; *Tatler*, No. 75; *Joseph Andrews*, p. 6; *Humphry Clinker*, pp. 19–20; *Flim-Flams*, p. 39; *Modern Chivalry*, p. 115; and *The Thespian Mirror*, ed. John Howard Payne (New York, 1805–6), p. 116 — an anatomy of noses — and 202 — "Dissertation on Sneezing."

29. Quoted in *TS*, p. 219.

30. See also Rab., pp. 80, 85, 114, 206, and 211.

31. Ferriar, p. 112.

32. *Scriblerus*, p. 38.

33. See pp. 173 and 200. Breeches became the symbol of New Netherlands: the skirts of Stuyvesant's regimental coat "turned up at the corners and separating gallantly behind, so as to display the seat of . . . brimstone coloured trunk breeches" (*HNY*, 296–97). And a fort established on the Delaware River is named "FORT CASIMIR, in honour of a favourite pair of . . . breeches" of the governor's (290–91). After Peter's death, memorials to him were hung in his estate: "His brimstone coloured breeches were for a long while suspended in the hall, until some years since they occasioned a dispute between a new married couple" (454).

34. See particularly p. 214. For similar comic figures see Rab., p. 188; *Hudibras*, I.i.532; *TS*, pp. 63, 254, and 589; and *Scriblerus*, p. 116.

35. *The Waning of the Middle Ages* (London, 1924), p. 281.

36. Una Ellis-Fermor, *The Jacobean Drama* (London, 1943), p. 123.

NOTES

37. Pp. 29 and 82. See also *Spec.*, No. 32: "Its a Jest at *Harlem* to talk of a Shape under eighteen Stone. Their wise Traders regulate their Beauties as they do their Butter, by the Pound; and Miss *Cross,* when she first arriv'd in the *Low-Countries,* was not computed to be so handsom as Madam *Van Brisket* by near half a Tun"; and *Shoemaker's Holiday,* III.i, pp. 41–42 and V.ii, p. 100.

38. Pp. 41–42 and 100.

39. Political satire in *The History* does not show any real comic advance over that in *Salmagundi;* it is an increase rather than a growth. Moreover, *The History* is the only one of Irving's early works which has received a fair amount of critical treatment, and that has been largely devoted to the political allegory of Kieft's reign and, to some extent, its political satire.

40. The figure of the storm may owe something to *Tristram Shandy:* "From the first moment I sat down to write . . . has a cloud insensibly been gathering over my father. – A tide of little evils and distresses has been setting in against him. – Not one thing as he observed himself, has gone right: and now is the storm thicken'd, and going to break, and pour down full upon his head" (215). See also Rab., pp. 491 and 506.

41. *PMI,* I, 31.

42. Many specific parallels could be given, e.g., Crowdero's wooden leg, I.ii.141–42 and 914–16, and Stuyvesant's wooden leg; and the modern writer's complaint at the gratuitous slaughter committed by the epic poets for trivial reasons, I.ii. 11–22 and *HNY,* p. 367. For samples of Butler's methods of comic heroics see I.i.289–92 and 377–78, I.ii.211–18 and 417–26, I.iii.493–94, and II.i.13–16 and 777–81.

43. See *Hudibras,* I.ii.305–14.

44. I.i.309, 313–16, and 351–54. See also Rab., p. 96; and *Hudibras,* I.i.296 through 402, where the parallel between fighting and nourishment is constantly played upon, involving, among other things, a reinterpretation of the Round Table in terms of food.

45. See *Hudibras,* I.ii.107–10, 120, and 1117–26; and II.ii.593–658.

46. Grub's ballad is quoted in Huddesford, "Bubble and Squeak," p. 17, and D'Urfey, *Wit and Mirth,* III, 315–23.

47. See also the parallel between *Hudibras,* I.ii.781–82 and *HNY,* p. 361.

48. The Yankees obviously cannot meet the Dutch on the field of comic battle, considering what they represented for Irving as well as the rudimentary characterization they had already received in American comedy. In this section, however, they invade and overwhelm New Amsterdam in ways consistent with the character of the Yankee when he finally emerges in Native American Humor: stealthy encroachment and the ability to drive a shrewd bargain.

Chapter IX

1. *STW,* I, 130–31.

2. Ibid., 168–69.

3. *Washington Irving: Representative Selections,* ed. Henry A. Pochmann (New York, 1934), p. 80 (in citations, *RS*).

4. Baker, "Political Allusion," p. 1124.

5. Hedges, *Washington Irving,* p. 137, also sees Dame Van Winkle as a Yankee: she is "the spirit of industry, a *Poor Richard's Almanac* made flesh, a combination of puritan conscience and Protestant ethic."

6. The tag to this tale associates American dreaming with the activity of the inhabitants of James Thomson's "Castle of Indolence."

7. By not having *The History* in mind, Hedges reads the passage from "Sleepy Hollow" as the expression of Crane's desire for a home of his own (*Washington Irving,* p. 142). On the contrary, it expresses the Yankee's "rambling propensity."

8. Hedges, *Washington Irving,* pp. 141–42. Because Robert A. Bone interprets Crane as a serious "symbol of man's higher aspirations" — "Irving's Headless Hessian," *American Quarterly,* XV (Summer, 1963), 167–75 — he is forced to see Brom Bones, who frolics through the tale, as "the embodiment . . . of mercenary values which threaten to engulf the imagination."

9. The choice of the Hessian may have been an unfortunate one on Irving's part, if it reminds us of Paine's ravishers in *Common Sense,* although Franklin took a more sympathetic view toward these mercenaries. The choice of André strikes deeper chords of ambivalence. It must be significant that our first important Revolutionary drama, William Dunlap's *André,* should celebrate the death of a noble and virtuous, and innocent, British spy.

Chapter X

1. The question of what constitutes significant anticipation is problematic. I have used the distinction between fine and functional literature (in which I do not believe) in order to eliminate an often powerful body of political and religious prose from consideration to contain the argument of this chapter. Allowing that distinction, Irving's only rival in striking possible American notes in literature would be Charles Brockden Brown. I do not, however, believe that his fiction arrives at any definition, although it poses interesting problems within this context.

2. Brown also poses a number of unreasonable, un-American premises that touch on salient features of our major literature. In *Wieland,* for example, there are the choice of the Gothic mode for a country presumed to be free of Old World passion and evil, a choice which should have failed but, on the contrary, partially succeeded in that work and went on to prosper mightily; the contradiction between his desire to create a rational woman and his actual projection of a creature who often makes the very notion of rationality seem grotesque but more often exists in a state of hysterical confusion; and his refusal to treat nature in a country which had very little else to offer.

3. Cited in Walter Blair's *Native American Humor* (San Francisco, 1937), p. 14.

4. *The Roots of American Culture* (New York, 1942). Jefferson was not a Yankee, and he took a middle position in this early debate over whether or not America was a proper home for the fine or "useless" arts.

INDEX

INDEX

INDEX

INDEX

51, 54–55, 93
Journals and notebooks, 1803–1805,
chapter II *passim*, 73
Writing, middle period, 16, 45, 91
Irving, William, 17, 18, 19, 67, 123

James, Henry, xii, 17, 26, 175, 177
Jefferson, Thomas, 62, 65, 66, 69–71,
73, 75, 77, 143–44, 162, 170, 192,
193, 200
Jonson, Ben, 4, 75, 150, 188, 191
Josephus, Flavius, 125
Joyce, James, x, 6, 21, 115, 122
"Junius Philaenus," 192
Juvenal, 4, 7

Lawrence, D. H., 156
"Legend of Sleepy Hollow, The," ix,
16, 87, 146, 155, 156, 159, 161–68,
176–77
"Letters of Jonathan Oldstyle, The," 16,
25, 48, 61, 81, 143, 149, 193
Lewis, Sinclair, 170
Life of Columbus, xii, 154
Life of Washington, xii, 154
Literary Leisure, 83
Locke, John, 33
Looker-On, The, 68, 192
Lucan, 148, 194
Lucian, 7, 10, 98, 101, 118, 121

Macklin, Charles, 89
Malory, Sir Thomas, 148, 174
Marquand, John Phillips, 26
Massachusetts Magazine, The, 193
Mathias, John, 67, 191
McDowell, Tremaine, 22
McKillop, A. D., 21
Melville, Herman, xi, 6, 9, 10, 15, 40,
44, 79, 114, 148, 171, 175, 176, 178,
179, 180, 181
Memoirs of . . . Martinus Scriblerus, The,
95, 97, 98–99, 104, 106–107, 189,
191, 198
Memoirs of the Society of Grub Street,
190, 195
Miller, Henry, 176
Miller, Perry, 12
Molière, 4, 89, 97, 137
Momus, or The Laughing Philosopher,
189, 193, 194, 195
Monroe, Harriet, 44
Moore, Edward, 190
Moore, Thomas, 192, 194
More, Sir Thomas, 129

Morning Chronicle, The, 16
Murphy, Arthur, 195

Nabokov, Vladimir, x, 6, 85
Native American humor, 58, 94, 130,
134–35
Yankee, 109, 124, 143, 175, 199
Neal, John, 61
New York Magazine, The, 38
North Briton, The, 192

Ovid, 126

Paine, Tom, 62, 68, 69, 71–72, 97,
170, 192, 200
Paulding, James Kirke, 29, 33, 45, 64,
67, 80, 88, 93, 123–24, 125–26, 197
Payne, John Howard, 198
Peacock, Thomas Love, 194
Pédant Joué, Le, 137
Periodical serials, 28, 29, 31, chapter IV
passim, 87
"Peter Pindar" [John Wolcut], 95, 191
Plato, 97, 132
Plautus, 4
Pope, Alexander, 4, 20, 52, 97, 106,
195
Port-Folio, The, 69, 104, 189, 190,
191, 192, 195, 196
Pound, Ezra, 44, 115
Prince, Thomas, 115
Prince Hoare, 88
Psalmanazar, 95–96
"Punch and Judy," 82, 158
Pythagoras, 112

Rabelais, Francois, x, xiii, 5, 6, 7, 8, 9,
10, 12, 16, 76–77, 84–85, 94, 98, 101,
105, 106, 107, 110, 111, 112, 114,
115, 129, 130, 131–32, 133, 134–35,
136, 138, 139–40, 148, 149, 150,
165, 178, 181, 184, 189, 190, 193,
194, 195, 198, 199
Radcliffe, Anne, 22
Rinomachie, La, 137
"Rip Van Winkle," ix, 16, 85, 128, 143,
146, 155–61, 162, 167, 172, 176–77,
180
Rocky Mountains, The, xii
Romanticism, 29, 35, 37, 42, 67, 96,
173–74, 188
Rourke, Constance, 177

Salmagundi, x, 10, 12, 17, 18, 24, 25,
26, chapters III to VII *passim*, 114,

204

INDEX